Music
Autoethnographies

Making Autoethnography Sing / Making Music Personal

Edited by
Brydie-Leigh Bartleet and Carolyn Ellis

www.
AUSTRALIANACADEMIC**PRESS**
.com.au

First published in 2009 from a completed manuscript presented to
Australian Academic Press
32 Jeays Street
Bowen Hills Qld 4006
Australia
www.australianacademicpress.com.au

The contributions to this publication were blind peer-reviewed by a panel of international
readers, and sub-edited by Catherine Grant.

National Library of Australia cataloguing-in-publication entry:

Title:	Music autoethnographies : making autoethnography sing : making music personal / editors Brydie-Leigh Bartleet and Carolyn Ellis.
ISBN:	9781921513404 (pbk.)
Notes:	Bibliography.
Subjects:	Communication in music. Subjectivity in music.
Other Authors/ Contributors:	Bartleet, Brydie-Leigh. Ellis, Carolyn.
Dewey Number:	780.7

Images on front cover: (Top left) Brydie-Leigh Bartleet conducting at the Chia-Yi Cultural
Centre, Taiwan. Photographer: Alvin Fong. (Top centre) Pham Thi Hue learning *ca tru* from
Master Nguyễn Thị Chúc in Ngãi Cầu Village, Vietnam. Photographer: Huib Schippers. (Top
right) Elizabeth Mackinlay dancing with Rosie a-Makurndurna Noble at The University of
Queensland. Photographer: Franca Tamisari. (Bottom centre) Band, Way Out West.
Photographer: Sharka Bosakova. Background image: Dreamstime/Pixelgallery.

Music Autoethnographies is an initiative of Queensland Conservatorium Research Centre (QCRC), Griffith University, and embodies its commitment to diverse, innovative, and practice-based research with direct relevance to contemporary realities in the global musical arena.

Contents

About the Authors

Katelyn Barney, PhD, is Research Officer and Managing Editor of *The Australian Journal of Indigenous Education* at the University of Queensland. Her main research interests include collaborative research with Indigenous Australian women who perform in contemporary music contexts, representation and ethics, and reflective writing as a teaching and learning tool. She teaches a range of topics including music history, ethnomusicology, popular music, and Indigenous studies. She is also the Secretary of the International Association for the Study of Popular Music Australia/New Zealand Branch and National Treasurer of the Musicological Society of Australia.

Brydie-Leigh Bartleet (co-editor of this volume), PhD, is a Lecturer in Research and Music Literature at the Queensland Conservatorium Griffith University. For the past two years she has worked on the Queensland Conservatorium Research Centre ARC funded project, *Sound Links: Community Music in Australia*. She has also worked as a sessional Lecturer at the University of Queensland, and as a freelance conductor has worked with ensembles from Australia, Thailand, Singapore and Taiwan. She has published widely on issues relating to community music, women conductors, peer-learning in conducting and feminist pedagogy, and is currently co-editing two music-related books — *Musical Islands: Exploring Connections Between Music, Place and Research*; and *Navigating Music and Sound Education*. She is also on the editorial board for the *International Journal of Community Music*.

David Carless, PhD, is currently a senior research fellow in the Carnegie Research Institute at Leeds Metropolitan University, United Kingdom. His work focuses on the use of narrative and arts-based approaches to understanding mental health, identity and wellbeing in and through physical activity and sport.

~~

Kitrina Douglas, PhD, played golf on the Ladies European Tour for 12 years and has worked in broadcasting and the media. Since 1996 she has been conducting narrative and arts-based research in the areas of sport, exercise, and health and is currently an Honorary Visiting Fellow at the University of Bristol, United Kingdom.

~~

Peter Dunbar-Hall is an Associate Professor in the Music Education Unit of Sydney Conservatorium of Music, University of Sydney. His teaching covers classroom methodology, history and philosophy of music education, multiculturalism, and Balinese gamelan. His research focuses on music pedagogies used by Balinese musicians. Publications by Peter include *Strella Wilson: The Career of an Australian Singer* (Redback Press, 1997) and, with Chris Gibson, *Deadly Sounds, Deadly Places: Contemporary Aboriginal Music in Australia* (UNSW Press, 2004).

~~

Carolyn Ellis (co-editor of this volume) is Professor of Communication and Sociology at the University of South Florida. She has published four books — *Fisher Folk: Two Communities on Chesapeake Bay*; *Final Negotiations: A Story of Love, Loss, and Chronic Illness*; *The Ethnographic I: A Methodological Novel about Autoethnography*, and *Revision: Autoethnographic Reflections on Life and Work* — four edited collections, and numerous articles and stories. With Arthur Bochner, she co-edits the book series, *Writing Lives: Ethnographic Narratives*. Her work is situated in interpretive and artistic representations of qualitative research and focuses on autoethnographic stories as a means to understand and interpret culture and live a meaningful life. She enjoys dancing, hiking, gardening, and listening to music; her actual musical talents are minimal.

~~

Stephen Emmerson has been on staff at the Queensland Conservatorium since 1987 where he teaches courses in music literature and music research as well as piano, chamber music, and performance practice. He also convenes the Doctor of Musical Arts program there and is a member of the Queensland Conservatorium Research Centre. As a pianist, he performs regularly both as soloist and with chamber ensembles, most notably within the Griffith Trio, Dean-Emmerson-Dean and the Endeavour Trio. Over a dozen CD recordings of his playing have been released commercially.

＝

Catherine Grant is a doctoral student at Queensland Conservatorium. She is Membership Secretary of the Musicological Society of Australia, an executive committee member of the Australian Society for Performing Arts Healthcare, and a member of the reference team for an Australia Learning and Teaching Council Priority Project on tertiary musicians' health and wellbeing. Cathy enjoys giving pre-concert talks for The Queensland Orchestra and presenting a weekly radio program on 4MBS Classic FM, *Your Classical Collection*.

＝

Stacy Holman Jones is an Associate Professor at the University of South Florida. Her work focuses on the intersections of gender, performance, and storytelling. Her publications include *Torch Singing: Performing Resistance and Desire from Billie Holiday to Edith Piaf* and *Kaleidoscope Notes: Writing Music and Organizational Culture*, as well as articles in *Text and Performance Quarterly*, *Qualitative Inquiry*, and *Cultural Studies ↔ Critical Methodologies*.

＝

Peter Knight is a Melbourne-based trumpeter and composer who has gained wide acclaim for his eclectic approach, which traverses jazz, world music, and experimental traditions. He leads several projects of his own and appears as a soloist in a range of settings. He also composes for theatre and film, and has created sound installations. Peter is currently completing a DMA at Queensland Conservatorium and lectures in music part time at RMIT and NMIT in Melbourne. www.peterknightmusic.com

＝

Elizabeth Mackinlay is a Senior Lecturer in the Aboriginal and Torres Strait Islander Studies Unit at the University of Queensland where she teaches Indigenous Studies, Anthropology and Ethnomusicology. Liz works with Yanyuwa women in Borroloola on the Gulf of Carpentaria in the Northern Territory and also researches music and mothering, and music and gifted education. Liz is co-editor of *Music Education Research and Innovation* and *The Australian Journal of Music Education*.

＝

Chris McRae is a doctoral student in the Department of Speech Communication at Southern Illinois University Carbondale and is working at the intersections of performance studies, communication pedagogy, and intercultural communication. His research interests include questions about music performance as a communicative, cultural, and embodied practice.

Chris J. Patti is a doctoral student in the Department of Communication and a McKnight Doctoral Fellow at the University of South Florida. His interests include autoethnography, ethnography, and rhetorical criticism focused on cancer and Holocaust narratives. Musically, he has performed for the past decade in a band called *My Favorite Band*. He is currently recording with Phil Allen on a musical project called *Mr Radar*.

Margaret Schindler is a Senior Lecturer in Voice at the Queensland Conservatorium Griffith University where she has been a member of academic staff since 1995. Her vibrant professional profile combines a fulltime teaching practice with an active performance schedule as concert artist and member of Australian chamber music ensemble, Southern Cross Soloists. She is also undertaking a Doctor of Musical Arts at the Queensland Conservatorium Griffith University. Her research focus on the role of the performer as teacher has been shaped by more than 25 years of performance experience as an opera singer and recitalist at a national and international level.

Huib Schippers is founding Director of the innovative Queensland Conservatorium Research Centre at Griffith University and President of the Musicological Society of Australia. His long and profound engagement with musics from various cultures has led to a slightly unconventional but successful career, including performance and teaching, music criticism, the record trade, arts policy, research, academic leadership, and the realisation of a $20 million World Music & Dance Centre in Rotterdam in 2006. From 2009–2013, Professor Schippers is leading a research team from seven countries in *Sustainable Futures for Music Traditions: Towards an Ecology of Musical Diversity*, a five-year, $5 million ARC-funded project to empower communities across the world to forge musical futures on their own terms, realised in partnership with the International Music Council and seven universities in Australia, Europe, the United States and the United Kingdom.

Karen Scott-Hoy is an independent scholar who is passionate about using visual arts, performance and evocative autoethnography to interrogate her research topics, ethnography in general, and herself as a researcher, allowing multi-perspectival reflection on phenomena. It is her hope that these projects assist "ordinary people" to explore, understand and improve their everyday lives. Her current research interests include social justice, parenting, and community development. Author of numerous conference papers, book chapters and journal articles, she also paints visual ethnographies, several of which have been featured on book covers. Karen lives in rural South Australia with her husband and sons.

~~~

Lexine Solomon is from North Queensland and is of Torres Strait Islander and South Sea Islander descent. She has been a solo singer, choral director and backing vocalist for more than 20 years and has released two albums, *This is Woman* and *Strike a Pose*. She is currently completing a Bachelor of Arts in Adult Education and Community Management at University of Technology Sydney, and continues to perform Australia-wide and frequently internationally.

~~~

Jodie Taylor completed her PhD entitled *Playing it Queer: Understanding Queer Gender, Sexual and Musical Praxis in a "New" Musicological Context* in 2008. Following this, Jodie took up a postdoctoral fellowship with the Centre for Public Culture and Ideas, Griffith University, in 2009. In this role she continues to work and publish on themes relating to queer identity and cultural practices in addition to contributing to the centre's Creativity and Social Inclusion initiative. In the past Jodie has worked as a sessional lecturer at the Queensland Conservatorium Griffith University where she taught music technology theory and aesthetics.

~~~

Colin Webber is a composer and educator based in Brisbane. Having created a wide range of music for media, theatre and film over 20 years, he now teaches music technology and audio production at tertiary level. Colin has been engaged in examining his composition and collaborative practice over the past several years, a process that was given significant sideways impetus by his diagnosis in 2005 with Asperger's syndrome. He has now devoted his doctoral research at the Queensland Conservatorium Griffith University to reconciling his autistic traits with his musical life.

~~~

Wang Yuyan is currently balancing an active freelancing career with a Doctor of Musical Arts degree at the Queensland Conservatorium Griffith University. After studying at the Shanghai Conservatory of Music, Wang Yuyan joined the Guangzhou Symphony Orchestra, touring Asia, Europe, Africa and Australia. Wang Yuyan also held the principal timpani and percussion position in the Lanzhou Symphony Orchestra. In Australia, she has been offered the principal timpani and percussion position with the Gold Coast Symphony Orchestra, and is regularly doing casual work with The Queensland Orchestra. Wang Yuyan also has a strong interest in traditional Chinese percussive arts, as her research shows.

Making Autoethnography Sing / Making Music Personal

Brydie-Leigh Bartleet and Carolyn Ellis

"I don't think I found autoethnography; I think autoethnography found me. In fact, I think it saved me," Brydie says to Carolyn, who thinks she knows just what Brydie means. Brydie has come to Melbourne to see Carolyn present her work at LaTrobe University. She has taken Carolyn's workshop there in preparation for Carolyn's visit to the Queensland Conservatorium a year later. The two are sharing a cup of coffee over breakfast the next morning, getting to know each other. "Autoethnography allowed me to end a very significant musical phase in my life; a phase filled with such darkness, dissonance and angst, it was strangling me. I had reached a point in my conducting career where I had become completely consumed by personal and musical insecurities and anxieties, I was ready to throw it all away," Brydie continues, swallowing hard. "But, instead of running away from this situation, I decided to face it head on with an autoethnographic study." Gently moving her hands in a circular motion and bringing them to a slow halt as though she is conducting the end of an intense musical phrase, she almost spills her coffee. "Autoethnography challenged me to find the cadence point, to breathe, and to listen to the reverberations of my pain and sadness. Autoethnography helped me to hear the beauty and vulnerability in that phrase and understand the reasons for its dark timbre, competing melodies, and restless pulse."

"Autoethnography saved me too," Carolyn responds, thinking how much she is enjoying sharing her love for autoethnography with Brydie, a musician and autoethnographer, who is fast becoming a friend and colleague through their joint efforts to connect music and autoethnography. "Personal writing saved me from being less than passionately involved in my career and from being so mired in grief that I couldn't breathe. Doing autoethnography made me feel that my work was worthwhile, that I could contribute to making the world a better place, show my students alternative ways to survive grief and reframe their lives, and equip myself to make sense of the life I was living."

Hearing Carolyn's admission, Brydie feels the courage to continue. "Before I began doing autoethnography, I was a young conductor teetering on the edge of career suicide. I'd been conducting for just over ten years and clocked up a string of performances with ensembles from Thailand, Singapore, Taiwan and Australia. My career was soaring, but a deep dissonance and restlessness was building inside me as I struggled to come to terms with issues about my musical identity, ability and shortcomings as a conductor. The more I stood on the podium, playing the role of 'conductor' and guiding my musicians from one work to the next, the more I felt like a fraud, a fake, a failure. My feelings of charlatanism were exacerbated by the fact that I no longer had time to play my trumpet. Conducting had become the dominant melody in my life, and my trumpet-playing had slipped quietly into a deafening silence. I dashed from one rehearsal and performance to the next, improvising my way through a massive amount of music, and dancing to a tune that left me exhausted. I couldn't see a way out of this situation; this phase felt like it would never end. I tried to cover up what I was feeling and act like I was enjoying the challenge of its competing and discordant elements; like I was somehow in control of this unruly improvisation. I hoped my musicians wouldn't see the struggle going on inside me, although I suspect they did. I'm sure my revealing face, yearning gestures, and vulnerable performances gave away what I was feeling. I had to do something. I knew I couldn't keep playing this worn out tune much longer." Brydie pauses for a moment, feeling slightly self-conscious about what she has divulged to Carolyn. The supportive expression on Carolyn's face lets her know that Carolyn understands where she is coming from, and again it gives her courage to continue. "So I decided to start an autoethnography to try to come to terms with why I was feeling so distressed on the podium. I knew a little about the method, having encountered it while doing ethnographic research for my doctorate. As I read more, I began to realise that this approach could offer me a way to pause, listen and come to appreciate this difficult musical phase in my life."

Carolyn notices how Brydie's face reveals her emotions as she talks — first her struggle, then her yearning, and finally the light that bursts onto her face. "I also went through a sad period prior to writing autoethnography," Carolyn relates, feeling amazingly comfortable with Brydie though she has known her for such a short time. "At first, the reasons were personal. My brother died in a commercial airplane crash in January 1982 on his way to visit me (see Ellis, 1993). In the summer of 1984, I tore the anterior cruciate ligament and meniscus in my left knee while playing basketball, which demanded surgery, and sent me into a midlife crisis. My body was failing me for the first time. Little did I know that there would be many other 'midlife crises' to follow!" Carolyn rolls her eyes and chuckles, then becomes serious. "And during this time, my romantic partner entered the final stages of chronic emphysema. I was a mess. Immersed in personal suffering, I couldn't figure out how to work my way through the pain."

Brydie looks knowingly at Carolyn, unsure of how to respond. She's read the autoethnographic stories that stemmed from these tragic events in Carolyn's life; she can certainly relate to the overwhelming feeling of being submerged that Carolyn is describing. "I think I know what you mean," Brydie adds, wishing that she had more comforting words to offer. She relates her own experience for companionship. "My inescapable absorption in conducting became my autoethnographic starting point. Although it was painful to be facing these issues head-on, it was also strangely comforting to finally acknowledge them. It was a relief to admit to the darkness of my experience with music, instead of trying to mask it with my professional conducting persona. I began recording and reflecting on my weekly musical experiences through journals, videos, recordings, and photographs. Over the months that followed, with time and constant reflection, I started to see musical patterns, meanings and insights. I started to understand how my feelings of musical inadequacy and dissatisfaction with conducting were tightly linked to the notion of the 'all-knowing' conductor upheld by my profession. Trying to fit that role was taking me further and further away from the pleasures of music-making. As I vulnerably shared some of my autoethnographic journal entries with other musicians and saw the rawness and understanding in their reactions, I came to realise that I couldn't know it all; I couldn't possibly understand everything hidden in this particular musical experience, or the scores I conducted on a weekly basis. I began to see that my humanity, with all its vulnerabilities and insecurities, was not a sign of musical weakness, but actually my greatest asset on the podium. Acknowledging my limitations as a human-being allowed me to relate more deeply to the music I conducted and appreciate the musicians with whom I was working. As I contextualised my experiences alongside those of other conducting colleagues, I realised I wasn't alone in my musical struggles. This awareness and sharing with others gave me reason to hope again, and showed me the very powerful space that music and autoethnography combined could create, both for musicians and autoethnographers alike."

"My personal and professional lives were linked as well," Carolyn says. "Flashbacks of my brother's death and my ongoing inability to 'get over' my loss were interrupted in real life by my partner gasping for breath while I hobbled as fast as I could to untangle his oxygen hose. In this context, the scientifically respectable survey of jealousy among undergraduates I had been working on seemed insignificant and I began to question the sociology I was doing. Instead, I wanted to understand and cope with the intense emotion I felt about loss and deterioration. On July 14, 1984, I began keeping notes about these experiences, focusing on my partner's situation, our relationship and coping with illness and dying. Writing these notes was therapeutic for me and I thought sociologically insightful as well. I wasn't sure initially what to do with all these pages; I just knew I had to write. Later the notes became the basis for a book, *Final Negotiations* (1995a), which described in the form of creative nonfiction how my partner and I coped (or didn't) with his illness and the effect it had on our relationship. As your work did for you, writing this story and getting responses from others helped make me feel that I was not alone, that others had had these feelings and experiences of loss, and they had survived. That was important — to find a way to believe that I would survive what was happening."

Thinking about her own difficulties with writing autoethnography, Brydie silently wonders what it must have been like for Carolyn to release *Final Negotiations* into the public realm, in terms of revealing so much of her life. She responds, "When I first presented my conducting autoethnography at a musicological conference in 2006, the experience was both terrifying and exhilarating." Carolyn nods in recognition. "I was terrified about revealing my vulnerabilities in front of my colleagues. I even had a nightmare the night before my presentation where the audience turned their backs on me, and I had to pour ice cold water on their heads to make them listen to me. But the exhilaration I felt as I delivered that presentation confirmed for me that I was on the right track with both my conducting and autoethnographic work. Sharing my personal story in this way encouraged others to do the same. After my presentation, the heartfelt words I heard from colleagues facing similar dark issues and the e-mails I received from others who revealed that they'd decided to begin their own journal writing showed how this presentation resonated beyond my own autoethnographic tale. I later reworked the paper into an article that looked at the process of using autoethnographic writing in my conducting practice (Bartleet, in press). I also started exploring other music-related autoethnographic projects with close colleagues. These autoethnographic articles examined diverse musical topics, such as peer-learning in professional conducting (Bartleet & Hultgren, 2008), feminist pedagogy in musicological classrooms (Mackinlay & Bartleet, 2008a), postgraduate supervision in music (Mackinlay, Bartleet, Barney & Monk, 2007), and friendship and sisterhood as the foundations of musicological and ethnographic fieldwork (Mackinlay & Bartleet, 2008b). Now a number of my postgraduate students also are exploring autoethnographic writing and composition in their musical projects. These collaborative ventures into music and autoethnography seem to have snow-balled since my first encounter with the approach."

"That's the way autoethnography often works," Carolyn says. "One autoethnography leads into another, for you and the people around you. I followed *Final Negotiations* with a story about my brother's death, and many other stories about personal loss (for example, Ellis, 1995b; 1998) and about collective trauma, such as the terrorist attack on the World Trade Center on September 11, 2001 (Ellis, 2002) and Katrina, the disastrous hurricane in New Orleans (Ellis, 2007). My goal became connecting the best of social science ethnographic research with the aesthetics of the creative arts. Given that I had been educated as a social scientist, initially my emphasis was almost all on how to bring elements of creative writing to social science writing. In 1996, Art Bochner and I published *Composing Ethnography: Alternative Forms of Qualitative Writing*, which included exemplars of autoethnography, dialogue, poetry, short stories, multi-voiced texts, theatrical performances, and photographic ethnographies. Then in 2001, we had the opportunity to give keynote addresses at the Graduate School of Multicultural Art Education at the University of Art and Design, Helsinki, Finland. It was there that we began to see the possibilities that autoethnography and narrative research had for all the arts. We also began to see the possibilities that the creative arts had for the work we were doing, and to think about integrating autoethnography and narrative with all the creative arts (see Bochner & Ellis, 2003). From that conference and the workshops we gave later in Jyvaskyla, Finland, Art and Marjatta Saarnivaara edited a special issue of *Qualitative Inquiry* called 'The Arts and Narrative Research: Art as Inquiry.' Then Art and I contributed to several edited collections published in Finland that connected narrative, autoethnography, and the creative arts, for example, 'Our Writing Lives: An Introduction to Writing and Research — Personal Views' (2004)."

Nodding her head in acknowledgement, Brydie continues, "I think those sources are incredibly useful for musicians wanting to explore the creative possibilities of this approach. They provide rich and imaginative models that lend themselves well to musical contexts. However, my sense is that there is still a musical dimension that remains open for further investigation in autoethnography; this is a dimension that goes beyond text and moves into the auditory word of musical sounds and relationships. We started this discussion in a workshop at the Queensland Conservatorium Griffith University in 2008, where my colleagues and I explored a range of examples of how autoethnography could be used in a musical context. We listened to beautiful compositions which served as autoethnographic narratives and heard moving autoethnographic accounts of people's musical experiences, relationships and creative processes. We looked at the ways in which autoethnography can allow musicians to explore their own creative practice in culturally insightful ways. Carolyn, your work also provided us with great inspiration," Brydie says smiling. "It was an exciting and evocative discussion that I hope we can continue exploring when you visit Brisbane in 2009."

"I can't wait until then to continue this discussion," Carolyn says, looking at her watch. "Let's start it now. I have the time."

"Good. I'll jot down some notes. We might want to publish something together," Brydie suggests, beaming from ear to ear. Carolyn and Brydie talk; Brydie jots. During the next few months, they pass this manuscript back and forth at least a dozen times.

Making Music Personal

The experiences we have just described are not unique to us. In fact, a wave of self-reflexivity is sweeping across the music profession and is gaining momentum in a number of areas, such as music practice, research and pedagogy. This wave is being fuelled by increasing numbers of musicians wanting to examine, understand and communicate the personal stories behind their creative experiences. In practice-led research, composers and performers are uncovering the ways in which their personal lives and cultural experiences intertwine in the creation and interpretation of musical works (see for example, Mio, 2005; Bartleet, in press). In musicology and ethnomusicology, researchers are sensitively exploring the interconnectedness between their lives and their areas of study, and the relationships they share with those in their fields of inquiry (see for example, Cottrell, 2004; Feld, 1990; Mackinlay, 2008; Wong, 2004). In music learning and instruction, teachers are reflecting on themselves as learners and critiquing the values and relationships they embody in the classroom with their students and subject matter (see for example Conway, 2003; Dunbar-Hall, 2006; Barrett & Stauffer, 2009). Likewise, musicians are reflexively exploring the ways in which they learn and acquire musical skills (see for example, Sudnow, 2001; Bartleet & Hultgren, 2008). With this wave has come an increasing desire for methodological approaches that assist musicians to navigate these personal explorations and that complement the creative and cultural contexts in which they find themselves.

As our opening entry suggests, the autoethnographic approach has emerged in recent years as a compelling possibility. Autoethnography is an autobiographical genre that connects the personal to the cultural, social, and political. Projects in this genre are distinctly characterised by a focus on "intimate involvement, engagement, and embodied participation" in the subject matter one is exploring (Ellis and Bochner, 2006, p. 434; see also Ellis and Bochner, 2000). Usually written in the first-person voice, autoethnographic work appears in a variety of creative formats; for example, short stories, music compositions, poetry, photographic essays, and reflective journals. While some creative art forms, such as performance (e.g. Holman Jones, 1998, 2002a; 2007; Pelias, 2004; Saldaña, 2008) and the visual arts (e.g. Ellis, 2008; Liamputtong & Rumbold, 2008; Saarnivaara & Bochner, 2003; Scott-Hoy & Ellis, 2008) have gained increasing prominence in the field of autoethnography, musical ventures in this area have remained relatively uncharted. This absence seems to be indicative of a widespread lack of musical voices in the burgeoning conversations about the arts in qualitative research more broadly (e.g. see collections by Knowles & Cole; 2008; Leavy, 2009; Liamputtong & Rumbold, 2008; Saarnivaara & Bochner, 2003). Leavy (2009; see also Daykin, 2004) suggests that music, along with dance (but see Cancienne & Bagley, 2008; Cancienne & Snowber, 2003; Ylönen, 2003, among others), still remains one of "the least-explored art forms with respect to arts-based methods, more frequently serving as a subject of social inquiry rather than a tool through which to conduct social research" (p. 106).

However, there seems to be a growing recognition that music can indeed provide "rich and powerful models for perception, conceptualisation and engagement for both listeners and performers," that have the potential to cultivate dynamic "processes and products of qualitative research" across a range of areas, including autoethnography (Bresler, 2009, pp. 8–9; see also Bresler & Stake, 1992; Jenoure, 2002; Leavy, 2009, p. 117). As these comments allude, the synergies between music and autoethnography are promising, ready to be fully realised. This edited volume tries to realise this potential by presenting work in which the relationship between these two areas is explored through the eyes, ears, emotions, and stories of music and autoethnography practitioners. Our goal is to write in such a way that a musician's musical identity can be fulfilled through research rather than restrained by it (see Jenoure, 2002, p. 76; Leavy, 2009, p. 110), and to think and feel in such a way that autoethnographers open themselves up to the possibilities offered by music.

Music and Autoethnography: A Meeting of Two Worlds

As we have discovered, music and autoethnography have much in common. At the heart of both is the desire to communicate engaging and personal tales through music and words, which inspire audiences to react, reflect, and, in many cases, reciprocate. In terms of process, many musicians spend their daily lives moving through cycles of creation, reflection, refinement and performance. These cycles often occur in communion with a wide range of sources that inspire and inform the creation of the work. Such processes involve complex layers of consciousness, meaning, and significance that vary from musician to musician, and autoethnographer to autoethnographer. These processes cannot be reduced to a simple formula. What these processes have in common, however, is a "unique ability to convey complexity and ambiguity" (Bresler, 2008, p. 229). As Ellis and Bochner write, autoethnographers

> look through an ethnographic wide angle lens, focusing outward on social and cultural aspects of their personal experiences; then, they look inward, exposing a vulnerable self that is moved by and may move through, refract, and resist cultural interpretations. As they zoom backward and forward, inward and outward, distinctions between the personal and cultural become blurred, sometimes beyond distinct recognition. (2004, p. 38)

Likewise, musicians move back and forth between the different layers of their musical consciousness in the interpretation and creation of musical works. In this creative process they draw on a wide range of musical experiences, memories and reference points, so that distinctions between the personal and musical become entangled.

As such, these processes are somewhat "unruly, dangerous, vulnerable, rebellious, and creative", and are certainly not under the control of reason and instrumental logic (Ellis & Bochner, 2006, p. 431; see also Holman Jones, 2002b). The resulting creations, whether they are presented in written text, scores, performances or recordings, are full of unique "colloquialisms, reverberations ... and emotional expressiveness" (Gergen & Gergen, 2002, p. 14). These personal creations also are representative of something bigger than themselves, and show a dynamic relationship between the self and their social and cultural context of creation (see Reed-Danahay, 1997, p. 3).

Musicians and autoethnographers grapple with the challenges of communicating and writing about their lived experiences. As these experiences are always dynamic, relational, embodied and highly subjective, they are difficult to express, particularly from a musical perspective where words are not the primary form of communication (see Cobussen, 2007, p. 23). However, as our opening section suggests, autoethnographic methods offer a way of working through this complex situation. Autoethnography frees musicians from writing dry descriptions or reports of musical experiences. Rather, this approach encourages them to convey the *meanings* of vibrant musical experiences evocatively. The focus becomes telling a tale that readers can enter and feel a part of (see Ellis, 2004, p. 116). The aim becomes to inspire others to critically reflect upon their own music experiences in relation to the autoethnographic tale being told (see Spry, 2001, p. 710). The product of the process thus becomes "something to be used; not a conclusion but a turn in a conversation; not a closed statement but an open question; not a way of declaring 'this is how it is' but a means of inviting others to consider what I (or they) could become" (Bochner & Ellis, 2003, p. 507).

Viewing their lives autoethnographically, musicians and other creative artists are concerned about what their work "awaken[s] or evoke[s] in the spectator, how it creates[s] meanings, how it [can] heal, and what it [can] teach, incite, inspire, or provoke" (Bochner & Ellis, 2003, p. 507). This leads them to ask: "To what uses could art [or music] be put? What new conversations would open for the viewer [or hearer]? What hidden possibilities would be unveiled? What dormant desires would be awakened?" As Bochner and Ellis (2003) suggest,

> These sorts of questions do not fit snugly within the scope of traditional canons of research that emphasize the delivery of a research product that is passively received by a reader, viewer, or hearer. To use art [or music] as a mode of narrative [and autoethnographic] inquiry [is] to move toward a new research paradigm in which ideas become as important as forms, the viewer's perceptions as important as the artist's intentions, the language and emotions of art [or music] as important as its aesthetic qualities. (p. 507)

The process becomes somewhat improvisational in nature, involving an unexpected interplay between a script and exploration, between tradition and innovation (see Bresler, 2009, p. 18).

A further parallel between music and autoethnography can be found in relation to the body. Just as the work of a musician is inherently corporeal, an autoethnographer also draws on and works from embodied knowledge and experiences. This focus frees the voice and body from the conventional and restrictive mind–body split that continues to pervade traditional academic writing. Within an autoethnographic paradigm, the corporeal knowledge of a musician's body and the physical act of music-making can be at the centre of the autoethnographic enquiry and used to explore both the creative process and the musical output (see Borgdorff, 2007, p. 5). This approach also acknowledges the deeply performative nature of autoethnography and music combined. Through performance, the meanings and stories behind the music autoethnographies gain further significance, as the audience is challenged to actively engage with them on a number of different levels, from the intellectual to the embodied to the emotional (see Holman Jones, 2002a, p. 51).

As musicians and autoethnographers explore their sense of selves, they also face the potential darkness of vulnerability that comes with revealing their stories, lives, and creative decisions. This is no small challenge, particularly for musicians who have been so accustomed to keeping such personal characteristics and problems hidden from public view. As Ritterman (2004, n. p.) explains: "for many musicians, the thought of subjecting one's own practice to deep critical reflection which is then publicly shared, is disconcerting." Like autoethnographers, musicians grapple with exposing their secrets to the world, knowing that once they are out there these secrets cannot be taken back. Moreover, they fear that consciously monitoring what they are doing can lead to a loss of inspiration and freedom (see Cobussen,

2007, p. 21). We suggest that although revealing the personal and vulnerable parts of their creative lives may feel risky to musicians, it also can be highly inspiring and rewarding, especially when the autoethnography is itself lyrical and musical.

〜

Making Autoethnography Sing

"We've talked and written notes about the ways that music can benefit from autoethnography," Carolyn says to Brydie. She takes a drink of coffee and grimaces because it has long ago gotten cold and bitter. She chooses her words carefully. "But I want us not to neglect the ways that autoethnography can benefit from music." Brydie nods in agreement, curious to see what Carolyn will say. "Music has been viewed as a mode for qualitative research," Carolyn continues. "Music also has been seen as a cultural text to be analysed."

Brydie replies, "I can think of several examples of both of those. There's Daykin (2008) who writes about the expressive qualities of music and how these can be used in an arts-based qualitative research project. Also, Leavy (2009) who showcases how arts-based researchers are presenting creative ideas, experiences and information in new and innovative ways" (see also Jenoure, 2002; Eisner, 2002). Then there's Holman Jones's (2002a, 2002b, 2007) extensive work on torch singing as a complex social phenomenon."

"And there's more," Carolyn says. "We need to integrate method and music, and write lyrical, personal, and cultural texts, blending social science and creative arts."

Brydie nods. "I can envision an edited book where we would include stories by and/or about musicians and music. Maybe you and I could do it together."

"What a wonderful idea," Carolyn responds. "Our goal would be for readers to hear as well as see the words, to feel as well as recognise them, to engage tests written from the heart, mind, and body about hearts, minds, and bodies ..."

"And to engage in the texts with *their* hearts, minds, and bodies," Brydie interrupts, getting very excited about the conversation.

"Exactly. We want readers to enter into the melodies, as well as the plot lines," Carolyn continues, now smiling, her voice growing louder and more excited, "to feel the 'riffs' that punctuate each idea (Jenoure, 2002, p. 78), hear the harmony of voices and join their voice with the voices in the text, feel the spaces, take the breaths, interpret the silences, respond, applaud, laugh, cry, find themselves, push away, and then come back again. We want our texts to have rhythm, to change tempo, have dissonance, be loud and then soft, change tones, fluidly flow through the reader." Carolyn stands now, both hands in the air, like a conductor cueing the different sections of an ensemble.

"The texts we include would have inventive forms and structures that push the creative boundaries of our disciplines," Brydie responds, scribbling notes madly as she talks, her eyes following Carolyn as she walks around the table. "We also want them to be spontaneous and improvise on a theme. They would capture the excitement, complexity, vitality, and wonder of music-making. They also might have cadences, and moments where they pause so that our musical ideas can resonate in the minds and hearts of our listeners."

"We would want the readers of this volume to *listen* closely and *hear* the music in the stories that are shared," Carolyn says, now standing on her chair, moving her hands and body as though she is conducting a large symphony orchestra. Suddenly she looks around, realises people are watching, and slowly sits back down. Brydie laughs.

"By embracing this musical fluidity in our autoethnographic work, we can also make our readers and listeners sensitive to the fluidity of the personal and cultural experiences explored" (see Bresler, 2005, p. 169), Brydie answers. Both suddenly burst into giggles as they realise Carolyn has become the musician and Brydie the social scientist.

Carolyn nods her head, saying, "And the way we accomplish this is to bring autoethnography to music."

"And music to autoethnography," Brydie reminds. "Just like a musical call-and-response!"

"Yes. Exactly! A call and response!" laughs Carolyn, imaging choruses of horns and trumpets answering one another's calls. "We want to do more than tell about our performances, data, and experience. We want to write in a literary way ..."

"That tries to show what happened to us as musicians — professionally ..."

"And personally," adds Carolyn. After pausing for a moment, she then suggests, "We want the feelings and personal aspects of music to become central in our writing and performances."

"Yes!" Brydie interjects. "Those feelings that you're talking about have been absent from traditional writing about music for far too long. As a conductor, I want people to know what goes on behind the baton. I want them to understand and appreciate the personal journey that I have taken to be able to stand on the podium and deliver the performances that I do. I don't want to cloak them in silence; these musical stories need to be told!"

Seeing the passion in Brydie's eyes, Carolyn shouts, "Now you're cookin'!"

"By using music as a framework for our autoethnographies," Brydie adds, "we can go straight to the senses and emotions of the listener. As musicians, we bring our bodies, feelings, and intuition to our work, and this can evoke a powerful relationship with those who we're performing alongside, and those who are listening to us ..."

Carolyn adds, "This is how music and method come together in their goals: Autoethnography with its roots in systematic ethnographic methods reaches for feeling, evocation, and embodiment in its narrative presentation, and what it asks of the reader. Music provides an exemplar for how to do that. Music has both feet in the creative arts, in feeling and evocation. As it reaches now for a way to explore itself and add the personal to the professional, it turns to autoethnography to pave the way. Together the two provide a harmonious serenade."

"Or even a counterpoint," says Brydie, as they rise to leave.

"What does that mean?" asks Carolyn, as she picks up her heavy stack of papers and books.

"In music, counterpoint means that while individual voices may be different in rhythm and contour, they are interconnected when played together to form harmony."

"Yeah, that's it. Let's call it 'harmonious' counterpoint just to make sure everyone gets it," Carolyn suggests.

As they leave the coffee shop, Carolyn says, "I don't think of myself as musical though I played the clarinet in high school and I've been known to carry a tune. But really what I like to do is dance. Just a few bars of a Motown song and I'm on my feet."

"Really?" says Brydie. "I didn't know that about you. Do you know I was a serious ballet dancer for many years? I stopped dancing so that I could focus on my musical career, but when I'm on the podium conducting and moving to the music it feels as though I'm a dancer again!"

As they hurry down the street, they feel as if they could break into song and dance, like characters in *Mamma Mia* or the final dance scene in *Slum Dog Millionaire*, but they restrain themselves — for now anyway.

Autoethnography in Harmonious Counterpoint

Many of the chapters in this collection provide illuminating stories and analyses of how their authors have grappled with and moved through joys and challenges to come to new understandings of themselves as musicians, and ultimately as human beings. The chapters showcase a diverse and imaginative range of examples that explore how autoethnography can expand musicians' awareness of their practice, and how musicians can expand the creative possibilities of autoethnography.

In the first section, "Composing and Improvising", the authors explore how the creative processes of songwriting and improvisation can be used as powerful autoethnographic tools to tell stories and reflect on significant life experiences. David Carless's and Kitrina Douglas's chapter examines the ways in which songwriting provides insights and understandings about human experience, both in terms of their own lives and the lives of others. They explore the songwriting process through a collaborative autoethnographic story about the writing of one particular song. Using narrative theory and comparing their stories to those of other songwriters, they reflect on how songwriting contributes to knowledge. Karen Scott-Hoy's chapter continues the songwriting theme, and tells the story behind an original song, "Beautiful Here", composed by her teenage son, his band, and her in an effort to understand death and to celebrate life. This is also a story about mothers and sons, and offers insights into the important role of music in young people's lives, and the ways in which they write, rehearse and perform their music. This piece shows how music, like autoethnographic writing, is a medium for heartfelt reflection and learning, a way of understanding ourselves and our world and of communicating that understanding to others.

Following the interconnected themes of family relationships and songwriting, Chris Patti's chapter examines four songs he wrote over the past decade in response to the death of his father. He illustrates the ways in which autoethnographic songwriting allows him to explore the fragmented, subjective, and complex memories of his father. The progression of songs shows how his perspectives on life, death, and remembering have grown out of singing and writing about his dad. Continuing this thread of looking at the ways in which musical expression and autoethnography intersect with issues of personal identity, relationships and life experiences, Peter Knight's chapter takes the discussion into the realm of improvisation. He gives a personal account of the ways in which learning to improvise freed him from the dissatisfactions of his early musical experiences and allowed him to find an "authentic" voice as a musician. Through a fragmented and episodic approach to autoethnographic writing, Knight reflects on how this journey into improvisation essentially facilitated his journey into a career in music.

The second section, "Interpreting and Performing", highlights the diversity of experiences that musicians face in relation to singing, interpreting musical works, acquiring musical skills and losing their ability to play music through injury. Stacy Holman Jones's chapter draws on Roland Barthes's *A Lover's Discourse* as both inspiration and method for her assembly of a lamenter's discourse on loss, love, and song. The stories she includes are constructed in conversation with Barthes's lover and reflect on love, language and writing, and the sad songs she and her son can't stop singing. Stephen Emmerson's chapter looks at similar themes of love, loss and songs, through a discussion of his interpretation of Schubert's *Winterreise*, and the opening bars of the song "Frühlingstraum". He reflects on the potential of the song's opening phrase to convey a psychological state so much more complex than its simple materials might initially suggest. Emmerson also considers how to balance the song's apparent cheerful simplicity with its potential for irony and nostalgia that grows from awareness of its context.

Catherine Grant's chapter traces loss of a different kind. Contextualising her own experiences alongside the stories of other musicians, she explores the social, emotional, and psychological impact of her own performance-related injury. Using a layered approach, her chapter illuminates the complex and intimate connection musicians feel towards their instruments and the far-reaching impact that an injury can have on this relationship. Also focusing on the central role of the body in a musician's practice and identity, Chris McRae's chapter uncovers the changes that happened to his body as he shifted from playing the trumpet to learning the bass guitar. He looks at the ways in which these changes are specific to his experience, but also layered with cultural and social meanings. He considers how technologies, such as musical instruments, are connected to our experiences of the world at an embodied level, and how these connections shape the ways in which we know and live in the world.

The chapters in the third section, "Learning and Teaching", offer autoethnographic accounts of studying music in three diverse cultural and pedagogical settings, including Bali, the South of China and a Western conservatoire context. Peter Dunbar-Hall's chapter reflects on a decade of studying Balinese gamelan music with Balinese teachers in Bali. He explores the ways in which his research into Balinese music then stimulated further research into his own learning processes and a refashioning of his ideas on music as a pedagogue. His chapter reflects on how this study affected his professional role as a university teacher in both ideological and practical ways. Following the theme of learning within and across cultures, Wang Yuyan's chapter also tells an autoethnographic tale of musical learning in an Asian context. She reflects on the ways in which social, cultural and family pressures can influence a musician's learning opportunities in China. Having had major hurdles to overcome in order to be allowed to study music for most of her life as a young Chinese woman, she reflects on significant situations and people who helped her on her journey to the renowned Shanghai Conservatory of Music. Also speaking from a Conservatoire setting, but in this case in a Western context, Margaret Schindler's chapter traces her personal and professional journey as a singer, in order to shed light on her current practice, values and beliefs as a performer/teacher at the Queensland Conservatorium. She draws comparisons between her studio teaching practice and autoethnography, and looks at the ways in which both approaches value the uniqueness of one's personal story, encourage enduring musical and pedagogical relationships, as well as ongoing learning.

In the fourth section, "Researching Identity and Cross-Cultural Contexts", the authors use autoethnography as a means to describe and reflect on their experiences undertaking research in a range of musical and cultural contexts. Huib Schippers' chapter reflects on a life-changing taxi ride out of Hanoi that triggers a series of experiences and reflections that lead to a world-wide project dedicated to saving the world's musics. He tells the story of the decline of the *ca tru* song form, and uses this as an example to reflect on issues relating to the "ecology" of musical diversity, and how cultures can work consciously and effectively for and against the survival of specific forms of music. Continuing with a number of the principles and sentiments of this "applied" approach to cross-cultural research, Katelyn Barney's and Lexine Soloman's chapter gives an autoethnographic account of their collaboration as non-Indigenous and Indigenous music researchers. In their chapter they "look into the trochus shell" — a metaphor Soloman often uses from her Torres Strait region — to think about the joys, challenges and oftentimes complicated ethics of music research collaborations such as their own. Elizabeth Mackinlay's chapter then continues the discussion of the relationships and ethics associated with working with Indigenous Australian people in music research. In particular, she tells a moving and personal story of how her research as an ethnomusicologist in the remote Indigenous community of Borroloola has "died". Her chapter gives a layered account of how she has experienced this "death", grieved over the passing of significant people in this community, and ultimately made peace with her "loss" as a researcher.

Looking at issues of researcher identity and musical relationships, Jodie Taylor's chapter then examines musical and musicological performances of queer identity and queer life-worlds. She reflects upon her intimate relationship with musical practice and scholarship, exploring how and why she has used music to express her "non-normative gender" and sexual identity. Continuing the dialogue about issues of identity and its performance through musical autoethnographies, Colin Webber's chapter reflects on the ways in which his own heightened autistic traits affect his musical practice and autoethnographic research in composition and the collaborative arts. His chapter highlights three aspects that he has found himself confronting in his autoethnographic research, which resonate strongly with many of the chapters in this volume, labelling them the triple-headed dragon of "obsession, depression, and defence".

This arrangement of chapters offers one of many possible ways to "listen" and engage with the musical autoethnographies shared in this volume. The chapters stand independently as musical lines within themselves, but also are interconnected in a harmonious counterpoint. While they share many common themes and contours, they also provide contrasting rhythms and textures. Combined they produce an intricate and illuminating story that shows how music can inspire autoethnography to sing, and how autoethnography can inspire musicians to reflect on the personal.

Acknowledgments

Carolyn wishes to thank Arthur Bochner, with whom some of the ideas in this chapter were co-constructed in other published pieces, as well as the many creative and musically talented students and colleagues who have energised her over the years. Brydie wishes to thank all the musicians and research colleagues she has worked with over the years, who have provided her with inspiration for this chapter. Carolyn and Brydie both wish to thank Arthur Bochner for his advice and assistance in the editing of this chapter.

References

Barrett, M., & Stauffer, S. (Eds.). (2009). *Narrative inquiry in music education: Troubling certainty*. Dordrecht, The Netherlands: Springer.

Bartleet, B. L. (in press). Behind the baton: Exploring autoethnographic writing in a musical context. *Journal of Contemporary Ethnography*.

Bartleet, B. L., & Hultgren, R. (2008). Sharing the podium: Peer learning in professional conducting. *British Journal of Music Education, 25*(2), 193–206.

Bochner, A., & Ellis, C. (2003). An introduction to the arts and narrative research: Art as inquiry. *Qualitative Inquiry, 9*, 506–514.

Bochner, A., & Ellis, C. (2004). Our writing lives: An introduction to writing and research — Personal views. In M. Saarnivaara, E. Vainikkala & M. van Delft (Eds.), *Writing and research — Personal views* (pp. 7–19). Jyvaskyla, Finland: Publications of the Research Centre for Contemporary Culture, University of Jyvaskyla.

Borgdorff, H. (2007). The debate on research in the arts. *Dutch Journal of Music Theory: Special Issue: Practice-based Research in Music, 12*(1), 1–17.

Bresler, L. (2005). What musicianship can teach educational research. *Music Education Research, 7*(2), 169–183.

Bresler, L. (Ed). (2007). *International handbook of research in arts education.* Dordrecht, The Netherlands: Springer.

Bresler, L. (2008). The music lesson. In J. G. Knowles and A. L. Cole (Eds.), *Handbook of the arts in qualitative research* (pp. 225–237). Thousand Oaks: Sage.

Bresler, L. (2009). Research education shaped by musical sensibilities. *British Journal of Music Education, 26*(1), 7–25.

Bresler, L., & Stake, R. E. (1992). Qualitative research methodology in music education. In R. Colwell (Ed.), *Handbook of music teaching and learning* (pp. 75–90). New York: Schirmer Books.

Cancienne, M. B., & Bagley, C. (2008). Dance as method: The process and product of movement in educational research. In P. Liamputtong & J. Rumbold (Eds.), *Knowing differently: Arts-based and collaborative research methods* (pp. 169–187). New York: Nova Science Publishers, Inc.

Cancienne, M. B. & Snowber, C. (2003). Writing rhythm: Movement as method. *Qualitative Inquiry, 9*(2), 237–253.

Cobussen, M. (2007). The Trojan horse: Epistemological explorations concerning practice-based research. *Dutch Journal of Music Theory: Special Issue: Practice-based Research in Music, 12*(1), 18–33.

Conway, C. M. (2003). Story and narrative inquiry in music teacher education research. *Journal of Music Teacher Education 12*(2), 29–39.

Cottrell, S. (2004). *Professional music-making in London: Ethnography and experience.* Aldershot, England: Ashgate.

Davis, C., & Ellis, C. (2008). Autoethnographic introspective in ethnographic fiction: A method of inquiry. In P. Liamputtong & J. Rumbold (Eds.), *Knowing differently: Arts-based and collaborative research methods* (pp. 99–117). New York: Nova Science.

Daykin, N. (2004). The role of music in an art-based qualitative inquiry. *International Journal of Qualitative Methods, 3*(2). Retrieved 1 June 2009, from http://www.openj-gate.org/Browse/Articlelist.aspx?Journal_ID=104454.

Daykin, N. (2008). Knowing through music: Implications for research. In P. Liamputtong & J. Rumbold (Eds.), *Knowing differently: Arts-based and collaborative research methods* (pp. 229–243). New York: Nova Science.

Dunbar-Hall, P. (2006). An investigation of strategies developed by music learners in a cross-cultural setting. *Research Studies in Music Education, 26*, 63–70.

Eisner, E. W. (2002). *The arts and the creation of mind.* New Haven: Yale University Press.

Ellis, C. (1993). 'There are survivors': Telling a story of sudden death. *The Sociological Quarterly, 34*(4), 711–730.

Ellis, C. (1995a). *Final negotiations: A story of love, loss, and chronic illness*. Philadelphia: Temple University Press.

Ellis, C. (1995b). Speaking of dying: An ethnographic short story. *Symbolic Interaction*, *18*(1), 73–81.

Ellis, C. (1998). I hate my voice: Coming to terms with bodily stigmas. *The Sociological Quarterly*, *39*(4), 517–537.

Ellis, C. (2002). Shattered lives: Making sense of September 11th and its aftermath. *Journal of Contemporary Ethnography*, *31*(4), 375–410.

Ellis, C. (2004). *The ethnographic I: A methodological novel about autoethnography*. Walnut Creek, CA: AltaMira Press.

Ellis, C. (2007) Stray cats and Katrina's displaced: Dealing with society's expendables. *Cultural Studies-Critical Methodologies*, *7*(1), 188–201.

Ellis, C. (2008). Homeless in New York City. *Visualizing Social Science: Photos by Rachel Tanur*. New York: Social Science Research Council.

Ellis, C., & Bochner, A. (Eds.). (1996). *Composing ethnography: Alternative forms of qualitative writing*. Walnut Creek, CA: AltaMira Press.

Ellis, C., & Bochner, A. (2000). Autoethnography, personal narrative, reflexivity: Researcher as subject. In N. Denzin & Y. Lincoln (Eds.), *The handbook of qualitative research* (2nd ed.) (pp. 733–768). Thousand Oaks: Sage.

Ellis, C. & Bochner, A. (2006). Analyzing analytic autoethnography: An autopsy. *Journal of Contemporary Ethnography*, *35*(4), 429–449.

Feld, S. (1990). *Sound and sentiment: Birds, weeping, poetics, and song in Kaluli expression* (2nd ed.). Philadelphia: University of Pennsylvania Press.

Gergen, M. M., & Gergen, K. J. (2002). Ethnographic representation as relationship. In C. Ellis & A. Bochner (Eds.), *Ethnographically speaking: Autoethnography, literature, and aesthetics* (pp. 11–33). Walnut Creek, CA: AltaMira Press.

Holman Jones, S. (1998). *Kaleidoscope notes: Writing women's music and organizational culture*. Walnut Creek: AltaMira Press.

Holman Jones, S. (2002a). The way we were, are, and might be: Torch singing as autoethnography. In C. Ellis & A. Bochner (Eds.), *Ethnographically speaking: Autoethnography, literature, and aesthetics* (pp. 44–56). Walnut Creek, CA: AltaMira Press.

Holman Jones (2002b). Emotional space: Performing the resistive possibilities of torch singing. *Qualitative Inquiry*, *8*(6), 738–759.

Holman Jones, S. (2007). *Torch singing: Performing resistance and desire from Billie Holiday to Edith Piaf*. Walnut Creet, CA: Altamira Press.

Jenoure, T. (2002). Sweeping the temple: A performance collage. In C. Bagley & M. B. Cancienne (Eds.), *Dancing the data* (pp. 73–89). New York: Peter Lang.

Kisliuk, M. (1997). (Un)doing fieldwork: Sharing songs, sharing lives. In T. J. Cooley & G. F. Barz (Eds.), *Shadows in the field: New perspectives for fieldwork in ethnomusicology* (pp. 23–44). New York: Oxford University Press.

Knowles, J. G., & Cole, A. L. (2008). *Handbook of the arts in qualitative research: Perspectives, methodologies, examples, and issues*. Thousand Oaks: Sage.

Leavy, P. (2009). *Method meets art: Arts-based research practice*. New York: The Guilford Press.

Liamputtong, P., & Rumbold, J. (Eds). (2008). *Knowing differently: Arts-based and collaborative research methods*. New York: Nova Science.

Mackinlay, E. (2008). Making space as white music educators for Indigenous Australian holders of song, dance and performance knowledge: The centrality of relationship as pedagogy. *Australian Journal of Music Education*, *1*, 2–6.

Mackinlay, E., & Bartleet, B. L. (2008a). Reflections on teaching and learning feminism in musicological classrooms: An autoethnographic conversation. *Outskirts: Feminisms along the edge*, 18, available at http://www.chloe.uwa.edu.au/outskirts

Mackinlay, E. & Bartleet, B. L. (2008b). Friendship as research: Exploring sisterhood and personal relationships as the foundations of musicological and ethnographic field-work. *29th National Conference of the Musicological Society of Australia*, Melbourne.

Mackinlay, E., Bartleet, B. L., Barney, K., & Monk, S. (2007). Finding your voice: Exploring the process of writing and research in musicology. *Combined Conference of the Australian and New Zealand Musicological Societies*, Brisbane.

Mio, V. (2005). *Concerto in two paradigms: An autoethnography in words and music.* University of Toronto (Canada).

Pelias, R. (2004). *A methodology of the heart: Evoking academic and daily life.* Walnut Creek, CA: AltaMira Press

Reed-Danahay, D. (1997). *Auto/ethnography: Rewriting the self and the social.* Oxford: Berg.

Ritterman, J. (2004). Knowing more than we can tell: Artistic practice and integrity [Public Lecture]. Queensland Conservatorium Griffith University.

Saarnivaara, M., & Bochner, A. (Eds.) (2003). The arts and narrative research: Art as inquiry. *Qualitative Inquiry*, 9(4, Spec. Ed.).

Saldaña, J. (2004). *One-man autoethnodrama, second chair.* Arizona State University.

Scott-Hoy, K., & Ellis, C. (2008). Wording pictures: Discovering heartful autoethnography. In A. Cole & J. G. Knowles (Eds.), *The handbook of the arts in qualitative social science research* (pp. 127–140). London: Sage.

Spry, T. (2001). Performing autoethnography: An embodied methodological praxis. *Journal of Contemporary Ethnography*, 7(6), 706–732.

Sudnow, D. (2001). *Ways of the hand: A rewritten account.* Cambridge, MA: MIT Press.

Wong, D. (2004). *Speak it louder: Asian Americans making music.* New York: Routledge.

Ylönen, M. E. (2003). Bodily flashes of dancing women: Dance as a method of inquiry. *Qualitative Inquiry*, 9(4), 554–568.

Section One
Composing and Improvising

Chapter 1

Songwriting and the Creation of Knowledge

David Carless and Kitrina Douglas

According to Elliot Eisner (2008), "not only does knowledge come in different forms, the forms of its creation differ" (p. 5). Through our personal lives as well as through our research, we have experienced some of the ways in which knowledge and understanding can be created through varied and diverse arts-informed writing practices such as fiction (Carless & Sparkes, 2008; Douglas & Carless, 2008a, 2009), poetry (Sparkes & Douglas, 2007; Carless & Douglas, in press) and autoethnography (Douglas, 2009; Carless, in press). Songwriting has been a cornerstone of our work: it has provided us with insights and understandings regarding human experience, both in terms of our own lives and the lives of others (see Douglas & Carless, 2005, 2008b). We therefore consider songwriting a productive and useful way of "coming to know" because its processes offer an alternative means of knowledge creation which are distinct from the more typical analytic and interpretive approaches of the social sciences.

Lori Neilsen (2008) writes that, "The challenge in arts-informed inquiry has always been epistemological: How do we come to know and how do we express that knowing?" (p. 385). It is to this challenge that we address this chapter. We invite you to join us in a "collaborative autoethnography", which begins with a co-constructed story about the day David wrote a song titled *A Little Rain*. Later, through considering the story in relation to narrative theory and the accounts of other songwriters, we identify some more general processes through which songwriting can contribute to the acquisition or creation of alternative kinds of knowledge. We hope that by focusing on a specific example of the creative process, we might shed some new light on how, through artistic processes, we can come to know.

A Collaborative Remembering

David: I have been writing songs for around 20 years. I wrote my first song before I began undergraduate study and long before I wrote my first research paper. Throughout this time, my life has resonated to a line from a Bruce Springsteen song which I remember from my teens, where the singer describes learning more from a rock and roll song than he learnt in school. For me too, songs have long been a way through which I have learned about my self, my experiences, my relationships, the world. I have been aware for some time that songs bring some kind of companionable knowledge and hopeful understanding into my life. Looking back, I see that writing songs has allowed me to create personal stories which map my life and fit my experience. Through writing songs I have been able to create, in Patrick Lewis's (2006) terms, "stories to live by".

I wrote the song *A Little Rain* on the morning of the May 16, 2004, while I was in Cornwall with my close friend and research colleague, Kitrina. We had scheduled a few days to work on a collaborative project, surf, walk, and play some music.

Kitrina: We were staying in a rented holiday house overlooking a tiny fishing village on the north coast. This particular morning was spectacularly bright, the sky huge and too blue to be real. Yet I was sad because David had announced it was time for him to leave for home. I wanted him to come for a surf, to stay another day, but he seemed uneasy, unreachable and edgy. I worried that I had done something wrong and was feeling a little upset with myself. I sensed a distance between us when my thoughts were interrupted by a telephone call: my uncle had died, in hospital, the previous day. I had visited him on the way down to Cornwall but didn't know or think that death was to be an imminent visitor and that was to be my last encounter with him, the last time I would touch his hands, see his face, share and make memories with him.

My uncle was a bear, I would disappear in his hugs, his hands shaped iron and wood, renovated houses, planted gardens. And now, he was no more ... gone ... like his wife, my aunt, my father's sister, who slipped from his powerful hands two years ago. They fed us with love the Christmas my father died. They attended my graduation. After my aunt died, he came away with me on trips, excitedly buying a wash bag for the night ferry trip to France, devouring white chocolate cheesecake in fancy coffee shops and shopping for jazz CDs. My father said "He kept his rugby boots, hoping for a son", but children never came. I wondered — was the love of ten nephews and nieces enough to fill that gap?

The news of my uncle's death brought a heaviness, which sunk my enthusiasm, a sadness that slowly enmeshed my body. I was frustrated that other relatives hadn't told me what was happening. But these were clouds raining in my head, not a conversation shared. I'd taken the call in the kitchen, then came into the sitting room to tell David.

David: I was sitting on the light-blue sofa and had been playing some songs on her guitar when Kitrina came in and told me the news. Although I didn't really know him, I had met Kitrina's uncle when he came to one of my gigs. After the show we chatted a little and he bought both my CDs. He told me that he had really enjoyed the music. It always means so much to me when I learn that a particular person likes my songs. It feels like a point of connection between us in some way, even if we have never met. I suppose I feel that person has come to know me a little through listening to my songs.

As Kitrina shared the news of his death I remember feeling, as my grandmother might have said, inadequate. I felt like I wanted to say something — something to help her with her sadness, something wise, something hopeful, something to make amends. But I couldn't think of anything to say. At those moments when I can't think of anything worth saying, I stay quiet. I don't remember whether or not I gave Kitrina a hug; I hope I did. If I didn't, I should have.

Kitrina: "Shall I go? Do you want to be alone?" David asked. What a stupid question! If I didn't want him to go earlier, I certainly didn't want him to go now! What was I supposed to "do" on my own? I wanted him to stay, but I didn't know what we were going to do either — a surf seemed inappropriate now too. I had nothing to say — so who goes first in these situations? How does a friend reach in? How can anyone know how to respond? "How close were you?" "Did he die in peace?" "Was it unexpected?" These, for me, would have been worse questions than the "Shall I leave you alone?" one. I probably wouldn't have been able to answer the "Are you OK?", "How do you feel?" questions either. I hated the barrage of questions I was asked by well-meaning people when Daddy died: "Was he ill?" "Had he heart problems?" "How old was he?" "How did it happen?" But David didn't appear to focus on my uncle. There was a chasm between us, now just deeper.

David: I sat there with the guitar, feeling sad for Kitrina but not knowing what to say or do. Somehow, it felt good at this time to just hold the guitar. From thousands of hours of playing, the feel of an acoustic guitar against my body has become a familiar and comforting one.

Kitrina's guitar is a beautiful instrument, handmade in Devon by people who — through this guitar — have become friends. A luthier named Simon designed this model, and its graceful curves are testament to his aesthetic sensibilities. Kitrina and I found it in a store in London and selected it in preference to an array of fine instruments from around the world. It has a deep golden spruce top and rich, heavily grained, honey-coloured rosewood sides and back. It was designed and made with love, and is lacquered and polished like a piece of jewellery. It is a unique instrument, one of a kind.

Kitrina: It was difficult to know what to do next, difficult for David to carry on singing as he had before. What does one sing or play when a friend tells you someone close has just died? Was it inappropriate to play or finger even a few chords? He became still, the guitar taking the weight of his body as he sat, his hands poised from their former business, a small furrow appearing in his brow — the way it always does when he shows concern — an acknowledgement of the situation, the passing of a life … The sun drew me to the balcony where my thoughts became lost in the vibrant colours of my pastels, something my hands could do, creating yellow flowers, feeling the chalk crumble as I pressed the pastels into the paper, feeling the warm sunshine, coffee my companion in thought.

David: What song could I possibly sing at a time like this? What lyrics would be appropriate? What song did I know — mine or another's — that I could pick which would not be insensitive or inappropriate at the moment of a family member's death? I couldn't think of one. Instead, I picked at some chords, feeling the wood reverberate against my body, the ebony fingerboard and silvered frets beneath my fingers, the clean bronze strings against my fingertips. Perhaps I began to lose myself in the tones coming from the instrument. Perhaps I became immersed in the notes and progressions that emerged without, it seemed to me, any conscious application on my part. These notes were not a part of some master plan — either mine or someone else's. They did not come from any discernable place and neither did they finish in any particular place. They had nowhere in particular to go. They were on no timetable and they held no obligations. The notes just were. They were there for the now and then they were gone. But the now was enough.

Kitrina: A short riff of about seven single notes followed by a sharp plucked chord echoed from inside; this sequence became a friend too, it came to me over and over, being affirmed and more obvious each time through. It was different to anything I had heard David play before. Because I know his music so well I can tell what song he is about to play from the first few chords, but this wasn't a chord progression I had heard. Initially it was only a background sound, it wasn't exactly music, but quite quickly there was a recognisable element which was being repeated while I became lost somewhere in my colours.

David: At some point during this process — it could have been after two minutes, it could have been after an hour — some words began to come. I was not aware of thinking the words, I was not aware of planning the words. I didn't even recognise the words as being my own, as being depictions or representations of my own thoughts. During our conversation earlier I could think of no words to say to Kitrina at this time, a time when she seemed sad, a time of loss. I could think of no pre-existing song lyrics that seemed appropriate. Yet I knew I wanted to say something, I wanted to speak, to communicate ... to not leave Kitrina alone at this moment. And yet, despite not knowing what to say, here were words:

> A little rain is gonna come your way
> A little dark ends every day
> A little cold might chill your bones
> A seed of doubt when you're on your own ...

Words were coming from my mouth along with a melody, a rhythm, and a sequence of chords and notes from the guitar. Yes, it was me who was playing the instrument. Yes, I knew the chord shapes: a variant on a G major, some kind of D, then a C major on the chorus. The dropped-D tuning is an acoustic guitarist's technique that I also knew and had used before. But somehow what was coming out of the guitar — through, perhaps, a combination of the instrument, what I knew about technique, and the energies in the moment — seemed to provide a platform which facilitated access to things I didn't know I knew, thoughts I didn't know I thought. The words came — not through deliberate thought — they just came:

> When the good things slip away
> What is there to do, what is there to say?
> Without a little love, a little faith
> A little joy and a bunch of grace
> A little smile, a simple song
> A floating raft to rest upon

I don't remember the specifics of *A Little Rain*, but usually when I'm writing a song words seem to just arrive — some stick and I sing them again, and some are lost. Some I like and write down, some I cross out, and some never even get written down. Words were coming from my body, for sure, but it felt like I merely chose which to keep and which to discard. The ones I kept, it felt to me, fitted the song, the music, the rhythm, and the story in the song. A story which, as always, was not one I had planned, but one which was seemingly emerging and taking form before me — as much of a surprise to me as to anyone looking on.

Kitrina: Every now and then sounds would penetrate my thoughts, then lyrics were added, created, appearing, or sometimes disappearing, were they not needed any more. Some lines wafting out put a smile on my face ... a little rain was going to come my way (and that was repeated a lot), later rafts appeared (which I liked), good times slipped away, but there was a little hope. Then, some time later, came a little magic ... tucked up my sleeve (which was especially magic on the first hearing). Even though the song touched on serious content, there was a lightness to it.

David: Later that morning — after 20 minutes, an hour, maybe two — the song was finished. To avoid losing it, I had captured the words on paper and the music on my old dictaphone tape-recorder. It felt OK to sing this song at this time. The words did not seem to diminish or trivialise a death. Kitrina had heard the writing process unfolding but had stayed on the balcony throughout. She hadn't spoken to me, she hadn't interfered, and she had expressed no judgment or opinion during the writing process. This was important — essential even. I can't remember how, but she made it clear that she liked the song. Perhaps she told me so, perhaps she smiled, perhaps she cried a little, perhaps she gave me a hug, perhaps she said "thank you". With her encouragement, I sang the song several more times that day. I have sung it many times since. I hope *A Little Rain* helped Kitrina that day. I hope it brought her strength and, maybe, a little hope. I hope her uncle would have liked it.

Kitrina: There was a bigger more magnanimous universe at the end of that time: I had a picture, David a song, and one that so "fitted" the mood, moment, situation, past, present and future that it was almost prophetic. We didn't and haven't talked about the song until now, when we decided to write about that morning. Whenever I hear the song I am surrounded by that moment and those events. The more I explore the lyrics the more amazingly meaningful they appear, the more appropriately they appear to capture what can be conveyed, the more they lessen the distance. I think at the end we were close because the song seemed to capture everything that couldn't be said at that time. How could David know what to say? What an amazingly wonderful thing. Strangely, although the situation that spawned the song was death, the song was new birth; therefore there was joy in that moment, despite the cultural expectation of singular sorrow. Some kind of healing — between us and between me and my spirit — had taken place.

What is to be Learned?

Leonard Cohen has said, "I don't know where the good songs come from or else I'd go there more often" (as cited in Zollo, 2003, p. 345). We don't know either. Yet reflecting on the preceding story, we recognise three interrelated characteristics or themes which inhabit our story of the writing of this particular song. We would like to explore these characteristics by offering an interpretation of our story, which through narrative theory draws parallels with (1) others' perspectives on performative and arts-informed inquiry, and (2) other songwriters' accounts of their creative process. Regarding the latter, we have focused selectively on published accounts of the songwriting process that resonate with our own songwriting experiences. These stories may not be consistent with every songwriter's experience, yet we hope that by discussing in general terms a creative process that is slippery and somewhat ambiguous, we may provide some insights into the ways in which knowledge may be produced through songwriting.

A Desire for Connection

For Ruthellen Josselson (1996), the ability to empathise underlies a desire to help: "We feel 'with' and then try to join or assuage or comfort or protect or cheer" (p. 211). In order to care, however, one must overcome the space that divides us. This point relates to the first theme we recognise in our story which we see as a desire to communicate, or connect in some way. This is evidenced in David's reaction to the news of death: "I felt like I wanted to say something" and "I don't remember whether or not I gave Kitrina a hug; I hope I did. If I didn't, I should have". Both comments are culturally situated responses to assuage or comfort someone experiencing grief. Alongside David's desire to communicate and lessen the distance between us, however, is a sense that conventional responses do not "fit" this particular situation.

In the story, an initial inability to find "the right words" to speak (to answer the question of "what to say?") comes with a sense of inadequacy as the desire for connection is thwarted and frustrated. A sense of these processes unfolding is also recounted by Kitrina; for example, when she says, "I hated the barrage of questions I was asked by well meaning people when Daddy died". Thus, the space between us was highlighted by both Kitrina (drawing on stories that had previously shaped her experience) and David (through his awareness that words could not capture an appropriate response that "felt right"). While feeling empathy, David could initially find no way to express these feelings.

Carl Leggo (2008) writes, "Our understanding, interpretations, responses, thoughts, and actions are all constructed and constrained by the discursive patterns and frames that society permits and authorises, on the one hand, and excludes and prohibits, on the other" (p. 168). In this regard, John McLeod (1997) suggests:

> The culture we live in supplies us with stories that do not fit experience, and experience that does not live up to the story. It may also fail to supply us with appropriate arenas for narrating whatever story it is we have to tell. The common theme across all of these circumstances is the experience of silence, of living with a story that has not or cannot be told. (p. 100)

This perspective moves David's inability to communicate, in part at least, away from him as an individual, unconnected being and into a socio-cultural space within which our stories are seen as being constructed through available narrative structures. In this space, the question of "what to say?" may be understood as problematic because — at certain times — appropriate narrative resources or maps are not accessible. From this perspective, the preceding excerpts of our story show how we both found the dominant modes of discourse concerning response to bereavement to be inadequate or unsatisfactory. The available narratives of bereavement feel "wrong" because they fail to "fit" our personal experience at this time. David's position of "not knowing" might therefore be seen as related to an inability to find or access appropriate narrative resources to guide his response at this moment. In this light, his impulse to write can be understood as a desire to find or create new knowledge and understanding — in short, an alternative story — that better "fits" and aligns with personal experience.

The answer to David's dilemma, of "what to do or say" is partly ontological as Andrew Sparkes and Brett Smith (2008) clarify: "Ontological narratives are used to define who we are: this in turn is a precondition for knowing what to do" (p. 300). In opening the preceding story, David began by sharing an ontological narrative with the reader: "I wrote my first song ... long before I wrote my first research paper". He then links who he is (a songwriter-scholar) with what he does: "Songwriting has been a way through which I have explored my self, my experiences and relationships". In this light, writing a song can be understood as a way for David to act that better "fits" with what he knows and how he comes to know. For him, an answer to the question of what to say or do when faced with silence is to become his songwriting-self in order to find something to extend or offer as a way of bridging the space between us.

For Gergen (1999), one of the problems of modernist tradition is the assumption that we have unified egos. In contrast, the transformational potential of narrative is that through self-reflexivity, evident when an individual recognises that available discourses are not working, we can embrace a polyvocal position that invites multiple meanings, multiple self-positions and therefore has the potential to generate a range of options permitting us to "walk on together." As Craig and Huber (2007) note, "the notion of narrative inquirers learning to walk together in good ways ... forms a dimension of the research text composed by narrative inquirers" (p. 271). In this case the compositional text was a song.

Discovering Alternative Stories

The writings of McLeod (1997) — as well as aspects of our own story — suggest that despite a desire for connection, silence (i.e., an absence of story) is a likely outcome when available narrative scripts fail to align with personal experience. In exploring this issue we have asked ourselves: What is it about the processes of songwriting that allows this silence to be broken and for us to — through the song—find a means of communication? How might the process of writing a song provide access to the kinds of understanding or knowledge that can act as a template for a 'new' story that better fits personal experience, one that feels authentic to the writer and hearer of the song? One answer, we think, centres on the ways in which the songwriting process entails some kind of movement away from conscious, controlled thought processes towards a more open sense of discovering alternative stories.

In the following passage, Neil Young describes how in order to write he must avoid, as he puts it, "thinking":

> **Interviewer:** When you get a song going, do you always stay there and try to finish it then or do you come back to it?
>
> **Neil Young:** Usually I sit down and go until I'm trying to think. As soon as I start thinking, I quit.
>
> **Interviewer:** What do you mean by that?
>
> **Neil Young:** I mean that I start consciously trying to think of what I'm going to do next. Then I quit. Then when I have an idea out of nowhere, I start up again. When that idea stops, I stop. I don't force it. If it's not there, it's not there and there's nothing you can do about it. (as cited in Zollo, 2003, p. 354)

David describes a similar process in his story of writing *A Little Rain*: "At some point during this process ... words began to come. I was not aware of thinking the words ... I didn't even recognise the words as being my own, as being depictions or representations of my own thoughts". For us, these excerpts suggest that for a songwriter to write, it is necessary, in Neil Young's terms, to avoid "consciously trying to think" or, at the least, to stop oneself from thinking in certain kinds of ways. Doing so allows what Paul Simon describes as a process of "discovering" through which stories, knowledge and understandings are realised. In Simon's words:

> You want your mind to wander, and to pick up words and phrases and fool with them and drop them. As soon as your mind knows that it's on and it's supposed to produce some lines, either it doesn't or it produces things that are very predictable. And that's why I say I'm not interested in writing something that I thought about. I'm interested in discovering where my mind wants to go, or what object it wants to pick up. (As cited in Zollo, 2003, p. 98)

We interpret the preceding excerpts from the perspective of narrative theory: that discovery entails seeing anew — making sense, understanding, knowing — in a way that deviates from, repositions, or challenges a dominant discourse. The sense of discovery arises when we realise something that is outside or counter to our mostly taken-for-granted assumptions. To achieve this, a first and necessary challenge is to somehow step outside the meta-narratives which writers such as McLeod (1997) and Leggo (2008) suggest shape and constrain both how and what we know.

But what is it about writing a *song* that might encourage an individual to step outside the dominant discourse? McLeod (1997) provides some clues on this when he suggests that some mediums promote an altered state of consciousness:

> Christian rituals involving fasting, singing, incense, long religious services, the reality-altering architecture of medieval cathedrals and vivid colour of stained glass, all contributed to the induction of altered states of awareness that served to release the person from the constraints and mind-set of ordinary everyday life. (p. 8)

We agree that alternative understandings and perspectives can emerge through an altered state of awareness, which in the story becomes possible for David through music itself — an integral and essential aspect of any song. Musicologists describe music as possessing a narrative or being drama unfolding (Levinson, 2004), in that music evokes an emotional dimension of human experience even when no words are present. For both the songwriter and those who hear a song, the impact of the music plays at least two important roles. At times music can act as a stage-setting ploy emotionally moving the songwriter and/or the listener, thereby preparing or readying them in some way for what is to follow. At other times music provides an important pause in a story so that the lyrics can be given consideration or be reflected upon. Once again, in our story, it is the musical element of the song that makes an appearance before the lyrical component, as these extracts illustrate:

Kitrina: A short riff of about seven single notes followed by a sharp plucked chord echoed from inside.

David: I picked at some chords, feeling the wood reverberate against my body … Perhaps I began to lose myself in the tones coming from the instrument. Perhaps I became immersed in the notes and progressions that emerged without, it seemed to me, any conscious application on my part.

An additional layer of explanation can be found in the work of Oscar Wilde: Wilde said that you can't believe in yourself if you're not being yourself, yet he urged people to be as artificial as possible. According to Peter Chadwick (2006), "The contradiction is resolved in the statement: 'give a man a mask and he will tell you the truth.' Via the masks we wear we multiply our personalities and eventuate the many different aspects and facets of ourselves" (p. 20). We suggest that the songwriting process might in this sense be understood as putting on a metaphorical mask. David has said that, for him, it is less a mask to "disguise" himself to others, more a mask to disguise aspects of *himself* to himself (Carless, 2007). Through temporarily escaping those ingrained narrative structures which articulate one's own prejudices and expectations, we suggest that songwriting can facilitate the discovery of insights and understandings that the writer might not otherwise be able to access.

Through the Body

We see one further — and central — process at work in the preceding story that permits or triggers the stimulus for discovery through songwriting. Leonard Cohen has said:

> My immediate realm of thought is bureaucratic and like a traffic jam … So to penetrate this chattering and this meaningless debate that is occupying most of my attention, I have to come up with something that really speaks to my deepest interest. (As cited in Zollo, 2003, p. 332)

In this remark, Cohen suggests *something* is required for him to be able to step outside his "immediate realm of thought". In our story, this thing is music itself. Implicit in and essential to this act are the symbiotic relationships between a musician's body, the body of the instrument and the music that comes out of and through both.

A sense of the *act* of playing music becoming a trigger for a new story is present in songwriter John Hiatt's description of writing:

> Interviewer: Does the guitar you use affect the song?
>
> John Hiatt: Absolutely. There are songs inside guitars. For sure. The question is, how you get them out of there.
>
> Interviewer: And what's the answer?
>
> John Hiatt: For me, it's to sit down and start playing, because its fun to play. If I'm lucky, something will hit me. If not, I keep playing. (As cited in Zollo, 2003, p. 647)

The physical-ness of playing music is also highlighted as important at several points in our story; for example, when David recounts: "Somehow, it felt good at this time to just hold the guitar. From thousands of hours of playing, the feel of an acoustic guitar against my body has become a familiar and comforting one". Later, "I picked at some chords, feeling the wood reverberate against my body, the ebony fingerboard and silvered frets beneath my fingers, the clean bronze strings against my fingertips". Finally, "… despite not knowing what to say, here were words … Words were coming from my mouth along with a melody, a rhythm, and a sequence of chords and notes from the guitar". At the core of these descriptions is a sense of *embodiment* which shows songwriting as ignited and sustained through physical, bodily processes that are realised through connection with a musical instrument.

What we are trying to suggest here is that the physicality of playing music — as an embodied practice — can be the "source" or stimulus of a new song and thereby new understanding. According to Liora Bresler (2008):

> Embodiment is at the core of music. Music is produced by physical movement — the voice or an instrument that functions as the extension of the body, where the performer unites with the instrument to produce sound. Embodiment is manifested differently in sight and sound. Whereas we see things "out there," the experience of sound, like touch and taste, is internal, "in here" … Sound penetrates us, engaging us on a bodily level in ways fundamentally different than the visual. (p. 231)

For us, some kind of embodied action — as opposed to disembodied cognitive thought — is part and parcel of the ways by which knowledge and understanding is created through songwriting. The physical "doing-ness" of playing music is tied to these insights. In this regard, Ronald Pelias (2008) observes that, "Unlike traditional scholarship where the body seems to slip away, performers generate and present their insights through the body, a knowing body, dependent on its participatory and empathic capacities" (p. 188). While Pelias is referring specifically to performative works here, we are also aware that humans are always, in some sense, performing — in our story *A Little Rain* was performed even as it was being written. Thus the process of coming to know evident in performance work in general resonates with the songwriter who, as Pelias observes:

> ... learns to trust what the body teaches ... The performer listens to what the body is saying and, based on what the body has come to know, makes judgements about performance choices ... At each step in the process, the performer relies upon the body as a location of knowledge. (p. 186)

From this perspective, we see interconnecting elements of music, the instrument and the musician's body, as supporting the *incorporation* of knowledge (Douglas & Carless, 2008c), which entails, literally, both *bringing knowledge into the body* and *bringing the body to knowledge*. Knowledge and its acquisition or creation through these forms cannot be seen as an entirely cognitive process. Instead, through songwriting we know in our bodies and we come to know *through* our bodies. In the context of a wholly embodied creative process, a host of biographical and material factors can also be seen as holding potential significance. In the story, for instance, David ascribes meaning to this particular guitar, the person who made it, their relationship, and so on. We suggest these biographical and material factors can be significant in the context of a songwriting process that necessarily involves the creation of meaning. Through a desire for connection combined with the opportunity to discover through writing, we see songwriting as a meaning-making process in which new knowledge and understanding can be accessed or created. A personally meaningful "prop" — in this instance, a guitar — can therefore be more than an essential tool; it can also be an effective way to help bring embodied meaning to the creative enterprise.

Closing Thoughts

In attempting to write about the relationship between art and research, Donald Blumenfeld-Jones (2002) describes his work as "an essay about the impossibility of speaking about the impossibility of art which makes everything possible but of which we cannot speak" (p. 90). With this chapter, we have traversed the same impossible territory. We accept that a degree of ambiguity and paradox (both inherent in the creative process itself *and* generated through telling a story of the creative process) implies that precise conclusions concerning songwriting are neither possible nor desirable. We do not wish to suggest that the themes in our story are universally representative of *every* songwriting process. Bob Dylan has said about songwriting: "There's no rhyme or reason to it. There's no rule. That's what makes it so *attractive*" (as cited in Zollo, 2003, p. 72). Indeed, no sooner is a "rule" of process suggested then someone goes and breaks it — sometimes with magnificent results. By trying to "explain" or "make sense" of songwriting we risk imposing reason on a process which may itself be devoid of reason. Thus, we offer our reflections on process with caution because we want to avoid doing "symbolic violence" to a creative process that arguably has a degree of disorder and chaos at its core.

For us, however, these risks are worth taking because songs and songwriting are part of an artistic canon that enables us, as researchers, "to know something about feeling that cannot be revealed in literal scientific statements" (Eisner, 2008, p. 8). In this regard, Eisner suggests that science states meaning, while art expresses it. We might add that as well as expressing meaning, art also contributes to its creation. Just as poetry "creates or makes the world in words" (Leggo, 2008, p. 166), songwriting helps create or make the world in music. It is on this basis, we believe, that songwriting merits inclusion within the work of autoethnographic, performative, narrative, and arts-informed researchers.

Acknowledgments

We thank Paul Zollo and Da Capo Press for kindly granting permission to quote from the interviews published in the book Songwriters On Songwriting, Expanded Edition. The featured lyrics from the song A Little Rain are reproduced with permission and the song can be heard in its entirety at www.myspace.com/davidcarless.

References

Blumenfeld-Jones, D. (2002). If I could have said it, I would have. In C. Bagley & M. Cancienne (Eds.), *Dancing the data*, (pp. 90–104). New York: Peter Lang.

Bresler, L. (2008). The music lesson. In J. Knowles & A. Cole (Eds.), *Handbook of the arts in qualitative research*, (pp. 225–237). Thousand Oaks, CA: Sage.

Carless, D. (2007, May). Hope: A performance ethnography. Paper presented at the *Third Congress of Qualitative Inquiry*, University of Illinois, IL.

Carless, D. (in press). Who the hell was *that?* Bodies, stories and actions in the world. *Qualitative Research in Psychology.*

Carless, D., & Douglas, K. (in press). Opening doors: Poetic representation of the sport experiences of men with severe mental health difficulties. *Qualitative Inquiry.*

Carless, D., & Sparkes, A. (2008). The physical activity experiences of men with serious mental illness: Three short stories. *Psychology of Sport and Exercise, 9*(2), 191–210.

Chadwick, P. (2006). Wilde's creative strategies. *The Wildean, 29,* July, 28–39.

Craig, C. J., & Huber, J. (2007). Relational reverberations: Shaping and reshaping narrative inquiries in the midst of storied lives and contexts. In D. Clandinin (Ed.), *Handbook of narrative inquiry* (pp. 251–279). Thousand Oaks, CA: Sage.

Douglas, K. (2009). Storying my self: Negotiating a relational identity in professional sport. *Qualitative Research in Sport and Exercise, 1*(2), 176–190.

Douglas, K., & Carless, D. (2005). *Across the Tamar: Stories from women in Cornwall.* [CD]. Bristol, UK: Self-produced.

Douglas, K., & Carless, D. (2008a). The team are off: Getting inside women's experiences in professional sport. *Aethlon: The Journal of Sport Literature, 25*(1), 241–251.

Douglas, K., & Carless, D. (2008b). Nurturing a performative self. *Forum Qualitative Sozialforschung/Forum: Qualitative Social Research, 9*(2), Art. 23, Available at http://www.qualitative-research.net/fqs-texte/2-08/08-2-23-e.htm

Douglas, K., & Carless, D. (2008c). Using stories in coach education. *International Journal of Sports Science and Coaching, 3*(1), 33–49.

Douglas, K., & Carless, D. (2009). Exploring taboo issues in professional sport through a fictional approach. *Reflective Practice, 10*(3), 311–323.

Eisner, E. (2008). Art and knowledge. In J. Knowles & A. Cole (Eds.), *Handbook of the arts in qualitative research*, (pp. 3–12). Thousand Oaks, CA: Sage.

Gergen, K. (1999). *An invitation to social constructionism.* Thousand Oaks, London: Sage.

Josselson, R. (1996). *The space between us: Exploring the dimensions of human relationships.* Thousand Oaks, CA: Sage.

Leggo, C. (2008). Astonishing silence: Knowing in poetry. In J. Knowles & A. Cole (Eds.), *Handbook of the arts in qualitative research* (pp. 165–174). Thousand Oaks, CA: Sage.

Levinson, J. (2004). Music as narrative and music as drama. *Mind and Language, 19*(4), 428–441.

Lewis, P. (2006). Stories I live by. *Qualitative Inquiry, 12*(5), 829–849.

McLeod, J. (1997). *Narrative and psychotherapy.* London: Sage.

Neilsen, L. (2008). Literacy genres: Housecleaning — A work with theoretical notes. In J. Knowles & A. Cole (Eds.), *Handbook of the arts in qualitative research*, (pp. 385–395). Thousand Oaks, CA: Sage.

Pelias, R. (2008). Performative inquiry: Embodiment and its challenges. In J. Knowles & A. Cole (Eds.), *Handbook of the arts in qualitative research* (pp. 185–193). Thousand Oaks, CA: Sage.

Sparkes, A. C., & Smith, B. (2008). Narrative constructionist inquiry. In J. Holstein & J. Gubrium (Eds.), *Handbook of constructionist research* (pp. 295–314). Guilford Press, London.

Sparkes, A. C., & Douglas, K. (2007). Making the case for poetic representations: An example in action. *The Sport Psychologist, 21*(2), 170–189.

Zollo, P. (2003). *Songwriters on songwriting* (expanded ed.). Cincinnati, OH: Da Capo Press.

Beautiful Here
Celebrating Life, Alternative Music, Adolescence and Autoethnography

Karen M. Scott-Hoy

> I have never thought of writing for reputation and honour. What I
> have in my heart must come out; that is the reason why I compose.
>
> Ludwig Van Beethoven

July 2007: Discovering a Riff and Breaking Down

The driving bass reverberates along the concrete slab, heaving its way
under the soft leather lounge. The boys have been practising for nearly
three hours now and the continual barrage of sound is taking its toll.
In spite of our efforts to contain the noise, (lining the downstairs room
with acoustic foam, carpet and egg cartons at great expense) the waves
of sound squeeze feverishly through every crack, travelling along every
straight surface until they collide with my ears, overpowering and
dominating the strains of the ABBA song "Thank you for the music"
playing on my *Mamma Mia* CD. The rapid driving beat of their music
is the antithesis of the serenity I have sought after a hard day of
washing clothes, cleaning bedrooms, shopping and meal preparation.

I'm irritated by the noise. I can't call it music; there's no melody, no
patterns to follow. The noise sounds angry, a cacophony of agitated
monotonous sounds, banging, scraping, squealing. I know Saarikallio
and Erkkila (2007, p. 99) found in their study of adolescents that kids
sometimes play "their" music loudly to annoy their parents, as a way
of expressing their emotions, but the boys aren't doing this; they have
simply forgotten about me and are just enjoying making music together.

Sometimes I wish they'd find something else to do. Then I recall what it was like when Vaughan, my youngest son, had nothing else to do. The boredom, the gloom, blackness, I think he called it, that was heavy upon him; the sneaking out, wandering the streets at night, the smoking, the drugs; and that's just what I know about! From about the time he was 14 I watched as my beautiful, happy fourth son changed into a sullen, withdrawn shadow that hung in the house. Suspicion coloured our conversations, as I screened his words for truth, and he chose his words ever so carefully to conceal his actions and divert my attention. Soon the conversations ended. Shrugs replaced words. My son, who was once an intimate part of my body and life, had become a stranger. Shame crept into our relationship. I was ashamed of my son's choices, and afraid of what others would think of me as a mother. I felt that his years defined me as much as him (Pelias, 2002). I felt both strong love and hate for my child, something I found disturbing. I was grieving the loss of my living son.

I can't recall exactly when things changed between us, but I clearly remember the setting. We were seated at a small table in a cafe having lunch. He was talking animatedly about his role as a theatre technician in a school music production. I remember telling him how good it was to have him talk to me again and how much I had missed that. He hung his head, lifted his eyes, and said, "Mum, I am so sorry I couldn't talk to you last year. I just had too much to hide".

Soon after that conversation, Vaughan, who is not quite 17, changed the social group he hung out with and formed a band. His brother was already part of another band that practised at our home and I encouraged this, offering to have band practices at our house, as I was aware of how important music is to young people (see Bloustein, 2007; Saarikallio & Erkkilä, 2007).

Vaughan's band plays alternative music, what they call "metal" and even more frightening for a parent, "death metal!" I looked the term up on the Internet and found the website was owned by *evilmusic*. That scares me! Some of the pictures on the CD covers are horrific, depicting violence and death, and many bands seem to incorporate death or dying into their names: "As I lay dying", "I killed the Prom Queen", "Every Time I Die". I often find offensive the lyrics that filter into my world from his room. Vaughan says he doesn't listen to the lyrics (see Ali & Peynircioglu, 2006);[1] he just enjoys the energy of the music. But is that energy harmful? What if this type of music *is* evil? What if this negative energy infiltrates their subconscious and encourages violence or teenage suicide? I have read studies about music like this and wonder whether I should intervene (e.g. Arnett, 1995; Kahn-Harris, 2002). Yet I notice that music improves his moods (see Christenson & Roberts, 1998, pp. 47–49; DeNora, 1999; Laiho, 2002, 2004; North et al., 2000; Roe, 1985; Sloboda & O'Neill, 2001; Wells & Hakanen, 1991 cited in Saarikallio & Erkkilä, 2007, p. 90), provides thrills, and inspires movement, especially when he plays the music so loud he can physically feel it. That annoys me as the sound invades my home space and I also worry about hearing damage. However, the appearance of little yellow spongy ear-plugs in the washing show he is careful of his hearing.

I loved the classics and learned flute, voice and harp. My sons also had the opportunity to learn musical instruments. They have played in school bands, jazz bands, church music groups, yet it is alternative music that seems to energise and bring them out of themselves. Their teen years have been a turning point for their musical preferences, as they discovered a world of different ideas, cultures, people and music. In our culture, in particular, this choice of music seems to have important social consequences. Levitin (2008) links this with the evolutionary idea of music as a vehicle for social bonding and societal cohesion. He explains that we listen to music that our friends listen to, and when we are young and in search of our identity, we form bonds or social groups with people we want to be like, or with whom we have something in common. Other scholars agree that music and musical preferences become a mark of personal and group identity and of distinction (Bloustein, 2007; Fornas, Lindberg & Sernhede, 1995; Kahn-Harris, 2004; Levitin, 2008; Williams, 2006).

There certainly have been changes Vaughan's appearance recently. Black seems to feature in his clothing colour choices, his hair is long and carefully groomed into "messy" styles. He never wears his jeans high enough to cover his underwear! I can't tell the difference between Emo, Goth, Straightedge and whatever they are. He picks up subtle differences that are lost on me. He hates wearing a school uniform, and yet has adopted his own uniform of sorts. So as the lads arrive at our home for band practice they are similarly dressed, often wearing T-shirts bearing the logos of their favourite bands to further reinforce this identification with their music.

I've had some good conversations with Vaughan about his music and why he likes it so much. I recall one when we were driving back from Adelaide one afternoon with the radio playing. "Mum, it's like this," said Vaughan, "Pop music, like what you're listening to on the radio is the popular approach to the music *business.*" He spat out the word *business* like it left a nasty taste in his mouth, then continued, "Pop music is written to entertain others. They want to sell music. I reckon artists in pop music focus outwardly, thinking about how they can appeal to their fans; manipulating words and music to create emotion. They decide how they want you to feel after listening to their music. This means that they'll hold back some of their thoughts and share only some of their intimate details."

"Sure, I can see that, but how is what you do any different?" I asked.

"Alternative music isn't written with entertainment in mind. What drives the music is art, not business. Alternative musicians mostly choose to ignore whoever they think is listening. They, you know, think inwardly and embrace their own emotions. I guess you would say they use music as 'personal reflective material,' like keeping a personal diary," explained Vaughan.

I smiled as I noted his use of my words. It was good to know that my work as an ethnographer, my passion for people and justice, was having some impact. Being a mum and a researcher, autoethnography appealed to me because of the way the method values the stories of "ordinary" people (see Ellis, 2007; Scott-Hoy & Ellis, 2008). "Listen and observe," I told my kids. "Ask who, why, what, when, how and where? Uncover the full story. Pay attention to physical feelings, thoughts and emotions. It doesn't matter whether it's a movie, a book, or a rumour in the school yard, keep digging deeper, asking 'What's going on here?' When you think you know, look inward and ask what does this mean to/for me as an individual. Then focus outward and ask what does this mean to my family, my community and the wider world." I insisted. "Sometimes," I explained, "you won't like what you learn as you reflect. It may be painful, but the insights you gain about yourself and the world around you make the pain bearable, perhaps even worth it, as you work through ethical struggles and develop coping strategies for life" (see Ellis, 2004, p. xx).

I was beginning to see from this conversation that music is for Vaughan what writing is for me; a medium for reflection and learning, a way of understanding ourselves and our world. However, I was both intrigued with and concerned by his attitude towards audience. When I write I am always mindful of my audience, of ways to open up my work and allow my audience to enter into my experience. Like Bochner and Ellis (2003) I expect my projects to evoke a response, inspire imagination, give pause for possibilities and new meanings, and open new questions and avenues of inquiry. I feel it's important that my audience see me; that I not hide behind the mask of storyteller, distant and protected (Scott-Hoy & Ellis, 2008, p. 135). I wanted to ask Vaughan if ignoring your audience doesn't somehow make these musicians' motives more selfish but I didn't, because I was trying not to judge, and wanted to keep our conversation going.

"A diary," I responded reflecting on his explanation.

"You've got to remember a person's diary contains lots of different things, not only will you see the words on the page but the style of writing, pictures, blots of ink, torn out pages, holes, cuts, stickers, tears, string, colour, black and white, doodling and more … These tiny little extra details can tell you more about how that person was feeling that day, than the writing itself. A diary is raw emotion," Vaughan continued. "No details are left out. It contains stuff, not scripted that comes straight from the heart. It's not formalised like you'd find in an essay."

I was reminded of the graffiti-like tags that are in his school diary. It's a sign of protest and rebellion too, I thought, knowing how he has used his diary in ways that are not approved by the school. But it does tell you a lot about how he's feeling in a particular week.

I am brought back to the present with a jolt. A sound like a pig squealing shatters my thoughts. I stand and move toward the double glass doors. I've had enough! As my hand connects with the polished wooden door knob, it is pushed away as Vaughan comes hurtling through.

"Wow! Sorry mum! Didn't see you," he pants. He has no shirt, and sweat runs off his young taut body. "We just wrote another song," he begins, but is cut short as his friend Sherman ambles through the doors.

"Hey! Got a drink? Oh! Hi Mrs S-H," he adds. "I reckon we need to redo that last riff …"

"The one before the bridge?" asks Vaughan becoming animated.

"Nah! The last one …"

"No! That's great … What about the breakdown …?"

They move towards the kitchen, their voices animated and defensive as they convey to each other their different ideas and feelings.

I'm left standing by the door, the smell of hot teenage boys still hanging in the air. I close the door and return to my seat on the lounge. A song; so that's what they call it. What's a riff or a breakdown? I studied music at high school. We learnt about concerto form, and had to memorise themes from symphonies and concertos. We learnt to harmonise, but never breakdown! It's a whole new language and for an outsider, it's quite frightening. How can I relate to this?

I recall Varese (as cited in Levitin, 2006, p. 14) describing music as "organised sound" and I guess avant-garde composers challenged what most of us think music is, using sounds from daily life like jackhammers, trains, and waterfalls, playing with their pitch, and combining them into "an organised collage of sound with the same type of emotional trajectory — the same tension and release — as traditional music" (p. 14). Is that different to the boys who use growls, screams, drums, and distorted guitars to create their music? Perhaps if I embrace the tension and release, I'll come to appreciate this organised sound ... this music.

February 2008. Lyrics: Building a Bridge of Words

Vaughan is sitting with his headphones on, staring at the computer screen intently. Wondering if I should disturb him, I hesitate before deciding to enter the room. I tap him on the shoulder. He turns and smiles, hits the pause button and removes his headphones.

"Was it a good band session today?" I inquire, unsure of what it is I really want to know, but realising I seek an emotional connection. Perhaps watching these boys, well young men really, come and go through our lounge room most of days of the week makes me realise Vaughan won't be living here much longer, and I wrestle with sadness and guilt at that thought. Constraints of time, energy and the ongoing demands of life with four sons meant that I have not given him the quality time I imagined I would all those years ago when I was a new mother. Now I have more time to offer, I feel I am not needed; as if I am competing for my son's precious time.

"Yeah! Sherman and I got down the whole song. I'm editing it now," Vaughan says turning back to the screen.

"What's it called?" I ask.

"I don't know," he snaps. "The boys are calling it the Emo song ..."

"I thought you guys thought Emo was bad! I'm confused. Is Emo good now?" I sigh.

"Nah! Emo like black and miserable is still bad. What the guys want is an emotional thinking, positive song," he hesitates. "Gee, I don't really know either. It's not my problem. I don't write the lyrics!" Vaughan states defensively as he replaces his headphones, attempting to end the conversation.

I'm surprised, not realising the band members had such clearly defined roles. I've heard how tough they are on each other and how they call each other to account for their mistakes or not getting something right. They volunteer for, or are assigned different aspects of the composing, playing and administration of the band. It reminded me of some studies (Fornas, Lindberg and Sernhede, 1995; Jaffurs, 2004) I'd read about kids roles in a garage band and how students said they felt they could engage in rock music without anxiety or feelings of inferiority (Gracyk, 1993, p. 56). I admire or perhaps envy that.

"So, if lyrics aren't your problem, whose are they?" I respond as I remove the headphones, not too gently. "Surely you need words?"

Vaughan shrugs.

"Is this the piece you were working on as a tribute to *The Red Shore* members?" I inquire more gently, referring to a horrific road accident that left two band members dead.

"No," Vaughan answers. "I'm still working on that. That's my own piece. I don't want to share that with anyone, not even the band. At least not yet," he adds thoughtfully.

I realise he's still processing his grief, and long to hold and protect him, but know I cannot take away this hurt. Knowing how therapeutic I find writing, I hope he will find comfort and understanding in his music.

Vaughan attended the *The Red Shore* performance in Adelaide a couple of days before the accident. He was very disturbed by the deaths and was confused about the emotional and physical connection he had made with the band members, touching their hands while moshing. "I touched them," he told me with tears in his eyes, "and now they are dead". The media frenzy and outpouring of emotion by both supporters of and those opposed to death metal had further heightened his reaction and grief. Some people saw irony in the young men's deaths while on their *Christmas Carnage* tour. I just felt sick. Although many of their album and song titles are about death, I doubted those young men were ready to die. Surely "the commodification and commercialisation of death, the pervasive presence of images of death in all forms of visual entertainment, had withered sensibilities and transformed the experiences of death and the dying into abstractions and simulations" (Manning, 1999, p. 103).

Tonight, as I stand silently watching the patterns the sound waves make on the screen and marvelling at Vaughan's ability to write, record, and mix his own music, I wonder if the mothers of the dead band members had also marvelled at their sons' talent. What does it feel like to lose a son? Our children are supposed to be our legacy to the world. They are supposed to carry on the family name and genetics, when our lives have finished. What is left when they die before us?

"Mum." Vaughan's voice calls me back.

"Yes?"

"Do you think you could write the lyrics for this? The guys do need some words to sing ... you're right. Matt would look bloody stupid as a lead singer with no words," he began to laugh, lightening the atmosphere in the room.

"What did you have in mind?" I ask. I'd helped with lyrics before, even though I disliked their style of music. It was my way of re-entering my son's world, of finding a common bond, a passion we could share; the need to communicate feelings and thoughts with those around us.

"Well, I want to write about a car accident. I had this idea about starting the track with the sound of crashing glass, then ambulance sirens ..." he begins.

I catch my breath, jolted by surprise. Hadn't he just told me the band wants a positive emotional song?

"I want to talk about death experiences and how death can make you value life. You know; like in that book you gave me to read," he says.

"*90 Minutes in Heaven?*" I ask (see Piper & Murphey, 2004).

"Yeah, that one," he replies.

"What do the others think about that idea?" I ask quietly.

"They don't like it. Reckon it's too negative. Matt says he'll refuse to sing it. He doesn't do negative! Gerr doesn't go much for thinking about anything, let alone death, and Sherman, well he's just worried that it's uncool and people won't like it ..." Vaughan trails off.

"But you want to give it a go," I reply distractedly, still thinking about the opening passages in the book, where the man is pronounced clinically dead at the scene of a car accident, but then revived.

"Sure. It's been bugging me. Ever since those guys were killed, I can't stop thinking about the kinds of things that would have gone through their heads at the end. And because I'm a musician, I see the music they left behind as a summary of what kind of people they were. So when I think about my life, I wonder what I have to show for myself. If I died how would people remember me; especially if they only know me through my music?" He pauses. "You know, I want to reach people: people my age. I want to share what I feel. I have to make sure that I don't make a mistake by not doing this. Don't laugh, but," he hesitates, "I had a dream and I heard *this* piece, I can't really explain it. It's just I know how well it would work: this sort of idea in a song. It's what our band needs: a song to challenge people to think beyond the ordinary. I don't think this piece has to be negative: it can be positive; encouraging people to do more with their lives while they can. But I just can't put it down in words!" Vaughan exclaims in frustration.

I hesitate, not because of the task — for song writing as Hirschhorn (2004) says involves "observing life and all we see around us", like ethnography — but because of the subject matter. *The Red Shore* deaths had already caused me to dig up memories I'd hidden for many years; memories of a close friend's death in a car accident. I had been working through my feelings and helping Vaughan with his, rereading Carolyn Ellis' account of her brother's death (1993) and recalling the discussions I had with her about her students' reactions to grief and loss. In Carolyn's course 'Communicating Grief and Loss', she found students were enthusiastic and passionate in the beginning but towards the end, they slackened off to a much greater extent than happens in other classes she teaches. Having gotten the point of the class — that loss is painful, ubiquitous, and there is value in writing and talking about it — students say they'd rather celebrate life. Like Vaughan's mates, her students argued, "We don't have to think about this now!" (Ellis, 2008, p. 154).

Could I write something that encourages young people to think about death now? According to one study I read (Saarikallio & Erkkilä, 2007, p. 100), young people respond to lyrics that arouse meaningful thoughts, ideas and feelings, and encourage and facilitate mental imagery and contemplation giving kids new ideas and insights. How could I marry my words to Vaughan's music to achieve this? I recall reading about what Gattenstaetter (2007, p. 4) calls "a state of musical listening, which is not simply devoted concentration, but involves critical engagement with this devotion or devotion within critical engagement". I'll need to sense and engage with what Vaughan felt as he wrote the music, to understand what it is he wants the music to evoke. Because, as he has told me, his music is like a personal diary, I realise this will be an intensely intimate task, and one of trust. I take a deep breath.

"Okay," I mumble. "I'll try."

Vaughan copies the music onto a flash drive for me.

The next afternoon, I sit at my computer and insert the flash drive. What seemed so foreign to me a few months ago is now more familiar. I am no longer alienated from this music, but have tried to understand it and am now becoming intimately involved in its creation. I close my eyes; the music and sounds dictate to me. It jars and disconcerts. I try to connect with the tension and release, and follow its emotional trajectory.

The words begin to flow and I am taken back to the time when I opened my door to find two police officers standing there; to the numbness and disbelief I felt as they told me my friend had been killed in a car crash on the other side of the world. Closing my tear-filled eyes I see the yellow sticky notes he left in the house we shared, reminding me to water his plants until he came back: but he never came back. I recall the discussions with my pastor, as I tried to make sense of his death. Would I see him again in heaven? How could I know what he felt at that moment of death? Did he see a bright light of love at the end of a tunnel as many people have described? I am amazed at how fresh the memories are of this event which happened almost 30 years ago ... Tears and words intermingle as trembling I type.

～～

"Mum!" Vaughan's voice rings through the house.

"Here!" I call from the lounge where I'm folding underwear.

"Have you done it?" he asks breathlessly.

"Yes," I reply as he races to the cupboard in search of food. I note that today his excitement about the lyrics has come before, "What's there to eat?"

Now as Vaughan sits expectantly in front of my computer, his two-minute noodles go untouched next to the screen. "Whoa!" he mutters. He reaches over and shovels a forkful of noodles into his mouth. I am unsure if "Whoa!" is good or bad.

"Is that what you wanted?" I ask.

"I won't know until I see how it works with the music," he mumbles as he gulps yet another mouthful of food, removes his flash drive and heads to his workstation in his room. As he turns and leaves, the success of my lyric writing remains unresolved. Disappointment rises within and I realise how much emotional energy I have invested, not just in writing words, but in restoring a relationship with my son. I want the words to touch him and show him that I understand what it is to deal with grief, to experience the anger associated with death snatching away someone so young. The scab has again been knocked off my wound, and I am bleeding silently, within.

The Next Day. Mixing and Mastering: Life and Death

At 3.35 the next afternoon, I hear Vaughan crashing through the door and heading straight to his room. I register the sound of his computer booting up. A few minutes later, Sherman, Matt, and Gerr arrive. I am closest to the door so they greet me as they scoot through the hall. They all know their way around our house. There is a sense of anticipation and excitement as they pile into my son's small bedroom. Vaughan, anxious to share the song, begins to speak. I lean against his bedroom door jamb, keen to see this first hand.

"Okay. I know you guys didn't like my idea to start with, but I've worked on it, remixed it and I want you to shut up and listen and then tell me honestly what you think," he says. He pushes the play button. A keyboard melody sets a calm and peaceful scene.

"This isn't the Emo song," Gerr says impatiently as he tries to stand. Vaughan glares at him and he sits again. Vaughan has mixed two tracks that use interrelated chord progressions: a previously recorded keyboard interlude and the Emo song. As the music continues to play the sound of screeching car tyres jars into the music at twice the volume. Two of the boys in the room jump. The screeching roars closer, and the sound of metal crunching, glass shattering and fire crackling follows. The keyboard music stops. I shift uncomfortably, awful images flooding my mind. The silence is broken by a car horn, a crash, and an explosion. Matt closes his eyes. Gerr looks at the carpet. Sherman and Vaughan stare into space. The melodic keyboard returns quiet and distant, easing through the noises. A whining siren shrills into my consciousness, then a flowing bass riff descending and ascending. The boys recognise the Emo song's introduction. Vaughan turns the screen towards his audience, the recently arranged lyrics clearly visible. He reads the lyrics over the music, changing the timbre and volume of his voice, employing pauses and silences.

> *Beautiful Here*
>
> **Verse 1:** Floating above this eerie scene,
> No-one hears me when I scream!
> If that's my body trapped down there,
> Tell me, Tell me, I am where?
> Is this heaven?
> Feels like hell ...
>
> **Chorus:** Not ready to die today! (Shouted)
> That's what I heard them say.
> It's so beautiful here.
> I've seen a light so pure and clear,
> Music, Peace, and Love divine.
> Let me in, one more time!
>
> **Verse 2:** Metal breaking, crunching glass,
> Lights are flashing, faces pass.
> My body's broken, I'm bruised and sore,
> I don't wanna' live no more.
> If this is earth,
> it feels like hell!
>
> **Pre-Chorus:** What are they doing? They're taking me away!
> Then I heard this voice divine say:
> "Don't throw those pearls amongst the swine."
>
> **Chorus**

Bridge: Your life is precious, like a pearl,
Don't lose yourself in this downward whirl!
Tell others what it is you saw,
Tell them that, tell them more.
Tell of my love and tell of my peace,
How you felt complete release.
Tell of your sorrow, remorse and pain
Tell them of your precious life regained.

Coda: Like a pearl ...
It's so beautiful here.
Seen light so pure and so clear,
Music, Peace, Love divine.
Send me out, one last time.

I am proud of the way Vaughan reads the lyrics. He has amended them, made them his own. Nobody speaks. No-one interrupts. No-one objects. Matt wipes a tear from his eye. I leave, my heart racing, my mind full of confronting images, tears rolling down my cheek.

August 2008. Performing/Transforming

As the boys developed from a group of friends into "the band," they learned to use the Internet to promote themselves, uploading their music and the lyrics onto the band site. A friend designed a logo and they added photos of performances, and practice sessions. In doing these tasks the boys learned networking, collaboration and trust; "aspects that make the risky creation and representation of the self, and a sense of belonging in a shifting world, seem more manageable and worthwhile" (Bloustien, 2007, p. 495).

The band has developed quite a following and has been asked to perform at school assembly. Their excitement is palpable as they gather today to rehearse. They place great importance on rehearsing, as they perfect the skills needed to give what Bloustien (2007, p. 455) calls the ultimate authentic performance. It's not just sharing the music that makes a performance exciting but the way in which "the body becomes the locus and primary symbol of acquiring, articulating and negotiating particular understandings of the world, firmly linking image, gesture and style to cultural expression and identity" (Bloustien, 2007, p. 451).

Sherman learned to swing his guitar around his large torso without hitting himself in the head, something that required a lot of practice and a cricket helmet for protection initially! Vaughan learned the relaxed posture and laissez-faire facial gestures that are required of the drummer, even when he is working extremely hard playing rapid double kicks with both his feet and toms and cymbals with his hands. Gerr learned the stooped stance, jumps and stretches required of the bass player. Matt learned actions like throwing a mike stand down without hitting the guitarist, swinging his hips and of course, the guttural screams that help convey the music's passion to their audience.

They have elected to sing "Beautiful Here", and I am keen to hear from each band member their take on the song.

"Can I have a minute?" I ask Sherman as he enters the room. "I just want to know what it is about 'Beautiful Here' that inspires your performance."

"This is for me our most meaningful piece of music. I love those strong, direct chord progressions mixed with lyrics telling about that death experience. It's great the way the guitar begins the chorus strongly with a 'C minor' chord which instantly hits the listener with a serious sort of feel," he mimes the playing of his guitar as he speaks. "Then the music builds with a series of major chords creating a positive feel. It's important the students get it, so we've decided to put the words on the screen behind us when we play."

Sherman looks down at me, lowering his voice, "Since we finished the recording process, 'Beautiful Here' means even more to me. Listening to the whole piece through Vaughan's stereo made me more aware of the lyrics and what they meant, compared to just playing it at band practice. My attitude toward death and dying has changed writing this song. Now I reckon that there really is something else out there and it doesn't have to be all bad, you know hell, the devil, and that sort of thing." He pauses as Gerr enters the lounge carrying his bass guitar.

"What you talking about?" Gerr asks.

"'Beautiful Here'," Sherman replies.

"It's changed the way I think about music, about how diverse music is, and," he pauses, "I never really thought about lyrics before! These lyrics really get to me. They're so powerful and really emphasise what that guy went through ..." He looks embarrassed, unsure of what to say next.

"Did they make you think about what it would be like if it happened to you?" I ask quietly.

"Yeah! Like how horrific death could be and all the people who would be devastated that you're not there anymore, and how that there's so much in life that you haven't done," he states animatedly.

"Matt puts so much raw emotion and the passion in the vocals," Gerr says shaking his head.

"What's that about me?" Matt asks as he races through the door to the kitchen before returning with a glass of water.

"We were just discussing the song," I reply.

"Man, I really like that song. It just made me cry again."

I smile as I recall reading how adolescents search for strong emotional experiences from music and how they really enjoy surrendering to plays, feeling thrilling sensations and deep emotions (Saarikallio & Erkkilä, 2007, p. 98). "I hear you are going to speak before the band play."

"For sure," Matt replies. "Music is like one of the biggest ways of connecting with people and we get to perform this awesome song and show them what we are on about. You know, get people to think about the meaning and purpose of their lives and what happens to you when you die," Matt enthuses. "I felt the music was amazing even before it had lyrics! Imagine the impact when we actually perform it for them. Powerful stuff!" Matt sighs and leans back, his arms behind his head. "It's like a great way to evangelise. I really want them to get it. I really want to share my faith with people, but it's so hard because as soon as you try to talk, I mean really talk to people, you get shot down and called a 'loser'. If I can do it through this song it would be so cool." Matt sits forward his head cupped in his hands.

Sherman returns carrying his guitar. Gerr stands, picks up his bass, and they head out the front door.

"Matt! Matt! Come on ..." Vaughan calls as he charges up the stairs and sinks into the lounge next to Matt. "Hey, you sang great this arvo." Vaughan punches Matt in the arm. "I was so moved by it."

"Me too," laughs Matt pretending to blow his nose and wipe his eyes. "Do you know how hard it is to sing with a lump in your throat?"

Vaughan grabs his own throat and pretends to sing while being strangled. We laugh.

"No seriously, this song is something! Fresh and original, it expresses all the feelings I wanted to share," says Vaughan. "That's why I find music so great!"

He turns and looks at me, "You know Mum, I had that idea, that song, in my mind and having to make it real, you know, get it down, was real hard but now it's done, it feels amazing!"

"Great! I get the same feeling when I write and I find that as I return to a piece I see new things in it, which continue to amaze and challenge me. When you compose something, I bet you'll find it will have different meanings for you every time you go back to it, because you will be in what Flemons and Green (2002, p. 92) call a different place. That's what's so exciting about the creative process; it's vibrant and alive, never static."

"Speaking of creative process, I need the lead vocalist," Vaughan says as he stands and drags Matt away.

As they leave I smile as I recall the way things have changed in the last few months. Although the noise levels are still a problem, and I tire of answering the front door, as they wander in and out, I love having the lads here. They are no longer just dark shadows who steal silently in and out of the front door. We've crossed the generational divide of "them" and "us" and created more of a sense of partnership. We now negotiate practice times to allow them time "to play all out" without upsetting me, and I've found like Bloustien (2007) that "far from seeking independence from parental, familial and older social networks, [these] young people realise that the fastest route to success is through mentors, family members, cultural networks and creative pathways" (p. 452) and have been happy to negotiate with us and include us in most of their plans. This may sound like they are using us to get where they want but I know that I am not just the provider of a physical place for the band to practice, but also an emotional place where they can test their ideas for the band and their lives. At times, it feels like walking a tight rope: balancing being a supportive friend/mentor with the need for parental discipline, caution, and restraint, all the time moving slowly forward toward your goal, buffeted by things out of your control. In sharing Vaughan's passion for music, I've lost much of the fear I had, because much of the unknown has become known, and what I don't know, I'm not afraid to ask. I'm sure there are still things Mum will never know, but that is okay, for I have those secrets too.

June 2009. Coda and 'Dead'-ication

A feeling of heaviness hangs over me tonight as I sit on the lounge in the quiet empty room. I look down at the shiny cream-coloured order of service in my hand. "In Loving Memory of ..." The smiling face of a 19-year-old boy seems so out of place under those words. Yet it is not one, but two, faces that merge and interchange under these words, as my tears fall silently for the two teenaged lads from our small country town who have lost their lives in separate car crashes, these past two weeks.

Vaughan and the band have just left for a gig in Adelaide. I helped pack their cars full of the music equipment, and told them to drive carefully as darkness descended and the rain began to fall. What do I hope when I say that? What is careful to a young man? "Careful," I called out to my two-year-old as he skipped along the footpath. "Careful," I say to the elderly man I help down the footpath and across the street. "Careful." Both interpret that word differently. One knows no danger; one has seen a lot of danger. "Careful."

I am careful. Full of care and concern for these young men, our young men, my young men. Our community has held meetings to try and understand what it is we can do to stop the road carnage. There, that word again, *carnage,* the word that brought Vaughan and me to a place where we had to confront grief and our fears about death, and ended with the composition and performance of the song "Beautiful Here".

I try to imagine how the boys will feel tonight as they perform that song. How do you sing when you are in mourning? Matt told me he is really angry with God. Perhaps his screams will be more real tonight. Gerr feels like he's been kicked in the gut. Will he attack his bass guitar strings to relieve that pain? Vaughan can't understand why they are angry with God. He feels closer to God right now. Perhaps that will allow him to keep a steady beat on the drums as the tension rises and falls.

"As time goes by …" Rod Stewart's husky voice trails off as I look at the clock, waiting anxiously for Vaughan to return. He is late. I text and he responds that they have car trouble. As I sip soothing camomile tea I hear Vaughan return. The gig was a hit, he tells me. They have been asked to play again.

"How did it feel to perform 'Beautiful Here' tonight?" I ask, finally able to voice the question that has been haunting me all evening.

"Great! We dedicated it to the boys who were killed," he replies. "Then we sang our guts out! There were lots of kids from school there, and others in the audience came up to us and said they had read about the deaths in the newspaper. I reckon they all felt it with us."

As he wishes me good night and wanders into his room, I am left wondering how many songs it will take to stop the road toll rising. In composing "Beautiful Here" Vaughan set out to talk about death experiences and how they can make you value life. Tonight I find myself trying desperately to come to grips with what it is that makes a life well lived. Is it the numbers of years? No, I don't think so. Is it the number of people we touch? Perhaps. Is it whether we leave the world a better place than when we entered it? How can we judge that? I feel an ebb and flow of thought, of pain and joy, life and death, tension and release, music and silence.

My eyes are getting heavy now. I look once more at that smiling face on order of service for the funeral. How do I make sense of all this? I open the cover and read "Cling to the memories and let them find their way to heal you ... the love and laughter, the joy we shared will make us strong."

I guess the band have found the answer. We dedicate ourselves to remembering, to honouring, to learning, to desperately trying to improve lives, and we keep on composing and making music, telling and writing stories, screaming and singing our guts out until we are filled with the joy of life.

Acknowledgments

The author wishes to thank Carolyn Ellis for helpful comments on an earlier version. I also wish to thank Vaughan and his band members for their willingness to share and delve deeper with me into their love of music and life.

Endnote

1   Ali & Peynircioglu (2006) found in their study that melodies were more dominant than lyrics in eliciting emotions.

References

Ali, S. O., & Peynircioglu, Z. F. (2006). Songs and emotions: Are lyrics and melodies equal partners? *Psychology of Music, 34*, 511–534.

Arnett, J. J. (1995). *Metalheads: Heavy metal music and adolescent alienation.* Boulder, CA: Westview Press.

Bloustien, G. (2007). "Wigging people out": Youth music practice and mediated communities. *Journal of Community & Applied Social Psychology, 17*, 446–462.

Bochner, A., & Ellis, C. (2003). An introduction to the arts and narrative research: Art as inquiry, *Qualitative Inquiry, 9*, 506–514.

Dietz, M. L., Prus, R., & Shaffir, W. (Eds.) (1994). *Doing everyday life: Ethnography as human lived experience.* Toronto, Canada: Copp, Clark Longman.

Ellis, C. (2004). *The ethnographic I: A methodological novel about autoethnography.* Walnut Creek, CA: AltaMira Press.

Ellis, C. (1993). "There are survivors": Telling a story of sudden death. *Sociological Quarterly, 34*, 711–30.

Ellis, C. (2007). *The ethnographic I: A methodological novel about autoethnography.* Walnut Creek, CA: Alta Mira Press.

Ellis, C. (2008). *Revision: Autoethnographic reflections on life and work.* Walnut Creek, CA: Left Coast Press.

Flemons, D., & Green, S. (2002). Stories that conform/ stories that transform: A conversation in four parts. In A. Bochner & C. Ellis (Eds.), *Ethnographically speaking: Autoethnography, literature, and aesthetics* (pp. 87–94). Walnut Creek, CA: Alta Mira Press.

Fornas , J., Lindberg, U., & Sernhede, O. (1995). *In garageland.* London: Routledge.

Gattenstaetter, C. (2007). Semantical Investigations: From the Acoustic Signal to the Musical Event Sketches Towards a Compositional Poetics (W. Hoban, Trans.). *MusikTexte, 113*, 19–26.

Glassner, B., & Hertz, R. (Eds.) (1999). *Qualitative sociology as everyday life*. Thousand Oaks, CA: Sage.

Gracyk, T. (1993). Romanticizing rock music. *Journal of Aesthetic Education, 27*(2), 43–58.

Hirschhorn, J. (2004). *The complete idiot's guide to songwriting*. New York. Alpha.

Jaffurs, S. E. (2004). The impact of informal music learning practices in the classroom, or how I learned how to teach from a garage band. *International Journal of Music Education, 22*(3), 189–200.

Kahn-Harris, K. (2002). Death metal and the limits of musical expression. In M. Cloonan & R. Garofalo (Eds.), *Policing popular music* (pp. 81–99). Philadelphia, PA: Temple University Press.

Kahn-Harris, K. (2004). The 'failure' of youth culture: Reflexivity, music and politics in the black metal scene. *European Journal of Cultural Studies, 7*(1), 95–111.

Levitin, D. (2008). *This is your brain on music*. London: Atlantic Books.

Manning, P. (1999). Five minutes. In B. Glassner & R. Hertz (Eds.), *Qualitative sociology as everyday life* (pp. 97–107). Thousand Oaks, CA: Sage.

Pelias, R. (2002). For father and son: An ethnodrama with no catharsis. In A. Bochner & C. Ellis (Eds.), *Ethnographically speaking: Autoethnography, literature, and aesthetics*, (pp. 35–43). Walnut Creek, CA: Alta Mira Press.

Piper, D., & Murphey, C. (2004). *90 minutes in heaven: A true story of death and life*. Grand Rapids, MI: Revell.

Saarikallio, S., & Erkkilä, J. (2007). The role of music in adolescents' mood regulation. *Psychology of Music, 35*(1), 88–109.

Scott-Hoy, K., & Ellis, C. (2008). Wording Pictures: Discovering Heartful Autoethnography. In J. G. Knowles & A. L. Cole (Eds.), *Handbook of the arts in qualitative research* (pp. 127–140). Thousand Oaks, CA: Sage.

Chapter 3

Musical Artefacts of My Father's Death
Autoethnography, Music, and Aesthetic Representation

Chris J. Patti

> Eight weeks after Dad passed away, we found eight shoeboxes in his closet. They were filled with scraps of paper, old envelops, napkins, matchbook covers, little blue spiral notebooks — even cash register receipts — all covered with ideas Dad thought were profound, interesting, or merely amusing.
>
> H. Jackson Brown, *A Father's Book of Wisdom* (1990, p. 3)

These words introduce *A Father's Book of Wisdom*, a book of quotes my older sister gave my dad for Father's Day, 1992. Today, 12 years after my father's death from melanoma, I still identify with the author's experience every time I run across scraps of paper, pictures, and memories of my father. These fragments are artefacts of Dad, though they ultimately fail to represent him as a whole. Music is another way of remembering my father. From the age of 17 to my current age of 27, I have written, recorded, and performed songs about Dad. How I remember my father has changed over the past decade and this is reflected in my music. These songs are aesthetic artefacts, holding insight into my experience of my father's death.

This chapter investigates four songs I have written about my father. I use an autoethnographic approach to explore the complexity of representing human experience (Crawford, 1996; Ellis, 1997, 2004; Krizek, 2003), as it relates to illness, life, and death (Ellis, 1993, 1995; Park-Fuller, 1995, 2008). Brown's (1990) discovery of his father's material artefacts is metaphorically like my process of *archeologically*[1] (Foucault, 1969/1972) excavating the songs about my father. I am attempting to unearth layered, complex fragments of my personal history. Each song paints a particular portrait of my father, my experience of his death, and my own subjective process of making meaning from lived experience.

Autoethnographic Context

In this "personal ethnography" (Crawford, 1996), I represent my lived experience as "an unstable/subjective self, ... the surfing of perspectives, the high-speed juxtaposition of the private and global ... precarious stories of various truths" (p. 168). My unstable/subjective self continually changes as I struggle to make meaning from my father's death. I feel the paradoxical growth and loss that have come from this experience. I surf between autoethnography and music, theory and personal experience, life and death. The intricacies of my private story simultaneously juxtapose global issues of human experience. This is a precarious, ever-changing story that I can never know or tell completely. I make this story up as I go along, and I try to tell it as "truthfully" as I know how, so that it resonates with my experience and hopefully with readers as well.

I treat autoethnography as a methodological art — an aesthetic representation that struggles to contextualise and translate the specificities of human experience in larger cultural, academic contexts. In this sense, I borrow from Kurt Vonnegut's (2007) final lines in his last book:[2]

> It's very simple. There are two sorts of artists, one not being the least superior to the other. But one responds to the history of his or her art so far, and the other responds to life itself ... What you respond to in any work of art is the artist's struggle against his or her limitations. (p. 135)

Autoethnography is an art that "responds to life itself" and struggles meaningfully against the limitations of representing and *translating* (Burke, 1968) lived experience: "Art is a translation, and every translation is a compromise (although, be it noted, a compromise which may have new virtues of its own, virtues not part of the original)" (p. 54). Music and autoethnography continue to help me remember and understand the life and death of my father. I create new virtues — memories, meanings, and insights — through these creative processes.

My (Father's) Story

I was 11 in the summer of 1993 — the year I learned my dad, who was 37 years old, had a rare, stage-4 melanoma. One Saturday afternoon my father said, "Chris, feel my stomach … do you feel that weird bump there?" Pressing his abdomen, my hand found a hard, golf ball-sized knot. I said immediately, "It's a tumor, you need to go to the doctor." That was the last I heard of it for a while.

At this point my parents had, by most accounts, an ideal marriage. We lived in the picturesque, upper-middle class suburb of Laguna Hills — a small city in southern Orange County, California. We had a large house at the end of a cul-de-sac in a community filled with lawyers, businessmen, and other successful professionals. Sometime after I felt the bump, my parents separated. Shortly after their separation, my dad invited my mom, sister, brother and me over to his half-empty house (half of the furniture had been moved to my mom's new house). We all collected in the barren living room and sat on my dad's remaining gaudy green leather couch and chair.

My dad told us he loved us very much, that he had a serious cancer, and had been undergoing chemotherapy for the past few months. He said he was a fighter and did not believe the statistics. "The statistics don't matter; they don't tell a person's will to live, and I have an unstoppable will to live." I believed him, and while I was scared, I knew that he would survive. After all, my dad was the biggest, strongest, and most alive person I'd ever known. He was the sort of archetypal father embodied by Chevy Chase in the *Vacation* movies — a traditional breadwinning alpha male, who was also loving and sensitive. Less than three years later, after a difficult and honourable fight, at the age of 39, my father passed away. I was 14.

Songs About Dad

Playing music and writing songs have often been the only ways for me to share the dangerous, painful, and hidden parts of my experience. For the past decade, I have performed professionally as a singer, songwriter, and bass player. My rock-n-roll band, *My Favorite Band*[3] went on multiple tours of California,[4] and we played many well-known clubs in southern California.[5] In 2006, we won the Best Buy/Sony Battle of the Bands.[6] Today, my musical career involves working with sound engineer and guitarist Phil Allen[7] on a recording project called *Mr Radar*. My perspectives as a working musician and academic influence my songs, analyses, and stories. In my analysis, I start with the most recent song, digging chronologically deeper into my fragmented memory.

My most recent song, *Ties (Lies) That Bind* (Patti & Allen, 2008, track 3), was recorded in response to a graduate seminar on ethnography I took in autumn 2008. I was conducting participant observation at cancer support groups in Tampa, Florida. Once again, cancer became my academic focus. My chest knotted with fear as I entered the hospital to find a support group. I rinsed the sweat off my face and was nauseated by the familiar smell of antiseptic soap. I thought, "Why can't I move on to a topic that doesn't force me to confront Dad's death and my fear that I too am genetically damned to get cancer?"

> *Ties (Lies) That Bind*
>
> **Verse:** Undo this / and clean away /
> These fragments / of memory /
> All that was yours /
> I know for sure / of this secure /
> Quicksand and tides / the lies that bind /
> Behind your smile / while all the while /
> There lies a core / of nothing more /
>
> **Chorus:** I can't / stand back / stand up / react to this cross /
> You lied / you died / your heart and mine crucified /
> For what / for now / forever and no I can't count
> To three and wake me from this dream /
>
> **Verse:** I know for sure / there was no cure /
> For you and I / the ties that bind /
> And since the day / you went away /
> I've learned much more / there's no for sure /

Sonically, the song is ethereal and dark. Keyboard, bass guitar, and guitar melodies weave in and out, meandering from the background to the foreground. My musical influences span a wide range of bands and artists such as Led Zeppelin, *Weather Report*, *Tower of Power*, *Red Hot Chilli Peppers*, *Foo Fighters*, Chris Cornell, and *Jellyfish*. While I have been heavily influenced by musical genres such as rock, jazz, funk, blues, punk, and pop, the most recent song attempts to deconstruct and forget genre entirely, to be post-genre — an impossible task. The more I write music the more limiting genres become. The more I think about the experience of my father's death the more unknowable it becomes. My postmodern thoughts about human experience parallel my musical expression.

The lyrics speak to the complexity of life and contrast the simple (four major chords) sonic landscape. Rhetorically,[8] this sonic/lyric tension adds "perspective by incongruity" (Burke, 1954) to the song. This same technique is used in Bruce Springsteen's (1984) anthem "Born in the USA": Sonically, the song is a proud power-ballad, yet the lyrics tell the intimate tale of the struggle of a Vietnam veteran.

The first lines, which speak about cleaning away the fragments of your memory, represent my frustration with being unable to stop grieving. The notion that I am trying to "clean away" my memories of Dad is dangerous and something I rarely express to my friends or family directly. Music and autoethnography allow me to express forbidden feelings that I sometimes want to stop thinking about my dad, stop hurting, and stop confronting cancer.

Further, artistic expression is one way to access the unconscious mind, which often surfaces hidden, shadowy images[9] (Jung, 1947; Rushing and Frentz, 1995). Music, according to Jung (1947), "contains ... a material which it very well adapted to bring into play the abundance of ancient symbolic possibilities, latent in the human mind" (p. 391). The archetypal images and words used in my music represent windows into my unconscious mind/memory/emotion/creativity.

The first song exposes a central tension in my music: trying to let go and be at peace while also trying to hold close and honour my dad. The lyric, "these fragments of memory, all that was yours" inspired this chapter. Today, 12 years after my dad's death, all I have are bits and pieces of him — his gold ring, Swiss Army watch, and leather jackets (all of which I still wear). While these fragments cannot create a complete image of my dad, they are still meaningful. The line "all that was yours" shifts the focus from my fragmented memories to my dad's lost memory. I will never know all the things that he knew. I can never reconstruct a complete image of him. All I can do is attempt to assemble a complex, unique, and nuanced collage.

Later in the first verse I sing "the lies that bind, behind your smile, while all the while, there lies a core, of nothing more". The word "lies" is used twice. Again, I am using art to express that which is dangerous and difficult to say. I accuse my father of lying about surviving cancer. He promised to survive and broke that promise. In the second verse the words change from "lies that bind" to "ties that bind", symbolising the connections our lies create. *Lies are an essential and binding aspect of human life.* In Burke's (1961) words, "[Human beings] can give a *wrong* answer. At least in their *mistakes*, then, they will be 'creative'; and to that extent they will be really free" (p. 282). This idea opposes traditional, Western morality, based on the ability to find and know Truth. Through our subjective limitations to understand and represent (through our lies) we attain creative expression and freedom. Crawford (1996) argues that our subjective limitations — our lies, instabilities, and insecurities — are rich with insight. Our lies make us interesting, they connect us, and further, from a postmodern autoethnographic perspective, lies are all we have.

In the chorus I sing about the unbearable pain and helplessness I felt when I realised my father was dying. My family and I, along with the latest cancer treatments, could offer no help. I watched my dad's body deteriorate from a powerful 6'2", 200-pound frame to a fragile skeleton weighing scarcely more than his 14-year-old son. As Dad put it, "Cancer is an effective diet, but I wouldn't recommend it". The chorus likens the burden of cancer patients and their families and friends to Jesus' crucifixion. "I can't stand back, stand up, react to this cross. You lied, you died, your heart and mine crucified." Here, the influence that Christianity has had on me is clear. Symbolically, Jesus' crucifixion represents one of the most archetypal images in Western culture (Jung, 1947; Burke, 1961). I am suggesting that those who die from cancer are tragic saviours, like Christ (blasphemy?). Their stories are mythical in proportion and should be treated as sacred. Perhaps I feel my father's story should redeem me from my own sins and guilt? Perhaps marginalised stories have that power redeem us from our collective guilt?

The second verse shows the influence of Buddhism in my life. The words symbolise a release of attachments, as well as an acceptance of uncertainty: "and since the day, you went away, I've learned much more, there's no for sure." In a broader, theoretical sense, Buddhism is symbolic of Eastern, non-modernist perspectives.[10] Not knowing for *sure*, not knowing Truth, is tied to my autoethnographic epistemology.

The second song, *Words You Say* (Patti & Allen, 2006, track 2), was written in response to ethnographic work I did in Long Beach, California at a peer-led cancer support group. For eight months, I was a participant observer and eventually created a 30-minute play using verbatim interviews from the members of the support group.[11] Pat (pseudonym), the main character of the play, had three types of cancer and was considered "terminally ill" for over a decade. I was immediately drawn to him and his wife Lori (pseudonym), and they became like family to me. At the wake following Pat's funeral, my script sat in the middle of a shrine dedicated to his life. Pat's story overlapped with my Dad's story and this is represented in the song.

Words You Say

Verse: I can hear 'em talk / everything they say /
The man who isn't walking now / his wife and family /
He can tell a tale / without saying a word /
The story wrote / on his face / the man with cancer's heard /

Chorus: On that day / I heard you say / a word to me /
And I won't / forget to / ride into the sun / you say /

Verse: The dust has fallen past and gone again /
It sometimes seems my only friend /
But I know that this is not the end / this is not the end /
Take your friendship with me now /
Save someone else with what you've found /
And I know that you are not around / you are not around /

The song opens with a lone Telecaster guitar playing a 16-count blues riff — heavy reverb. Pat, even weeks before his death, was a happy man who wore turquoise rings on every finger, a black cowboy hat, and a shirt from the "Grand Ole Opry". The first lines of this song represent the importance of listening to the stories of those dealing with cancer. "I can hear 'em talk, everything they say, the man who isn't walking now, his wife and family." The song has an old-West feel, both musically and lyrically, which invokes the archetypal image of the stoic cowboy (Rushing & Frentz, 1995). "The frontier myth ... is America's most enduring vision of the archetypal story ... that of the initiation of the boy into manhood" (Rushing & Frentz, 1995, p. 53). After my father's death, I felt I had been initiated into manhood. I had seen that even the strongest and healthiest person could die. Facing Dad's death at 14 forced me to mature. Symbolically, the cowboy lives isolated on the frontier in a world he knows is coming to an end (Rushing & Frentz, 1995). In a darker sense, the frontier is a metaphor for the isolation and imminence of death a cancer patient feels when labelled "terminally ill".

"He can tell a tale, without saying a word. The story wrote, on his face. The man with cancer's heard." This line comes from a memory of Pat as he lost his ability to speak. His demeanour told a powerful story of human struggle and dignity without saying a word. The last memory I have of my father overlaps with Pat's story. My father, medicated for pain and connected to medical equipment, gathered his family to say goodbye. He slipped in and out of consciousness as he lost his ability to speak. He even joked about his lack of lucidity: "I know I'm not making much sense." Yet his message of love for his family was viscerally clear. By collapsing my dad and

Pat's stories, this song suggests that autoethnographic expression can speak to the specificity of human experience while also to the experiences of others. Autoethnography exists on the *frontier* between self and other (Crawford, 1996; Ellis, 2004). Pat's and my dad's few words took on a preciousness that tapped into the depth of the human experience.

"On that day, I heard you say, a word to me. And I won't forget to ride into the sun." The archetype of the sun is repeated in many songs about my father and is symbolic of growth, power, transition, the cycle of life and death, and universality. "This image [the sun] was the first, and was profoundly entitled to become the symbolic carrier of human destiny" (Jung, 1947, p. 390). More specifically, my use of the word "sun" is a play on words that always comes to symbolise me as my father's son (a relationship influenced by Christian notions of The Father and The Son). Corroborating this Christian connection, the second verse begins, "The dust has fallen past and gone again". This line riffs on the Biblical saying "ashes to ashes, dust to dust".

The second verse continues, "Take your friendship with me now. Save someone else with what you've found. And I know that you are not around, you are not around." The lyrics speak of the obligation I feel to use the wisdom of Pat's and my father's lives to help others make sense of cancer. This ethical obligation is similar to the commitment guiding Conquergood's (1988, 1991, 2002), and many other critical ethnographers', work. Autoethnography, while focused on the intimacies of subjective experience, can also function critically to speak and give back to others. These lyrics imply that by listening to cancer patients it becomes possible to hear new stories about cancer, death, and dying (Rich, 2002).

The third song, *On My Way Home* (Patti, Allen, Malik, & Allen, 2003, track 8), was written in 2003 when my band was recording our album *Tyrannosaurus Rocks*. The song has a dark progressive-rock feel. The opening eighth-note bass melody is slow and sombre like a funeral procession. Glassy guitars punctuate the open sound, ringing like church bells. This song represents the paradox of feeling like my father is still alive while realising that he had been gone for — at the time this song was written — seven years. I was 21 when I wrote this song, just prior to my graduate education. The song shows my perspective prior to thinking of myself as an aspiring academic. *On My Way Home* falls neatly into the progressive-rock genre with its slow verse, powerfully distorted chorus, technically intricate double-time bridge, and resolving, four-part harmony outro.

On My Way Home

Verse: As I sit / I think of you / has it been so many years /
Since I waited / for you / to come home /
But still I find / myself awake / as I wonder where you are /
Now I cannot see / I've gone blind / looking at the sky / staring at
the sun /

Chorus: Thoughts in my head / painting a masterpiece /
Plastic / a hollow dream of you /
All the color / bright as your memory /
Is slowly fading away /

Bridge: It would be okay / if you're not here today /
You know I would be just fine /
Drifting through the night / I have lost my way /
Drifting through the night / I'll follow you home /

Outro: On my way home /
I'm on my way home /

The first verse of this song came from a night when I woke up, still half-asleep, and thought my father was returning home from work. Upon realising that I was dreaming, I thought about how long it had been since I had waited for him to come home. "Now I cannot see, I've gone blind, looking at the sky, staring at the sun." This line invokes the sun archetype and symbolises the futility and pain of trying to know what happened to my dad *after* he died.

The chorus of this song resonates with the theoretical ideas of this chapter. "Thoughts in my head, painting a masterpiece. Plastic, a hollow dream of you. All the color, bright as your memory, is slowly fading away." These words articulate my "hollow" attempts to reconstruct images of my father artistically. These artistic translations, in their limitations, are still masterpieces. Further, the frustration of realising the limitations of my memory is shown. This is a tragic understanding that, as I age, I will continue to lose the details and colour of my father's memory. Like death, the loss of memory is common to human experience. I fight against my loss of memory. My artistic expressions of Dad, synthesised here in my musical autoethnography, create an archive of memories. These songs and words unearth specific memories, retrieving and displaying the treasures of my experience. My art takes me back to places, times, and emotions. I look back through this archive and new meanings emerge as I contrast my current and former selves.

The bridge and outro of this song represent the back-and-fourth emotional journey of dealing with a loved one's death. The music here has a frantic pace, emphasising the energy and conflicting emotion in the lyrics. "It would be okay. If you're not here today. You know I would be just fine. Drifting through the night. I have lost my way. Drifting through the night. I'll follow you home. On my way home. I'm on my way home." The music resolves dramatically at this point into a four-chord outro. The last line resounds in four-part harmony and repeats four times. These words are positive and symbolise that I can still follow my dad's memory to a place of solace and safety. My father's memory, too, has a safe home in my music and scholarship.

The fourth song, *Justin Time* (Patti & Malik, 1999, track 4), was written when I was 17. This was the first and most raw song I wrote about my father. The music has a pop-punk feel and alternates between heavy guitar distortion and clean guitar picking. Soft "angelic" vocals are barely audible in the background. The title is an inside joke that my father used to have with my childhood friend, Justin Malik. Whenever Justin would visit, my dad would jokingly say, "Hey, Justin time!" Justin's father passed away from cancer five years after my dad. Justin was also the rhythm guitarist for *My Favorite Band* and the co-writer of this song. *Justin Time* makes a fitting close to my analysis of the songs about my father.

> *Justin Time*
> **Verse:** Last night / after I fell asleep /
> You were there / in my dreams /
> And things were how they used to be /
> When I awoke / I did see /
> It's different now / without you here /
> I've grown so much I feel you near /
> I notice you in everything I see /
> I know now you're part of me /
>
> **Pre-Chorus:** Now you live in my memory /
> I see you in all you teach /
> As time passes by / you grow stronger in my life /
>
> **Chorus:** I see you in a passer by /
> I feel you when I start to cry /
> I know you're still here with me /
> All your love eternally /
>
> **Verse:** I notice you in everything I see /
> I know now you're part of me /
> This is how / I made it through / the loss of you /
> I know someday I'll see you again /
> But I will never understand /

This song is prototypical of the rest of my songs about Dad. Memory and artistic representations are cyclical, self-referential, and constantly shifting — being transformed and recycled over time. The song contains the themes of dreaming, memory, growth, wisdom, sadness, and love. The first lines are very close to the first lines in *On My Way Home*. "Last night after I fell asleep, you were there in my dreams. And things were how they used to be." This is a bittersweet line signifying the happiness of my memories of my father and also the inability to relive those memories.

"When I awoke I did see. It's different now without you here. I've grown so much I feel you near." These lines show a realisation of life without Dad. There is also contradiction in the words "It's different now without you here. I've grown so much I feel you near". I am trying to show the sadness of losing my father and also the growth and connection that his death continues to create. Remembering and representing stories of illness, death, and dying celebrates life (Ellis, 1993, 1995; Hedtke & Winslade, 2004). Stories of death show the ongoing influence that loved ones continue to have on us, long after they are gone; they create a continuing conversation (Hedtke & Winslade, 2004). In the last lines of the first verse I sing, "I notice you in everything I see. I know now you're part of me." These lines come from seeing people on the street who looked like my father. For the first five years after his death, I would see people I thought were my dad everywhere. On occasion, I would even follow these people to make sure they were not him.

The second verse echoes the first but changes slightly towards the middle: "I notice you in everything I see. I know now you're part of me. This is how I made it through the loss of you. I know someday I'll see you again. But I will never understand." The last line was a struggle. I remember going back and forth in my mind about it. Half the time I wanted to sing, "then I will finally understand". Even when recording this song, the lyrics I wrote contained the more positive of the two versions. However, when I recorded the vocal, the negative version came out in the performance. In retrospect, this line speaks to my age — 17 — and my nihilistic, punk influences at the time. I wanted to be angry and I wanted to represent how impossible it would be to ever understand the death of my father. Today I still want to show the impossibility of understanding human experience; however, now I am inspired by my limitations. I live in the liminal spaces created through following the cracks in my story. I rejoice in the constant opportunity to create afforded by my limitations.

Remembering the End

This chapter celebrates my father's life and death and the depth of human experience. My creative expressions intertwine, informing one another. They synthesise as musical autoethnography. This form of artistic expression gives me a new vision of my creativity and life experience. I envision my songs, writing, and father anew. I hear my autoethnography differently because of my music. I see my music reflected in my theory and my theory reflected in my songs. I understand more about my music and autoethnography by combining the two, by fusing two forms of my artistic expression. I observe myself surfing between my memories and my present reality, between subjective and collective experience, between various levels of truths. I see my father in a unique light created through this specific process, aware now of the tragedy of his death and yet the grace and humour with which he handled it. I gain strength knowing that he is still a part of me. I see his influence in everything I create and I am able to more fully embrace the sadness I feel at his loss.

Each song lyric and analysis provides me with more insight about the life and death of my father, the connections between my experience and others', and the meaning that emerges through artistic creation. *Ties (Lies) That Bind* shows me at my worst: tired of grieving and afraid of confronting cancer again. The analysis offers a window into my unconscious mind, which links art to both individual and collective experience (Jung, 1941; Rushing & Frentz, 1995). In this sense, I connect Jesus' sacrifice and the redemption of humanity to the sacrifice of those who die of cancer. Collective redemption occurs by learning from marginalised experiences such as these.

I bring up the anger I held towards my father for lying about survival. This pain is released in the realisation that lies are an essential, binding aspect of human experience. I realise my father did his best to survive despite his cancer. Because human experience is always already too complex to understand, limited representations (lies) are all we have. Buddhism adds to this idea, representing an Eastern perspective that seeks wisdom as opposed to Truth. Theoretically, this is a goal of Ellis's (2004) perspective on autoethnography — to gain wisdom through writing about personal experience.

Words You Say combines my father's and Pat's stories as cancer took their ability to speak. Pat's cowboy demeanour and my dad's love of western novels inspired the sonic/lyric old-west feel of the song. This draws on the frontier myth in order to underline the triple frontiers of: (1) the initiation into manhood I felt following the death of my father;

(2) the imminence of death created when a patient is labelled "terminally ill"; and (3), the liminal space between self and other central to autoethnography.

Second, this song employs the archetype of the sun. The sun is a vital metaphor used repeatedly in songs about my father. Symbolically:

> The sun ... sacrifices its greatest strength in order to hasten onwards to the fruits of autumn, which are the seeds of immortality; fulfilled in children, in works, in posthumous fame, in a new order of things, all of which in their turn begin and complete the sun's course over again. (Jung, 1947, p. 391)

The sun represents the cyclical nature of human life and the torch my father has passed to me. He is fulfilled and lives on in my memory, work, and life.

On My Way Home shows tragically that as I age, my memories of my father will continue to fade. This is balanced with the idea that creative expressions of my father are masterpieces that create a home for my memories of him. This song, fitting neatly into the progressive-rock genre, also highlights the parallels between my musical genre-arc and theoretical arc. My music moves from pop-punk, to progressive rock, to contemplative attempts as writing post-genre music. This move mirrors my theoretical growth towards postmodern autoethnographic expression. My music and autoethnography are tied together. They mutually reference and inspire each other.

Justin Time takes me back to the beginning. I see Justin smiling as my father makes his dad-like pun: "Hey, Justin time!" I think of Justin as he lost his father to cancer. I remember how afraid I was when I wrote this song and the embrace I received from my band mates at hearing the lyrics. I think of a friend who also lost his father to cancer and the feeling I had when he told me that he listens to the song when he wants to think about his dad. Ultimately, this song is tied to the broader idea that stories of death create ongoing conversations with the ones we lose, keep them in our lives, and are celebrations of life (Ellis, 1993, 1995; Hedtke & Winslade, 2004).

Why do I continue to write songs and scholarship about my father? Because there's always more to say, explore, remember, learn. Because my father continues to influence my life. Because there is joy in remembering. Because there is a chance that the wisdom that comes from writing about Dad can help others to deal with similar losses. Because I have a need to create. Because I can't stop. As time has gone on, the frequency with which I write songs about my dad has increased. This reminds me of a lyric from *Justin Time*: "as time passes by, you grow stronger in my life." The more I write about Dad the more there is to know and express. My life and the memories of my father become richer through these expressions.

As I work to make sense of these thoughts, a new song emerges to synthesise the theoretical and aesthetic insights of this musical autoethnography. It is only right that this chapter should end in song.

Remembering the End

Verse: East and West / the winds of change are blowing again / And this buffalo head nickel's a piece of you / remembering the end / Ongoing fragments of a life that lives through me / An artefact / a peace of mind / is what you give / what you give to me /

Chorus: You said / to a fool / time brings age not wisdom / Well I'm no fool / the time has shown / more than Truth to me / As a man / your life and death / they continue burning / Like the sun / in my songs / I begin to see /

Verse: Once again / writing a song about you / New images reflecting in the warm glow / of a campfire's light / A circle of stories / surround the burning flames / Creating there a sacred space / where memories / memories remain /

Acknowledgements

I am grateful to the anonymous reviewer and Brydie-Leigh Bartleet for their generous and helpful comments in preparing this chapter. Carolyn Ellis was instrumental in guiding me through the writing process, thank you. I am grateful to Kenley Erickson for her love and emotional support. I would also like to acknowledge my peers Dave Steinweg and Katie Wegner for their contributions to this piece. My music and this chapter would not be possible without my band mates Phil Allen, Justin Malik, and Francis Allen—thank you. This piece is dedicated to my dad, Walter A. Patti, Jr.

Endnotes

1 Foucault's notion of archeology was a paradigm-shifting method of historical analysis focused on unearthing more complex, fragmented, and often contradictory notions of history, which challenged prevailing modernist theories of history (1972). Though Foucault was not concerned with personal notions of history, this work applies his ideas to that topic.

2 Vonnegut attributes this quote to his friend and graphic artist Saul Steinberg. He also mentions that Saul was the wisest person he ever met.

3 "My Favorite Band" seems to be an inherently autoethnographic name — although the band came up with the name long before I knew what autoethnography was.

4   The band's largest show was at Sonoma State University in front of approximately 3,000 people. We also played at California State University, Long Beach, University of California at Davis, and University of California at Irvine in front of more than a thousand people.

5   Most notably, the Whiskey and House of Blues in Los Angeles, Chain Reaction in Anaheim, and the Coach House in San Juan Capistrano.

6   In order to win this competition, we went through multiple elimination rounds, eventually winning the semi-finals at the House of Blues in Los Angeles (for a packed house of approximately 800), and then winning the finals at the famous Roosevelt Hotel in Los Angeles (an intimate show for a few hundred Best Buy/Sony management). Our reward was free recording time at the famous Los Angeles recording studio, The Chop Shop. However, we were unhappy with the results of the recording time and re-recorded the demo ourselves.

7   Phil Allen was the lead guitarist for *My Favorite Band*. He works for Blue Microphones as a product engineer. He graduated with a degree in sound engineering from the University of Southern California, where the five-time Grammy Award wining producer Glen Ballard mentored him.

8   Rhetorical criticism influences the textual analysis of this chapter. Specifically, Kenneth Burke's dramatistic vocabulary is used. Burke's work is seen as foundational to the field of contemporary rhetorical criticism. His dramatistic perspective emphasises the symbolic depth present in texts, which speaks to the worldview of the rhetor (in this case, me). Additionally, his perspective fits well with the aesthetic aim of this paper, emphasizing the dramatic, creative elements of human symbolic action.

9   Rushing & Frentz legitimised the use of Jungian archetypal criticism in the field of rhetorical criticism. This type of rhetorical criticism is also referred to as psychological criticism. The purpose of this type of analysis is to examine specific texts in order to explore archetypal symbols, which speak to larger cultural and theoretical exigencies. Their work deals specifically with bridging the theoretical divide of modernism and postmodernism. Most of their analyses are of popular films (e.g., *Terminator*); however, their work is also interested in bridging personal subjectivity with broader cultural and theoretical observations.

10 Modern/postmodern distinctions tend to be a Western phenomenon.

11 This play was then performed (with the help of five colleagues) for the support group and 200 members of the local and university community. A DVD of the videotaped performance was subsequently presented at the National Communication Associations conference, in Chicago 2007.

References

Brown, J. (1990). *A father's book of wisdom*. Nashville, TN: Rutledge Hill Press.

Burke, K. (1954). *Permanence and change: An anatomy of purpose*. Los Angeles: University of California Press.

Burke, K. (1961). *The rhetoric of religion: Studies in logology*. Los Angeles: University of California Press.

Burke, K. (1968). *Counter-statement*. Los Angeles: University of California Press.

Conquergood, D. (1988). Health theatre in a Hmong refugee camp: Performance, communication, and dialogue. *The Drama Review, 32*, 174–208.

Conquergood, D. (1991). Rethinking ethnography: Towards a critical cultural politics. *Communication Monographs, 58*, 179–194.

Conquergood, D. (2002). Performance studies: Interventions and radical research. *The Drama Review, 46*, 145–156.

Crawford, L. (1996). Personal ethnography. *Communication Monographs, 63*, 158–170.

Ellis, C. (1993). There are survivors: Telling a story of sudden death. *Sociological Quarterly, 34*, 711–730.

Ellis, C. (1995). *Final negotiations: A story of love, loss, and chronic illness*. Philadelphia: Temple University Press.

Ellis, C. (1997). Evocative autoethnography: Writing emotionally about our lives. In W. G. Tierney & Y. S. Lincoln (Eds.), *Representation and text: Reframing narrative voices* (pp. 115–139). Albany, NY: State University of New York Press.

Ellis, C. (2004). *The ethnographic I: A methodological novel about autoethnography*. Walnut Creek, CA: AltaMira Press.

Foucault, M. (1972). *The archeology of knowledge* (A. M. Sheridan Smith, Trans.). New York: Pantheon. (Original work published 1969)

Hedtke, L., & Winslade, J. (2004). *Re-membering Lives: Conversations with the Dying*. Amityville, NY: Baywood.

Jung, C. G. (1947). *Psychology of the unconscious*. New York: Dodd, Mead, & Company.

Krizek, R. L. (2003). Ethnography as the Excavation of Personal Narrative. In R. P. Clair (Ed.), *Expressions of ethnography: Novel approaches to qualitative methods* (pp. 141–152). Albany, NY: State University of New York Press.

Park-Fuller, L. M. (1995). Narration and narratization of a cancer story: Composing and performing 'A clean breast of it'. *Text and Performance Quarterly, 15*, 60–67.

Park-Fuller, L. M. (2008). How to tell a true cancer story. *Text and Performance Quarterly, 28*, 178–182.

Patti, C., & Malik, J. (1999). Justin time. On *Monkey business* [CD]. Laguna Hills, CA: Self-Produced.

Patti, C., Allen, P., Malik J., & Allen, F. (2003). On my way home. On *Tyrannosaurus rocks* [CD]. Long Beach, CA: Self-Produced.

Patti, C., & Allen, P. (2006). Words you say. On *To the moon* [CD]. Long Beach, CA: Self-Produced.

Patti, C., & Allen, P. (2008). Ties (lies) that bind. On *To the moon* [CD]. Tampa, FL: Self-Produced.

Rich, M. (2002). Memory circles: The implications of (not) grieving at cancer camps. *Journal of Contemporary Ethnography, 31*, 548–581.

Rushing, J. H., & Frentz, T. S. (1995). *Projecting the shadow: The Cyborg hero in American Film*. Chicago: University of Chicago Press.

Springsteen, B. (1984). Born in the USA. On *Born in the USA* [CD]. New York: Sony Music.

Vonnegut, K. (2007). *A man without a country*. New York: Random House.

Chapter 4

Creativity and Improvisation
A Journey into Music

Peter Knight

> There I am sitting in the corner of our living room in the armchair, headphones on, with Skyhooks blasting into my ears whisking me away into some other reality. I have that sensation of movement, of motion, which music can bring. I watch as if from a great distance as my mother comes into the room and silently mouths something at me, smiles, then walks away.

I am 43 years old now and I have made a career for myself in music. It sometimes seems incredible to me to think that I did that. Not because it's so remarkable in and of itself, but because it seems amazing, given the relationship I had with music throughout my school years, that I made that choice and that the choice I made stuck.

I loved music when I was young, I loved to listen and I loved to play. I used to sit and practise the cornet for hours, playing from *A Tune a Day* until my lips were sore. However, like lots of children, I was not really urged to take music seriously or to consider a career in music. Instead, I was encouraged to play the trumpet as a "hobby" and to study the sciences and mathematics because that way you "keep your options open". I wanted to do the "right thing" and so I chose those subjects even though I was consistently better at humanities. As a teenager I spent a lot of time thinking about what career I might follow. I went through phases of wanting to be a pilot, then a geologist, and then a journalist. I kept playing the trumpet right through this time, having lessons, playing in the school orchestra, but year-by-year my enthusiasm for the instrument waned. I still *liked* playing but the *drive* to play that I'd experienced as a young boy gradually vanished.

I enrolled in an arts/science degree at Melbourne University the year after I finished school. It was the first of three courses that I dropped out of in as many years.

~~

> There I am sitting in the band, enveloped by sound. The tenor horns, the cornets, the tuba, the euphonium — in front of me, behind me, beside me. I remember the smell of stale uniforms along with that indescribable odour which emanates from brass instruments left too long in their cases. The valves of my cornet sluggish under my fingers, the notes on the page — D, one and three — A, one and two but higher than E — C, under the stave with a little line through it — no fingers down ...

~~

Music did not open up for me until I was in my twenties. I had pretty much given up the trumpet upon leaving school, though it wasn't so much that I "gave up", more like I just didn't get round to playing. However, my relationship with the instrument and my feeling for music changed when I was introduced to the idea of improvisation. I can remember the moment: It was in the University of Melbourne cafeteria. I was in my second year of an arts degree, which I approached without much consciousness of what I was doing or where it was leading me. I ran into a guy called Steph who played trumpet with me in high school orchestra. We started talking about the trumpet, about orchestra, about our teacher, Bob. Steph mentioned that he had started improvising on the trumpet and I asked him how he did that. He told me that you simply take the notes of the scale in a key and start making up your own melodies. I think he actually began describing his discovery something along the lines of, "Did you know you can ...?" or, "I found out that you can ...". Emphasis here was on the notion of *permission*. And I think this is maybe why I remember this conversation — because I recall thinking that I had never considered this possibility and wondering why.

When Steph and I played 2nd and 3rd trumpets in the Melbourne Grammar School Orchestra the idea of improvisation was literally never mentioned and jazz was not taught at all. I enjoyed playing trumpet but I never connected this with my genuine love of music. The trumpet for me was an interesting technical challenge and the orchestra a fun social opportunity. It was all totally separate from my interest in bands like Midnight Oil, Pink Floyd, and the Sex Pistols et al.

The only time the two came close to meeting was when I discovered the album *Feels So Good* by trumpeter/flugal hornist, Chuck Mangione. I remember being amazed by his approach; by the melodies, the feeling of freedom, the grooves and, most importantly, the *sound* of the instrument so far removed from the limited conception of the trumpet expressed in the orchestral repertoire I had come into contact with. I took the tape into my next lesson with Bob and put it on. He didn't look impressed and merely said, "Chuck Mangione used to play better when he was in the army." I couldn't imagine how he knew that but unfortunately I respected him enough to take that as the last word on the matter until my conversation with Steph five years later in the Melbourne Uni caf.

⌐⌐

> I'm looking at my reflection in the bell of my new trumpet. My forehead is huge, my mouth sucked into a tiny pointed chin. I can make all kinds of sounds with the slide, my eye huge now in reflection as I listen to the air suck through the valves before it releases with a pop.

⌐⌐

Although my music practice now incorporates a large range of influences I studied jazz for years and spent much of my twenties soaking up the sounds of New Orleans, New York and all the other geographic and cultural focal points important in the development of the music. Like most young Australian jazz musicians, much of my listening went on in my bedroom (for me in Albert Park in Melbourne) and in a sense that listening was quite disconnected from my upbringing and from the culture through which I moved on a daily basis. I didn't, however, spend a lot of time thinking about this disconnect during those years and I think in some vague sense I actually enjoyed it. I relished the exoticness of jazz and of those far off places — so far from where I had grown up in country Victoria.

⌐⌐

From the time of my conversation in the Melbourne University cafeteria with Steph I was led deeper into music by a series of random accidents. There was no shining light of inspiration, no sense of inevitability. In fact, I am almost certain that I would have never again picked up the trumpet, never again had anything to do with music, if any one of a number of unconnected events had not happened. And I don't think this would have necessarily been a bad thing. I love music and I'm glad — grateful — for the way my life has turned out, but I'm sure there are many other lives I could have happily lived. I do though have a sense that I was driven towards some sort of creative expression. The discovery of improvisation in music was the key to my realisation that *music* could be an outlet for that expression.

⌐⌐

> Still. Quiet and still — fingers going like little pistons. A slight pressure on my spine as I lean back. The drummer is pushing the beat up behind me. Thermal puffs of bass — little updraughts to hang notes on, notes like kites ...

⌐⌐

One day, not long after my conversation with Steph about improvisation, I was speaking to another university friend studying law. She told me she was involved in organising the band for the annual Law Review. She remembered that I played trumpet and said they were looking for a trumpet player for the band. I volunteered, and it was a great experience for me at that time. I loved everything about it, loved working with a group of people intensively to bring a show to fruition. The sense of teamwork and esprit de corps gave me an energy and enthusiasm I had not felt since leaving school. But the thing I loved most was that at every performance I got to play an improvised solo on *Summertime*. I had no idea of what I was doing, but the musical director (now a well-known composer) was encouraging and constructively critical. And I *felt* like I had something when I was "making it up". I was able to find a space within myself that I hadn't hitherto known. I'm sure it sounded amateurish; however, the important thing was that I experienced an opening of possibility.

⌐⌐

> I often wonder whether music is, for me, an escape from the search for meaning or a way of searching for meaning.

⌐⌐

Jazz music seized my imagination as a young man because improvisation is integral to its form. I was also drawn to it both as a listener and player because it features the trumpet. Most important to me though is that the process of creation is in evidence in the performance of jazz. Even when we listen to jazz on a CD we can hear the musicians responding to one another, witness surprise and delight or frustration at the unexpected and feel the excitement when the music is really working. In improvised music success or failure depends entirely on the relationships between the performers; without these relationships, there is no music. This is not to say that relationships must be "good" or friendly for the music to succeed — in fact they could be antagonistic — but there must be a level of engagement. In improvised music process and outcome are inextricable.

Contrastingly, in pre-composed music there is, by definition, a greater emphasis on a pre-determined musical outcome. That outcome can be (and often is) sublime, but as Christopher Small observes in *Musicking* (1998), there is, in pre-composed music, also a greater tendency for performers to rely on the music to do the "work" for them. Small's perspective certainly resonates with my early experiences of music, and even though I didn't think about these issues in this manner when I was 15 I nonetheless believe my *feeling* about music has not changed much since that time. After years of stultifying boredom rehearsing the repertoires of brass bands and amateur orchestras, the discovery of improvisation and of jazz all of a sudden reconnected my love for the sound of the trumpet with the natural love of music I had experienced when I was a child.

∿

I first came into contact with the cornet when I was about seven or eight years old. My discovery of the instrument was a revelation. I went to my friend's house one day after school and his dad had one, I got my hands on it and was completely besotted with its shininess and its mechanical workings. I made up my mind there and then that I must play it and nagged my parents to let me join the Orbost Municipal Brass Band (we lived at the time in the small country town of Orbost). At first they thought I was too young but eventually they relented and signed me up, and I got a musty old cornet in a beaten-up case with tattered but sumptuous deep-green felt lining. I loved playing in the band at first; I especially loved the uniform with its shiny buttons and epaulettes. I did my first gig in the main street of Orbost on Christmas Eve in about 1976. I remember the uniform smelled of mothballs. It was too big and was scratchy on my skin. And I remember that I couldn't really play, I just kind of mimed along on 4th cornet, occasionally managing to get out a few notes while looking intently at the page on my lyre music stand and enjoying that sensation of being *inside* music.

I loved the cornet; I loved the sound of it. I also loved the sound of my own voice. I was a boy given to daydreaming about doing "important" things: being a pop star or a movie star. I loved being the centre of attention — somewhere in me I still do, though my relationship with this is complicated now — I drove everyone around me mad, incessantly talking, asking questions, making up stories, having temper tantrums when I couldn't get my own way. But of course I grew up — small country towns have a way of pummelling the exuberance out of you, of knocking you down to size. Of making everything that is different about you seem aberrant.

I loved the cornet and I loved the feeling of being enveloped by music. Though now, when I look back on my first musical experiences in the Orbost Municipal Brass Band, I can see how those experiences helped to set in train both positive and negative aspects of my relationship with music. It is clear to me today that the bandmaster was a limited and insensitive man who cared little for the young people under his charge, and, although I have developed a narrative about spontaneity and free spiritedness and improvisation, my inclination towards improvisation could also partly be a response to a fear of performing notes written on a page, which I developed in these formative experiences.

⚮

> There I am in the Orbost Municipal Brass Band at rehearsal. A big boy with a grown-up cornet just like the men — I'm in the band with all that sound around me, lifting my cornet, imagining that I am playing the most beautiful music ever created. Eyes closed. Making it up because I can't read my part. Suddenly, the band stops — the sound stops — except for a few braying notes from my cornet sustaining awfully over the instantly yawning chasm of silence. I open my eyes and the bandmaster is glaring at me red faced — "That sounds terrible, what do you think you're doing?"

⚮

Many young people expect that a vocation will reveal itself as an epiphany; that their destiny will arrive in a flash of inspiration. I expected that to happen to me but it didn't. I tried studying a few different courses at university but nothing really inspired me. I had never been encouraged even to consider a creative path as it didn't really count as a "legitimate" choice, and two years into university I was bored and doing not much of anything except drink and hang around with my friends going out to hear indie rock bands in St Kilda. The stint with the Law Review playing trumpet in the band really was a highlight of that year and I had no way of imagining how that might become anything longer term; though I missed it when it finished I fell quickly back into my uninspired loop. That year, 1984, I failed all my subjects, argued with my parents, and became skinny and unhealthy.

It wasn't until 1985 that things really started to change for me when one day, for no immediate reason, I decided to become a musician — to make a career for myself in music. I remember riding on a tram through the city. I remember the very moment with clarity. The tram was clanking across Swanson St Bridge, it was late on a gloomy winter afternoon and I was heading home to Albert Park after a few hours smoking cigarettes and drinking coffee in the Melbourne University Cafeteria. I was thinking about what I should do with my life and at that moment I just decided I would be a musician. There was no great moment of inspiration or of feeling "called" to music; I just couldn't think of anything else to do that I really liked, and I was desperate for a direction in life.

For some reason that decision stuck. I started to practise the trumpet every day. I kept it simple: *Play every day*. I didn't play for long and I wasn't very organised in how I went about things, and I wasn't very good, but I played every day. For some reason I could do that when I hadn't been able to manage even the most modest discipline for the study of chemistry or commercial law. I practised differently from the way I had when I was at school: Instead of endlessly banging away at etudes and exercises from *Arban* and *Clarke*, I improvised. And I liked it. I would put on Miles Davis, or Vince Jones, or some old blues record I found in a second hand shop and just play along. I had no idea at all about the workings of harmony — all I knew was what Steph had told me — but it was fun to just play along and make it up.

I don't really believe in fate but I do think we make our own luck and that for some reason, when we make clear decisions, and direct energy in a focussed way that things happen — so it was for me. I was hitch-hiking one night from Albert Park to St Kilda to hear a band. I was with my flatmate Meagan. We were walking along Danks St with our fingers out when a car pulled over and offered us a lift. I opened the car door and was greeted by a familiar voice — Margaret — I knew her from university. She was with two guys a bit older than Meagan and me. We got in the car and started talking and Margaret asked me what I had been up to, I began to tell her about the Law Review and playing in the band and one of the guys in the front asked me what instrument I played. I told him and he immediately said — "I've got a band and we're looking for a horn section, do you want to come along for a rehearsal?"

It was the heyday of Hunters and Collectors, and The Saints had just released an album featuring a horn section — horn sections in rock bands were certainly flavour of the month. I hadn't really thought about all of this too much but I jumped at the opportunity to play with other people again. Two weeks later I was in Sydney for the first time and I was "on tour".

～

> Sinking. Releasing all the air from my lungs in great silvery bubbles and sliding to the bottom of the pool. Save a little in puffed out cheeks so I can lie there for a few blissful seconds looking at all the bendy legs and splashing from far, far away. A lifetime in a breath of air — in a moment. Then I'm lying on my belly on the hot cement at the edge of the pool, with my head on my hands, watching diamonds of water on my tanned arms slowly shrink.

～

For years I listened to jazz incessantly. I listened to nothing else; I was desperate to unlock its mysteries. I listened and played along and after a while started to learn trumpet solos taking them apart note by note. I was driven to understand the music, to learn the language, the syntax, and the style. Something in jazz music resonated with me deeply. Importantly too, as I have mentioned, the exoticness of jazz was incredibly attractive; the sense that this music had travelled from a long way away (culturally and geographically). I heard the fierce refusal to conform in the music of Miles Davis, John Coltrane, and Thelonious Monk and I loved it. And I think in some small way I related it to the outsider sensation which I felt as an over-exuberant young boy growing up in a country town that expected conformity. Perhaps for the same reason I also loved (and still love) the rebelliousness of rock, but jazz for me was like rock and roll without the pervasive nihilism that seems to drive much of that music. And I *burned* to play jazz.

～

George E. Lewis writes about jazz improvisation and notes that its differentiating characteristics include "its welcoming of agency, social necessity, personality and difference, as well as its strong relationship to popular and folk cultures" (2004, p. 150). His words resonate with my experience of being drawn to jazz and also to my more recent experience of feeling a need to move away from it (at least in the sense of style). He goes on to say, "the development of the improviser in improvised music is regarded as encompassing not only the formation of individual music personality but the harmonisation of one's musical personality with social environment" (p. 150).

In this sense a musician's development as an improviser in the jazz tradition (or as Lewis would say, from an "Afrological" starting point) is about gradually allowing one's personality and culture to speak through music. The comparison between jazz improvisation and autoethnography is too obvious not to be touched upon here, though I am not the first to draw such a parallel. Stacy Holman Jones (2002) describes torch singing as a form of autoethnography, and Deborah Reed-Danahay writes that autoethnography and torch singing both enact a life story within larger cultural and social contexts and histories (1997, p. 9). Instrumental jazz, too, enacts life stories within social contexts and histories, or should if we follow Lewis's thinking. I am also reminded of my own development as an improviser and my experience of cultural dislocation when Reed-Danahay notes:

> The most cogent aspect to the study of autoethnography is that of the cultural displacement or situation of exile characteristic of the themes expressed by autoethnographers ... whether the autoethnographer is the anthropologist studying his or her own kind, the native telling his or her life story, or the native anthropologist, this figure is not completely "at home". (1997, p. 4)

She might have added to this list: the Australian musician struggling to find authentic expression in the context of idioms and forms imported from America and Europe. As I developed as a musician this feeling of not being "completely at home" became more acute and I have spent the last ten years working towards developing my own language as an improviser and my own forms as a composer. I think of myself now as an "improvising" musician (and a composer) rather than a "jazz" musician because I have consciously moved away from the sounds of idiomatic American jazz. At a certain point in my development I could not ignore the question of what American jazz music has to do with a boy who grew up in country Victoria and Melbourne listening to Sherbet and Gary Glitter and Skyhooks, and whose background in music performance consisted of brass band and school orchestra. To paraphrase Whiteoak (1999), I began to wonder what I was doing playing music that developed in a completely different physical, spiritual and social environment to that in which we live. Interestingly though, my journey follows the paradigm of Afrological improvisation that Lewis describes (and which he distinguishes from "Eurological"). In fact I am probably closer to his notion of "jazz" now than I was when I was "re-creating" the sounds of jazz in terms of musical style.

～

One day around the time of my conversations with Steph about improvisation, and the rekindling of my relationship with the trumpet during the Law Review, I met this slightly older guy called Gavin who played the trumpet. We were talking and he casually said something about

"Miles"…"Miles who?" I asked. He looked at me in utter disbelief. And I can't believe now that I managed to play trumpet all through school — the best part of 10 years — without anybody mentioning Miles Davis to me. Gavin was gracious enough not to patronise me; instead he made me a tape of *Sketches of Spain*.

＝〜

> It's late at night. I'm travelling to Orbost with my girlfriend to visit my parents. We're driving along a flat straight stretch of road between Traralgon and Sale and there's a flat mist hanging low on the road. It feels like we're flying. Other than the mist it's a clear night and there are no other cars on the road. The clatter of castanets in the opening of Concierto de Aranjuez quietens our conversation. "Wow what's this?" my girlfriend asks me. "Some tape this guy called Gavin made me," I reply as the orchestra enters and states the melody. A moment later against the hum of the road I hear the sound of Miles Davis' trumpet for the first time …

＝〜

Lewis describes the process of learning to improvise in the jazz context as, "commencing with the emulation of other improvisers" (2004, p. 156). It occurs to me that the process of developing as an improviser is one of moving closer to the source of your inspiration. Removing obstacles, psychological and technical so you can speak through music with your own voice, and so that your culture and social environment can also find a way of speaking through your music. Lewis argues that the "notion of the importance of personal narrative" (2004, p. 156) is one of the central aspects of Afrological improvisation. He seems to imply that it transcends "style" and idiom, and when one tries to make sense of the range of musical utterance described as "jazz" — from New Orleans traditional to avant-garde downtown New York — it is this perspective that helps thread these superficially disparate musical phenomena together. It also helps me to make sense of my path as an improviser from jazz and rock through cross-cultural music to abstract electro-acoustic collaboration.

＝〜

> I'm looking at my reflection in the screen of my laptop listening to the sound of the air suck through the valves of my trumpet before it releases with a pop. I sample the sound and reverse it — thump — wheeze — then process and texturise the sound and listen as it layers up over previously sampled clicks and exhalations …

＝〜

One of my primary motivations as a musician today is to find ways of making my music relevant to the time and place in which I live. Creating music that draws on my background in jazz without being bound by the idiom, music that embodies the "personal". But here it is that words fail us — when we try to use them to describe what we are driven to express in music it's almost impossible to do without chasing yourself around in circles — suffice to say that what I am attempting to achieve is that difficult to define quality of "authenticity". And I use the term "authentic" knowing that in some sense it doesn't mean very much or that its meaning is not, as Schippers points out, "as clear, stable and value free" (2006, p. 333) as it may appear. What is authenticity? Authentic to whom? And so on. But it is a useful word in describing my practice in the context of this chapter because it points to the fact that I am more concerned with creating music that "feels" right to me and that communicates something of my truth (whatever that is). Schippers reminds us of Mautner's *Dictionary of Philosophy* definition of authenticity: "The quality of being genuine, being true to oneself" (Mautner 1995, p. 39).

David Borgo offers an interesting perspective in a fascinating paper about free improvisation and music pedagogy (2007) in which he refers to Eric Clarke's (2005) notion of an "ecological" approach to music performance. It seems particularly relevant here especially given the context of my musical development, in which improvisation has been key. The "ecological" approach to which Borgo refers resonates with what I am trying to achieve in my music practice: the creation of music that is personal and that embodies spontaneity, music in which the composed elements and the idiosyncratic improvisatory languages of the performers are integrated, music that is shaped through performance and which privileges process over outcomes. Borgo writes, "Ultimately, learning is not a matter of what one knows, but who one becomes" (2007, p. 62).

References

Borgo, D. (2007). Free jazz in the classroom: An ecological approach to music education. *Jazz Perspectives*, 1(1), 61 – 88.

Clarke, E. F. (2005). *Ways of listening: An ecological approach to the perception of musical meaning*. Oxford: Oxford University Press.

Holman Jones, S. (2002). The way we were, are, and might be: Torch singing as autoethnography. In Y. S. Lincoln & N. K. Denzin, *Turning points in qualitative research; Tying knots in a handkerchief* (pp. 105–118). Blue Ridge Summit, PA: Alta Mira Press.

Lewis, G. E. (2004). Improvised music after 1950: Afrological and Eurological perspectives. In D. Fischlin & A. Heble (Eds.), *The other side of nowhere* (pp. 131–162). Middletown, CT: Weselyan University Press.

Mautner, T. S. (1995). *A dictionary of philosophy*. Cambridge, MA: Blackwell.

Reed-Danahay, D. (1997). Introduction. In D. Reed-Danahay (Ed.), *Autoethnography: Rewriting the self and the social* (pp. 1–17). New York: Berg.

Schippers, H. (2006). Tradition, authenticity and context: The case for a dynamic approach. *British Journal of Music Education*. 23, 333–349. Cambridge: Cambridge University Press.

Small, C. (1998). *Musicking: The meanings of performing and listening*. Hanover: Wesleyan University Press.

Whiteoak, J. (1999). *Playing ad lib: Improvisatory music in Australia 1836–1970*. Sydney, Australia: Currency Press.

Section Two
Interpreting and Performing

Chapter 5

⤳ Bye Bye Love

Stacy Holman Jones

In the matter of what happens in singing, in the proffering of I-love-you, desire is neither repressed ... nor recognised ... but simply: released.

(Barthes, 1978, p. 149).

If I picked you up, oh you'd slip right away ... baby, I think I love you too much.

(Knopfler, n.d., para. 9–10, 15–16).

A Lamenter's Discourse

Ode, *n.*

A poem intended to be sung. A lyric poem, typically one in the form of an address to a particular subject. (*Oxford English Dictionary [OED]*, 2008, paras. 1.a, 1.b).

Barthes's (1978) *A Lover's Discourse* assembles fragments on love, on loving, and on the lover. The lover's discourse is one of solitude, fashioned in the realm of the unreal, and absent community (Barthes, 1978, p. 1). The lover is forsaken and in need of affirmation — in need of confirmation and declaration — for such speech opens out into the realm of the possible. As written, the lover speaks, breathes, and sighs; the lover lives, hopes, and tries.

Barthes's affirmations are composed of texts of various origins that have been "put together" as an ode to love and to loving (1978, p. 8). His patchwork of citations performs "turns in textual conversations" between love, theory, and literature which "offer correctives to the supposed resistance of corporeality to language" and of text to the composition of the lover (Hamera, 2005, p. 17). This lover is not Barthes or Nietzsche or Goethe's *Werther*, but rather, a written subject, a textual, performative "I" who speaks and in doing so *becomes*, in and outside the languages of love (Pollock, 2005, p. 247). The lover's discourse creates a "syntactical-aria", a "mode of construction" in which the fragments "utter their affect" (Barthes, 1978, p. 6). This is Barthes's "third meaning": "immanent, obtuse, and erratic, in contrast to the 'obvious meaning' of semantic message and symbolic signification" (Stewart, 2007, p. 3). It is a speaking created in the act, a mode for singing a subject into being.

A Lover's Discourse offers an incomplete, uncertain speech. The text isn't written in the languages of correspondence, integration, fluency, or knowledge (Barthes, 1977, p. 7). The use and learning of languages, as we like to think of these activities, are undone in the contradictions of experience and the absence of poetic sense. The lover speaks instead by attention, desire, affect, and encounters with the "unforeseen" (Gingrich-Philbrook, 2005, p. 305). Her speech assembles a narrative invented within what the text provides. For the lover, "no transcendence, no deliverance, no novel" (Barthes, 1978, p. 7). But there is passion, there are sighs, and we do inhabit bodies touching languages touching bodies, trembling with desire (Barthes, 1978, p. 73).

And where a lover's discourse is text and makes speech, it is music that gets at the heart of (the) matter. Music is much more than metaphor for Barthes; it is a way out of a strict theory of signs (as a system of meaning and signification, contained and constrained) and into a process for discovering how language, rhythm, and matter collide to make a "body in a state of music" (Barthes, 1985, p. 312). Music conjures this body and gestures toward playing — participation and performance — rather than saying — a (strict) sense and comprehension. Seductive in its process of making, producing, creating — in its very possibility (Szekely, 2006, para. 37) — playing asks us to create a writing of action, emotion, embodiment, and introspection (Ellis, 2004, p. xix). Playing, we make a musical autoethnography.

A reader engages such writing by listening, though we listen not to decipher the grammars or structures of representational language. Instead, we search for feeling, movement, and relationships. The listening reader searches for "who speaks, who emits," creating an "inter-subjective space where 'I am listening' also means 'listen to me'" (Barthes, 1985, p. 246). Conceived in a passionate reaching toward intersubjectivity, this speech — this music — is for us, alone.

Inspired by Barthes' lover's discourse, I aspire to write my own lamenter's discourse,[1] fashioning a text that figures the possibilities wrought in spaces of loss, created between "imagined and entrenched realities" (Pollock, 2007, p. 247). A lament is sung in the speech of mourning, a song issued into silence (*OED*, 2008, para. 2). Though it sings the unrequited, it is not a story complete and instructive in the arts of sorrow, mourning, and loss. In your listening, you might answer. You might hear me speaking in the fragmented speech of an experience that *moves*. This speech performs "the sensation that something is happening — something that needs attending to" (Stewart, 2007, p. 5). It writes an affective performance "as if" something now happening is or could be otherwise, a plaintive asking after "what if?" (Pollock, 2007, p. 247). A lamenter's discourse creates a moving, speaking subject who is "always already about to fly off the page into being and becoming" (Pollock, 2007, p. 254). *And so it is a lamenter who speaks and who sings* (adapted from Barthes, 1978, p. 9):

Bye Bye Love

> Love, *v.*
>
> *trans. colloq.* (orig. *U.S.*). To show love towards, in the manner of a child; to embrace affectionately; to caress, fondle; to engage in love play with. (*OED*, 2008, para. 1.g).

1. Singing encourages language development. Singing teaches vocal imitation, grammar and vocabulary, phrasing, storytelling, pattern, rhythm, and rhyme (Buchman, 2005, para. 2). Singing to babies educates in the discrimination of languages. What is the language of love? The language of loss? How do we divine the difference?

2. We are deep into our bedtime ritual: taking a bath, reading books, and snuggling before sleep. We have put away the tales of Frog and Toad, two friends who take care of one another so kindly, so sweetly, their love makes us swoon. We push down into the covers and talk softly. I rub your arm as you tell the last of your story, languidly and in bursts of breath. Your eyes open and close, open and close, punctuating your sentences where your voice fails. And then, you stir, move toward me and breathe into my neck, "Mama, sing me a song".

3. Barthes (1977) writes that the "grain" of a voice is the "friction between music and something else"; language, yes, but not the *message* of the lyric (p. 273). The grain of the voice is "the body in the singing voice, in the writing hand, in the performing limb" (Barthes, 1977, p. 476). It engages in *love play*. It is a voice, body, and language, *choosing*.

4. I begin, "Bye bye love, bye bye happiness/Hello loneliness, I think I'm gonna cry ... Bye bye my love, good bye" (Bryant & Bryant, n.d., paras. 1–2, 5).[2]

5. Your eyes open. You draw in a sharp breath and say, "Mama, why do you only sing sad songs?"

"Oh, honey, I don't. Let me sing you another. 'You are my sunshine/My only sunshine/You make me happy/When skies are gray/You'll never know dear/How much I love you/Please don't take/My sunshine away'" (Davis & Mitchell, n.d., paras. 1–4).

"That song is sad, too." I stop. It is.

"My bonnie lies over the ocean/My bonnie lies over the sea ..." ("My Bonnie Lies Over the Ocean," n.d., paras. 5–6).

"That one, too."

"I guess I like sad songs."

"Why?"

"They make me feel something. Sadness, yes, but also something more. When you were a baby, I sang you to sleep. I sang the songs I remembered, and all the songs I remembered were sad songs."

"Did you think that singing sad songs to me would make me sad?"

"Oh no. I thought that if I sang the songs I knew — the songs that made me feel — you'd feel something, too. You'd feel how much I loved you."

Bye Bye Happiness

Happiness, *n*

Good fortune or luck in life or in a particular affair; success, prosperity. The state of pleasurable content of mind, which results from success or the attainment of what is considered good. (*OED*, 2008, paras. 1, 2).

1. I arrive at the school and park my car in the tree-lined lot. I cross the playground, already buzzing with children released from their work. I arrive at the door of the kindergarten and reach for the knob just as it bursts open. The children, including my son, rush toward the swings. Caroline, Noah's teacher, takes shape in the doorway.

"Noah says his heart is broken."

"What?" I say, trying to regain my balance.

"He says his heart is broken and all he does is cry."

"Did something happen today?"

"Nothing I noticed. Though he and Catherine seemed to struggle a bit."

"No longer best friends?"

"Oh no. They say they're getting married, and now the question is, where will they live?"

"Oh my. That does sound heartbreaking."

2. "The amorous subject suffers anxiety because the loved object replies scantily or not at all to his language ... In those brief moments when I speak for nothing, it as if I were dying. For the loved being becomes a leaden figure, a dream creature who does not speak" (Barthes, 1978, pp. 167, 168). Mourning becomes silence. Is silence. And then the lamenter speaks. The lamentation teaches another form of speech.

3. Later, when I ask Noah about his heartbreak, he explains: "I was feeling sad because Catherine said she didn't want to live in the castle with me, even though we're getting married. She said she wanted to live in a castle with her mom and dad and brother. She said I could visit her."

"And what did you say?"

"I said that I would live with you, Mama, and visit Catherine, even though my heart was broken."

"Why was your heart broken?"

"It wasn't."

"It wasn't?"

"No."

"So why did you say it was?"

"Because if I just said I was sad, Catherine wouldn't have paid attention to that. If I'd told Miss Caroline I was sad, she would just keep doing what she was doing, not even looking up, and she would have said, 'That's nice,' or something, not even listening."

"So if you say your heart was broken, Catherine and Miss Caroline will listen to you?"

"Yeah."

"Why?"

"Because that's a better story. There's no song that says, 'I'm sad.' There are plenty of songs that say, 'My heart is broken'."

Think I'm Gonna Cry

Cry, v.

To entreat, beg, beseech, implore, in a loud and emoved or excited voice, with the thing begged as direct object. To call aloud. (OED, 2008, paras. 1, 3).

1. Noah says, "Why is the song crying?"

   "Because the loved person in the song has someone new."

   "Who?"

   "The person walking away. Love."

   "Love is crying?"

   "The person telling the story, the person singing the song, is crying. Because of love. Lost love."

   "You're crying?"

   "No, not me."

   "But you're singing the song."

   "I am singing about love."

2. What I want to know (loss) is the "very substance I employ in order to speak (a lamenter's discourse)" (Barthes, 1978, p. 59, emphasis added).

3. Noah calls me crying. It is a night he usually stays over at his father's house. Noah's house too, just not mine. He says, "I want to stay with you. I want to, but Daddy says no. Will you come over? Will you kiss me goodnight?"

   I say, "Yes. Of course."

   When I arrive, he rushes into me and throws his arms around my legs. I bend to pick him up and he climbs me like a tree. He's big now, 6 years old, and he weighs nearly 50 pounds. I lean back to steady myself in his embrace. He puts his arms around my shoulders and presses his lips into my neck.

   "Mommy, I want you to stay here with me. Or I want to come and stay with you. I love you too much."

   "Let's get you tucked into bed. I'll snuggle with you and we'll talk."

   I climb into the twin bed and rest my forehead against Noah's. I say, "What's wrong, love?"

   "I want to stay with you."

   "Yesterday you wanted Daddy. You cried when he left."

   "When I'm with you, I want you, but I also want Daddy. When I'm with Daddy, I want you. I want us all to live in the same house. I want us to sleep in the same place."

   "I know love, and I'm sorry."

   "Daddy says that you tried to live together but you didn't make each other happy."

   "That's right. And even though I'm not here with you, I am thinking of you. And the same for Daddy."

   Noah says, "I hate leaving. I hate choosing."

4. Taylor (1999) writes of how lost love expressed in tango lyrics extends to subjectivities and the sometimes violence of human connections: "The disorientation of lost love ... becomes disorientation in the face of a savage order whose coherence and security rips apart human connections, leaving a chaos of aborted relationships, of blighted subjectivities, of broken bodies" (p. 63).

5. Taylor is speaking of how tango lyrics mirror the ways the dominant violently repress the rest of society. The metaphor is a technology of intimacy (Hamera, 2005, p. 19) and the intimacy is a technology of violence. Choosing — one home or another, one love or another — is a metaphor for my son's existence. Broken connections, a chaos of aborted relationships, blighted subjectivities, and broken hearts. Divorce is not the repression of the dominant. It is a technology of thwarted intimacy. It is a technology of violence for sons and mothers, for fathers and daughters. Isn't it?

6. Noah's father comes into the room and pushes in next to Noah on the other side of the slim bed. Noah is wedged between us. He transfers his stranglehold embrace from me to his father. After a few moments, I push myself up and stand next to the bed. Noah says, "A kiss!"

   I bend to receive his wet, sticky kiss and he throws his arms around my neck.

   "I don't want you to go! I love you too much! I need you! I want to come with you! He begins to cry, pulling away from me so he can throw his head back and wail. My heart pounds and my breath catches with each sob and denial.

   His father finally says, "I didn't know you'd be so upset. You can go with Mama."

   Noah closes his mouth. He reaches around my waist and pulls himself up against me. "Okay," he says. "Mama, let's go."

Sure Looks Happy

> Pusillanimous, *adj.*
>
> Of a quality, action, etc.: resulting from or manifesting a lack of courage or determination. (*OED*, 2008, para. 2).

1. Noah says, "Mama, will you sing a happy song?"
   I say, "I don't think I know any happy songs."
   He says, "Sure you do."
   "Okay, let me think."

He waits. I think, but nothing comes to mind. "I don't have any happy songs. Loan me one of yours."

He thinks. I wait. He laughs. "I don't have any happy songs, either. Why don't we just sing, 'Happy, happy, happy, happy'?"

I say, "Okay," and we do. "Happy, happy, happy, happy."

We stop and look at each other. Noah shrugs. "Maybe all the happy songs are boring. Maybe all there is to say is, 'Happy, happy, happy, happy.' That's why we don't know any happy songs."

Maybe.

2. "With regard to happiness, it would seem culpable to spoil its expression [if spoken]: the ego discourses only when it is hurt; when I am fulfilled or remember having been so, language seems pusillanimous: I am transported, beyond language ... The transport is the joy of which one cannot speak ... The fulfilled lover has no need to write, to transmit, to reproduce" (Barthes, 1978, pp. 55, 56).

I Sure Am Blue

> Blue, *a*.
>
> Said of the colour of smoke, vapour, distant hills, steel, thin milk. Of affairs, circumstances, prospects: dismal, unpromising, depressing. An off-pitch note. A clever, sensible woman. (OED, 2008, paras. 1b, 3c, 3d, 7).
>
> Blue, *v*.[2]
>
> To make a mess of, spoil, ruin. (OED, 2008, para. 1).

1. "Song is the precious addition to a blank message, entirely contained within its address, for what I give by singing is at once my body (by my voice) and the silence into which you cast that body" (Barthes, 1978, p. 77).

2. A torch song sings of lost, spoiled, love. "There goes my baby with someone new/She sure looks happy, I sure am blue" (Bryant & Bryant, n.d., paras. 6–7). As a musical form, torch singing developed in the United States during the 1920s. In addition to drawing on the musical traditions of English parlor songs, the French chanson, and US ragtime and swing, the torch song features the traditions of French cabaret, in which intimate and emotionally heightened ballads punctuated an evening of confrontational and provocative political satire, and US blues and jazz, music in which innovation in melodic structure and phrasing created spaces — openings — for audience interpretation and participation (Holman Jones, 2007, pp. 18–22). Heightened emotionality, critique, and

participation: A recipe for taking a standard form — a lament on lost love — and remaking it so it sings for you.

3. Noah has been writing epic torch songs for weeks. He begins with some forlorn line, "My heart is broken, I'll never love again", and he's off. He moves around the house, singing to the mirror, singing through the open windows, singing to the dogs, singing to himself. These songs go on and on and on, and Noah is lost in loss for hours.

4. Barthes (1978) says, "To know that one does not write for the other, to know that these things I am going to write will never cause me to be loved by the one I love (the other), to know that writing compensates for nothing, sublimates nothing, that it is precisely there where you are not — this is the beginning of writing" (p. 100).

5. When Noah first starting singing — when he began writing sad songs and performing them all over the place — I followed him, listening. But he stopped me. He wanted some privacy, to be alone with his sad lyrics and anguished performance. He said, "Stay there. Just listen." His torch songs became the soundtrack for our domestic bliss: Noah moving around the house singing of tragedy, me, humming along at his move into the power of story, us in a passionate search for words that speak.

6. I imagine myself a careful listener, one who gives her attention, as Engh (1993) writes, to "particularity, to specificity, to idiosyncrasy and detail" (p. 75). I listen to compose, to enter into a relation with what and who I am hearing. And "to compose, at least by propensity, is to give to do, not to give to hear but to give to write" (Barthes, 1977, p. 153).

7. Torch singing means voicing lost love, in all its melancholy and, yes, violence: lovers torn apart, lovers battered and beaten.[3] So why listen? Why sing along to a spoiled, wanting narrative? Because even within a sad, unsatisfying story it is possible to hear more, to hear and understand and sing something other, something else. This listening is not on the surface of things. It is not communicated in semantics or contained in signification. It is, instead, created in the unexpected sounding of a blue note, in a refusal to hit any note "straight", in a shifting, changing tone (Brackett, 1995, p. 65).[4] It is created in the call to participate in the narrative, turning listeners into singers and readers into writers, actively constructing meaning by voice, by body, by ear (Barthes, 1975). We sound a text that disrupts the lamenter's discourse — expected, mournful, dismal and

uncompromising — as written in code, in culture. We sing of loss without becoming lost.

8. I did as Noah asked and made some space around his lament, allowing it to unfold in his — in our — performance. I stayed close without touching. I listened with my voice, with my body and ear, without wanting to decipher the lyric, his text. I revelled in his torch song and in the blue images it made: vapor, distant hills, smoke.

That Might Have Been

> Knowledge, *v.*
>
> To confess to; to give thanks to, to praise. (*OED, 2008*, para. 1).
>
> Knowledge, *n.*
>
> The fact of knowing a thing, state, etc., or (in general sense) a person; acquaintance; familiarity gained by experience. Intimacy. To come to one's senses. (*OED, 2008*, paras. II.5.a, II.6.a, II.9.e).

1. "Is the scene always visual? It can be aural, the frame can be linguistic: I can fall in love with a sentence spoken to me: and not only because it says something which manages to touch my desire, but because of its syntactical turn (framing), which will inhabit me like a memory" (Barthes, 1978, p. 192).

2. Noah has stopped singing laments. His need for privacy, his need to write and bind his desires, has created a need for books. Just a few days ago, he asked if I would help him make a journal, a place to keep his secrets. I obliged, offering him a journal of my own, a black book with creamy white pages. When I opened the journal, I saw that I had used the first few pages to scribble some notes on Noah, trying to remember what he said at ages 3 and 4 and 5.

   "Oh," I say, "I'd forgotten that I'd written in this one."

   Noah says, "Can you take out those pages?"

   "Yes, but first, let me tell you what they say: Noah, 3: 'Mama, someone is lying on the radio. I think it is George W. Bush'. Noah, 4: 'Mama, I love you walking to the moon infinity times'. Noah, 5 (in a conversation about talking to God): 'What's his number?' Noah, 6 (after running up and down the sidewalk in front of our house): 'Mama, my legs are panting'."

   "I said all those things?"

   "Yes. And I wrote them down."

   "And now can you take them out?"

   I carefully cut the pages from the book, then hand it over. "It's yours."

Noah sets to work, pasting in photographs and crayon drawings, cutting desired people and objects from magazines and making them his own, writing captions, collecting himself. He puts together a collage of fragments and images that don't make sense, in terms of some kind of predictable narrative, in terms of offering discernable facts, in terms of a knowing understanding. His book is "indifferent to the properties of knowledge" (Barthes, 1978, p. 9). His book makes sense, though, as it creates a sensuous experience, a tactile intimacy, a confession that bestows value, praise, and yes, love, on its objects. His book, this collection, writes a life (King, 2008, p. 38).

3. Contradictions: When an interaction with someone or some thing we think we "know" goes wrong or bad: unknown, foreign, violent. Contradiction escapes our efforts to explain or analyze (Taylor, 1999, p. 119). Though contradiction can be "be evoked, enacted, and communicated by the juxtaposition of heterogeneous fragments within a text with its own contradicitons" (Taylor, 1999, p. 119).

4. Noah wants to fill all the pages of his journal, to inscribe an ending. But he loses patience, unable to completely inscribe the pages of his experience. I ask him to show me what he's made. He hugs the book to his chest. "No," he says, "It's not finished. And it's secret."

"Okay," I say. "But I helped you make it. I know what's in there."

"But you don't know how it goes."

And I don't. I clipped and trimmed the photos, I smeared the backs of images with glue, but I don't know how he's assembled them. Like a song for which I don't know the lyrics, for which I don't recall the tune, I cannot sing. Perhaps, this, too, is the silence of happiness, a fulfillment that does not give to do, to write.

5. Noah waits, reconsidering. He opens the book.

"Here's how it goes."

Here's how it goes: Noah's name, a magic wand, an empty table, a wedge of cheese, a powder compact, the "beautiful" Halle Barry. His book is a frame in which he has assembled his own becoming in name, in myth, in beauty, in absence, in sustenance, in desire. It is open, possible, waiting, refusing a conclusion. This book makes sense to no one but Noah, it makes sense to know one but in text. It is a lamenter's discourse in which desire is written in bursts, in exclamations that make language sing.

A Lamenter's Discourse

Lyric, *adj.* and *n.*

... meant to be sung; pertaining to or characteristic of song; short poems directly expressing the poet's own thoughts and sentiments. (OED, 2008, para. A.1).

1. When I turn to the lyric, a kind of self-talk, the kind of subjective discourse in which Barthes's lover is writing, in which the lamenter is writing, "this affiliation is, at the simplest level, one that links artifice to artifice, and kind of citational solidarity of things visibly, conspicuously 'made'": story, song, and the discourses of loss (Hamera, 2005, p. 17). The lyric is affirmation in the absence of a beloved other, community forged in words alone.

2. When I turn to the lyric, I am listening to the fragments, the silences, the incomprehensibility of my speech. I am saying: Listen to me, listen to my uncertainties and failures, listen to my love. I make music in the sounds of loss, letting myself "drop somewhere outside of language", outside of knowledge, possession, and understanding (Barthes, 1978, p. 233). I write to "let come ... what comes, to let pass ... what goes" (Barthes, 1978, p. 234). I write to try.

3. A lamenter's discourse is meant to be sung, meant to speak the languages of sorrow, grief, and melancholy on the way to an affective, sensual knowledge of something else. Out of this elsewhere, a possible subject is affectively being and becoming, about to fly off the page (Pollock, 2007, p. 254). A lamenter's discourse offers a lyric and lyrical conversation between and among language, theory, music, and experience. It writes a body in a state of music (Barthes, 1985, p. 312). A lamenter's discourse is an acquired dialect, one that makes language go, do, and write (Hamera, 2005, p. 17). It speaks of loss, but it is not lost. It recalls and re-members voice, throat, speech, and love. In figures, in bursts and in glimpses, it writes "a whole scene through the keyhole of language" (Barthes, 1978, p. 27).

4. It says, "Bye bye love". It says, "I love you too much". It says, "I love you walking to the moon infinity times". An ode in and to the language of love, it sings.

Endnotes

1   In addition to how this lamenter's discourse is inspired by — and constitutes an ode to — *Barthes's A Lover's Discourse*, this chapter is also inspired by Diane Schoemperlen's novel *In the Language of Love* (1997), which is composed of one hundred chapters,

each one based on one of the one hundred words in the Standard Word Association Test used to measure sanity (*Diane Schomperlen*, 2009).

2 Lyrics for "Bye Bye Love", written by the husband-and-wife songwriting team of Boudleaux and Felice Bryant. "Together, this talented couple penned many huge hits for the Everly Brothers and other artists, including 'Wake Up Little Susie' and 'All I Have To Do Is Dream'. The Bryants are credited with being the first songwriters to come to Nashville and make a living only by writing" ("Bye Bye Love", n.d., para. 2). Interestingly, nearly 30 artists, including Elvis, rejected the song before the Everly Brothers recorded it ("Bye Bye Love", n.d., para. 1). It became their first hit ("Bye Bye Love", 2008, para. 2). Out of rejection, happiness; out of disappointment, success.

3 The lyrics of "My Man", the quintessential torch song, include the lines: "He isn't true/He beats me too/What can I do?" (Willemetz & Jacques, 1996, p.114).

4 Brackett (1995) is commenting on Billie Holiday's singing style (p. 65).

References

Barthes, R. (1975). *S/Z: An essay* (R. Miller, Trans.). New York: Hill & Wang.

Barthes, R. (1977). *Image-music-text* (S. Heath, Trans.). New York: Hill & Wang.

Barthes, R. (1978). *A lover's discourse: Fragments* (R. Howard, Trans.). New York: Hill & Wang.

Barthes, R. (1985). *The responsibility of forms: Critical essays on music, art, and representation* (R. Howard, Trans.). Berkeley: University of California Press.

Brackett, D. (1995). *Interpreting popular music*. New York: Cambridge University Press.

Bryant, B., & Bryant F. (n.d.). Bye bye love. Retrieved February 20, 2009, from http://www.songfacts.com/detail.php?id=3254.

Buchman, R. (2005). Why singing is so important for your young child and you. *The Shepherd School of Music, Rice University*. Retrieved February 20, 2009, from http://music.rice.edu/preparatory/singing01.html

Bye Bye Love. (n.d.). Retrieved February 20, 2009, from http://www.songfacts.com/detail.php?id=3254.

Davis, J.H., & Mitchell, C. (n.d.). You are my sunshine. Retrieved February 20, 2009, from http://www.geocities.com/holidaysfun/sunshine

Diane Schomperlen. (2009). Retrieved February 20, 2009, from http://en.wikipedia.org/wiki/Diane_Schoemperlen

Ellis, C. (2004). *The ethnographic I: A methodological novel about teaching and doing autoethnography*. Walnut Creek, CA: AltaMira.

Engh, B. (1993). Loving it: Music and criticism in Roland Barthes. In R. Solie (Ed.), *Musicology and difference: Gender and sexuality in music scholarship* (pp. 66-79). Berkeley: University of California Press.

Gingrich-Philbrook, C. (2005). Autoethnography's family values: Easy access to compulsory experiences. *Text and Performance Quarterly 25*, 297–314.

Hamera, J. (2005). Regions of likeness: The poetry of Jorie Graham, dance, and citational solidarity. *Text and Performance Quarterly 25*, 14–26.

Holman Jones, S. (2007). *Torch singing: Performing resistance and desire from Billie Holiday to Edith Piaf*. Lantham, MD: AltaMira Press.

King, W.D. (2008). *Collections of nothing*. Chicago: University of Chicago Press.

Knopfler, M. (n.d.). I think I love you too much. Retrieved February 20, 2009, from http://www.metrolyrics.com/i-think-i-love-you-too-much-lyrics-mark-knopfler.html

My Bonnie Lies Over the Ocean. (n.d.). Retrieved February 20, 2009, from http://en.wikipedia.or/wiki/My_Bonnie_Lies_over_the_Ocean

Oxford English dictionary (Online ed.). (2008). Retrieved February 20, 2009, from http://dictionary.oed.com

Pollock, D. (2007). The performative "I." *Cultural Studies↔Critical Methodologies 7*, 239–255.

Schoemperlen, D. (1997). *In the language of love*. New York: Penguin.

Stewart, K. (2007). *Ordinary affects*. Durham, NC: Duke University Press.

Szekely, M.D. (2006). Gesture, pulsion, grain: Barthes' musical semiology. *Contemporary Aesthetics, 4*. Retrieved February 20, 2009, from http://www.contempaesthetics.org/newvolume/pages/article.php?articleID=409#FN40

Taylor, J. (1999). *Paper tangos*. Durham, NC: Duke University Press/Public Planet.

Willemetz, A. & Charles, J. (1996). My man (C. Pollock, Trans.; M. Yvain, music). In *The great American torch song* (p. 114). Miami: Warner Bros.

Chapter 6

Evoking Spring in Winter
Some Personal Reflections on Returning to Schubert's Cycle

Stephen Emmerson

> There is a melody, a simple but moving air, which she plays on the piano, with angelic skill. It is her very favourite tune, and the moment she plays the first note I feel delivered of all my pain, confusion and brooding fancies. Every word they say about the magical powers of ancient music strikes me as plausible. How that simple song enthrals me! And how she knows when to play it, often at times when I would gladly put a bullet through my head! The darkness and madness of my soul are dispelled, and I breathe more freely again. Johann Wolfgang von Goethe, *The Sorrows of Young Werther*, 1774.
>
> (Goethe, 1989, p. 46)

Frühlingstraum ("Dream of Spring"), the eleventh song from Schubert's *Winterreise*, opens with a four-bar phrase of disarming and perhaps deceptive simplicity (see Figure 1).

On its own, such an innocent phrase may not appear remarkable — it might even appear trite — but in performances of the work, these few bars have the potential to be among the most memorable moments in the cycle. In some cases, the passage can be unforgettable. But its impact, of course, depends to a considerable extent on how it is performed. This chapter hopes to illuminate some of what may lie behind these few simple bars from a performer's perspective. It reflects on my experiences with this song cycle and will identify some of the factors that have led me to play this particular phrase in particular ways. The chapter considers how myself and others have thought about it over years of engagement with it, what I wish my playing of it to convey, and how I have negotiated it in performance.

Figure 1
F. Schubert. "Frühlingstraum" ("Dream of Spring"), bars 1–4. Winterreise. (Schubert, 1895/1970)

Some Musical Context

Winterreise is a setting of a cycle of 24 poems by Wilhelm Müller completed in the penultimate year of Schubert's life (1827) and is considered by many to be the most remarkable of Romantic song cycles but also the most harrowing. It tells of a young man who, rejected by the girl he loves, embarks on a solitary journey across a frozen winter landscape. Laurence Kramer (2007) has referred to it as "an encyclopedic musical study of melancholy and depression" (p. 122).

> It raises one of the oldest aesthetic questions … How does the representation of pain give pleasure, particularly if the pain is strong and unrelieved? … How is it, then, that these unrelievedly, even pathologically bleak songs not only attract rather than repel audiences but also give an impression of beauty and strength? (p. 123)

For a start, it must be underlined that the particular beauty possible at the opening of "Frühlingstraum" can only be fully realised — its potential fully revealed — when heard in the context of the whole work. As Charles Rosen (1995) writes:

> The songs of *Winterreise* are only apparently separate works: even those which are effective outside the cycle lose in character and significance when so performed. The Schubert song cycle embodies a paradox: each song is a completely independent form, well rounded and finished, which nevertheless makes imperfect sense on its own. (p. 196)

So it is with individual songs, but the case is even more acute when the opening four bars of a song are taken out of their context as it is done here. Schubert's cycle of 24 songs is dominated by settings in minor keys, especially the first set of 12 songs, which were composed first, where only two are in a major key. The first of these is the fifth song, "Der Lindenbaum" ("The Linden Tree"). Then, six more songs in minor keys follow expressing various forms of heartbreak, misery, resignation and despair. In the last of these songs, "Rast" ("Rest"), the wanderer stops for the first time and tells, first, of the pain in his limbs but then of that in his heart. In performance we have had about half an hour of music not only dominated by minor keys but of rarely relenting anguish. After that song, the protagonist evidently falls asleep — though hopefully the audience does not. Following some moments of precious silence, the opening bars of "Frühlingstraum" must transport us far from all that precedes it and instantaneously evoke a beguiling dream of spring. Those bars on their own may appear somewhat ordinary but, in context, they carry a potential magic way beyond what their simple melody and harmonic progressions would otherwise suggest.

The text of the song is given with the translation by Celia Sgroi (n.d.; see Figure 2).

Of the six stanzas, the first three are each set to very different music. In the second stanza (B) the protagonist is rudely jolted back from his dream to the present, with music back in a minor mode, with a faster tempo and some violent dissonances. The music for the third stanza (C) returns at first to the major key, is at a slow tempo and, in any adequate performance, should be nothing less than heartbreaking. But, by the fourth stanza, he has evidently dropped back into slumber — an even more delightful one this time — and we return to the music with which the song opened. The notes are the same, but whatever loveliness was there at the start is now magnified, almost painfully. The words now speak of love requited and it must be evident that he is unlikely to experience such pleasures ever again. The fifth and sixth stanzas bring back the music of the second and third respectively. One might hope for the cycle could go around again — for another delicious dream, a further welcome delusion to follow — but even that small pleasure is denied. The end is devastating in his realisation that he will never know such love again. As Gerald Moore (1975) so quaintly put it: "I don't think there is a situation in all the cycle where the poor fellow is more crushed than this" (p. 121).

Some Personal Context

> Nun sitz' ich hier alleine
> Und denke dem Traume nach.
>
> Now I sit here alone
> And reflect on the dream.
>
> ("Frühlingstraum")

Frühlingstraum	Dream of Spring	Musical form and tempi
Ich träumte von bunten Blumen,	I dreamt of many-coloured flowers,	A
So wie sie wohl blühen im Mai;	The way they bloom in May;	Etwas
Ich träumte von grünen Wiesen,	I dreamed of green meadows,	bewegt
Von lustigem Vogelgeschrei.	Of merry bird calls.	
Und als die Hähne krähten,	And when the roosters crowed,	B
Da ward mein Auge wach;	My eye awakened;	Schnell
Da war es kalt und finster,	It was cold and dark;	
Es schrien die Raben vom Dach.	The ravens shrieked on the roof.	
Doch an den Fensterscheiben,	But on the window panes	C
Wer malte die Blätter da?	Who painted the leaves there?	Langsam
Ihr lacht wohl über den Träumer,	I suppose you'll laugh at the dreamer	
Der Blumen im Winter sah?	Who saw flowers in winter?	
Ich träumte von Lieb um Liebe,	I dreamed of love reciprocated,	A
Von einer schönen Maid,	Of a beautiful maiden,	Etwas
Von Herzen und von Küssen,	Of embracing and kissing,	bewegt
Von Wonne und Seligkeit.	Of joy and delight.	
Und als die Hähne krähten,	And when the roosters crowed,	B
Da ward mein Herze wach;	My heart awakened;	Schnell
Nun sitz' ich hier alleine	Now I sit here alone	
Und denke dem Traume nach.	And reflect on the dream.	
Die Augen schließ' ich wieder,	I close my eyes again,	C
Noch schlägt das herz so warm.	My heart still beats so warmly.	Langsam
Wann grünt ihr Blätter am Fenster?	When will you leaves on the window turn green?	
Wann halt' ich mein Liebchen im Arm?	When will I hold my love in my arms?	

Figure 2
F. Schubert. Frühlingstraum [Dream of Spring]. Winterreise (trans. Sgroi, n.d.).

I first played songs from *Winterreise* as an undergraduate student at the University of Queensland. I played many lieder at this time with a number of very good singing students, but I recall that the playing of these songs was among the musical highlights of those years. I did not do the whole cycle but a collection of about 10 songs. I remember being surprised with the difficulties I had playing "Der Lindenbaum", although I had been somewhat offended nonetheless when the singing teacher approached my piano teacher suggesting I needed help on it! Only years later did I realise just how immeasurably difficult the opening of that song is — not just to play the notes but to capture the elusive image beyond them. As ever, I needed all the help I could get.

Since then, my performance career as pianist has concentrated mostly on instrumental chamber music — notably with a piano trio for over a decade — and for too many years I did not play much lieder. And so in 2003 I welcomed the opportunity to do *Winterreise* with my friend and colleague Gregory Massingham, a fine tenor who is Head of Opera at Queensland Conservatorium. We have since performed the cycle several times, as well as other programs of lieder. To be playing such repertoire again has been deeply refreshing for me. There is a special bond between singer and pianist in lieder that is really like no other musical relationship I have experienced. Further, I was struck by how different the experience of playing lieder was from that of instrumental chamber music. In such repertoire it is more obvious that one's aim is to go beyond the notes, rather than primarily attending to all the detailed instructions in the score. The poetic imagery helps greatly to stimulate the imagination. Moreover, I would suggest that making music with an instrument that literally has to breathe is something all instrumentalists should continue to do, lest we forget.

The process through which Greg and I prepared for our first *Winterreise* involved nine months of preparation — an appropriate gestation period I suppose. We could have put together a respectable enough version in much less time but we knew that to forge our own concept of it — to conquer this Everest of song cycles — was going to take time. For that period, we met most weeks, if only for an hour or so, usually to rehearse a couple of songs at a time. Amid the hurly-burly of our jobs at the Conservatorium, those few hours a week were among the most precious and rejuvenating.

Much of our interpretation developed intuitively as we made music together over these months, though of course a range of interpretative details was discussed in rehearsals. These were mainly in terms of how the music could better underline the meaning of the words.

The bleak images of Müller's *Winterreise* have much in common with the German Romantic literary tradition. For example, there are many parallels with Goethe's *The Sorrows of Young Werther* (1774/ 1989), which probably more than any other work, established across Europe a virtual cult of melancholia. Although written some decades before *Winterreise,* the connections with Müller's poems were deep and at times quite specific. The character of Werther himself writes: "Indeed, I am nothing but a wanderer and a pilgrim on this earth! And what more are you?" (Goethe, 1974/1989, p. 97). Beyond recurring images of mountains, inns, churchyards, rivers, tears, and so on, several references to a linden tree (pp. 93–94, 128 and 162) underlined how specific Müller's allusions were to Goethe, references that his readers (and Schubert's listeners) presumably would not have missed. The world of *Winterreise* is unmistakeably close. In relation to "Frühlingstraum" the passage below offers striking parallels.

> Am I not still the very same man who once walked in excess of happiness, paradise before him at every step, with a heart that could embrace the world in the fullness of love? And now that heart is dead and no longer gives me joy, my eyes are dry, and my senses are not refreshed by heartfelt tears any more but furrow my brow with fearful worries. I suffer a great deal because I have lost the sole pleasure in my life … When I gaze from my window … oh! all the glories of nature are frozen to my eye … (Goethe, 1974/1989, pp. 110–111)

It is difficult to pinpoint exactly what observing such literary parallels contributes to one's performance but, at this stage, one might note the deep vein of nostalgia and irony which pervades that Romantic world of *Werther* and, as will later be evident, this does bear upon how one approaches the opening of "Frühlingstraum".

Interrogating Irony: Attaining simplicity

Daniel Barenboim (2005) tells the story of a 12-year-old girl who provided what he refers to as "a wonderful definition of Schubert":

> After hearing the *Unfinished Symphony* she said she liked the music so much because if the music is sad, she had the feeling it was smiling at the same time. And if it was cheerful, she felt that it still contained a tear.

There are very few smiles in *Winterreise,* but the opening of "Frühlingstraum" would be one of them. I am concerned here with how apparently cheerful music might evoke a tear. How is it that such simple music can communicate something so psychologically complex and potentially so moving? I wonder to what extent that tear is somehow written into the music or to what extent evoking such a response is dependent upon the performer delivering it in a particular way.

As the pianist Steven Lubin (2000) has noted of Schubert's late style, "He can step in and out of conventions, can use irony in complex and varied ways … [L]ayered meanings are subtle and varied — irony is no more than a catch-all term for them" (pp. 194, 196).

There is clearly considerable potential for complex irony in that deceptively innocent phrase that opens "Frühlingstraum". Richard Capell (1957) even suggested that the opening of the song is "the only suggestion of parody to be found in all Schubert's music" (p. 236)!

> *Frühlingstraum* begins with an amiable, old-fashioned tune in tripping 6–8 movement ... It is sweetly pretty; it is redolent of simple old provincial Germany. As a boy Schubert wrote such tunes in all seriousness ... In 'Die Schöne Müllerin' the *Frühlingstraum* air would not have caused a suspicion ... But appearing with its charming faded colours in the midst of the tragic 'Winterreise' music it conveys a mockery of the conventional songs of spring. A faint mockery. The tune is too graceful to be a caricature. (p. 236)

To begin to unpack further the potential irony here, one may note that the opening is not about experiencing happiness nor even just about dreaming of happiness. The dream is recalled while awake with some ironic realisation of its unreality. It is a memory of a dream. And so, beyond just innocent recollection, there is deep self-awareness as it is being played and sung (especially the fourth stanza) that such happiness is now lost, probably forever. As in "Der Lindenbaum", the song places in sharp juxtaposition entrancing memories beside the harsher present realities in a distinctly Romantic way. (Again *Werther* comes to mind.) As Rosen (1996) has observed:

> The most signal triumphs of Romantic portrayal of memory are not those which recall past happiness, but remembrances of those moments when future happiness still seemed possible, when hopes were not yet frustrated. ... Romantic memories are often those of absence, of that which never was. (pp. 174–175)

Such irony may be conveyed in performance by simply playing the phrase (and singing the first stanza) with a naïve innocence. With the rude awakening at the second stanza, the savage contrasts between dream and reality, between hope and despair, between pleasant delusion and awful realisation, are all underlined by such an approach. As Gerald Moore (1975) suggested, the opening may be "innocent and charming".

> There is a disarming simplicity about it ... The little tune flows along sweetly and unpretentiously with a graceful inflection at 2 and with unfussy feathery grace in 3. (p. 117)

Many performances and recordings seem to aim for that and most achieve it effectively (though in relation to his words, Moore's own 1972 Deutsche Grammophon recording with Fischer-Dieskau is surprisingly pensive at this point). Further, Moore writes:

> We must forget the anguish of the heart and bodily pain of the love-lorn man ... Only for fourteen bars will it last, so let him be sentimental if he will — there is hardly enough time for this slight extravagance to be perceived let alone criticized. (1975, p. 118)

I find the subtext underlying such language unsettling. For a start, the special beauty of these bars is largely due the anguish that surrounds them. This is not something to be forgotten but, I believe, can be reflected in the way it is played. Moreover Moore clearly considered sentimentality a weak if not forbidden emotion — an extravagance that, with some luck, one may escape mortal criticism because, being only a few bars, it will pass by quickly. But I really do not want this moment — what can be one of the most memorable moments of the cycle — to be passed over apologetically, marred by a regrettable indulgence one is hoping to get away with. And besides, it is not just 14 bars, because the musical setting returns at the fourth stanza and, as mentioned above, whatever was evoked at first is even more poignant the second time. (Barenboim in his live performance with Quasthoff, 2005b, here takes one's breath away ...)

Perhaps a direct simplicity is all that is required here. As András Schiff (1998) writes:

> Simplicity is one of Schubert's greatest virtues, and performance must reflect this. One must be extremely expressive and colourful but the music must flow naturally and be left alone. It is a bad sign when the performer's wilfulness becomes too obvious. *Rubato* must be carefully applied but an overdose of it could easily make the music sound sentimental. Schubert's world is never sentimental or too sweet; it only seems so ... in tasteless bad performances. (p. 208)

Many classical musicians — clearly Schiff and Moore among them — seem desperate to avoid the accusation of sentimentality in their playing. As it is here, that verdict is often inseparable from the damming but all too easy judgments of being "indulgent", "extravagant" or "tasteless". In my experience, such words only need to be enunciated in a rehearsal for an approach to be discarded — which, to me, is sometimes a pity. Such judgements are embedded deeply in the concept of *Werktreue* which, as Taruskin (1995) and others have argued, has too often suppressed the interpretative freedom and imagination of performers. Forbidding a performer's "wilfulness" or telling him/her that the music should be "left alone" is not the sort of engagement that I think is helpful.

While Schiff evidently admits the possibility of rubato, he clearly has serious concerns that it will too easily become "sentimental" and "tasteless". Rubato has always been a matter of taste — notoriously so — and, as Hudson (1997) has amply demonstrated, taste in this matter has been transforming over the centuries. (One hopes it will continue to do so.) But the judgments of musicians and critics are often put in absolute terms expressing a moral and self-righteous outrage when their personal boundaries of taste are crossed. This is regrettable insofar as fear of such judgments does not encourage performers to take creative risks or explore imaginative alternatives. I recall a pertinent debate in the journal *Early Music* (1997) in response to an article by David Montgomery, who had objected almost violently to the perceived liberties taken by Robert Levin in one of his Schubert recordings. Malcolm Bilson (1997) responded devastatingly well. "Critics who constantly set upon every player who endeavours to be creative are going to drive our all-to-often arid music-making still further into the dust" (p. 721). Bilson was deeply critical of what he refers to as "the art of 'Thou shalt not: Thou shalt not depart from the written text (p. 716)'" — again that *Werktreue* philosophy — which I hear resonating in Schiff's words and which remains prevalent across our classical music culture a decade later. One still hopes to attain a simplicity — a clarity — but to achieve that is in fact not simple at all and involves significantly more creative involvement from the performer than leaving the notes alone to speak for themselves. To me no one has reflected on this better than Wanda Landowska (1964) who writes:

> Simplicity can be that of a brute who only sees and plays what is written. But there is also that of the visionary who discovers, dreams, meditates, throws himself into foolish adventures, but comes back bloody, battered, with his heart wounded, though happy and richer. Then quietness pervades him gradually; everything becomes clearer; waste falls away; simplicity appears little by little. That simplicity has resonances; through it one hears all that has been felt and experienced. (p. 402)

Living with Recordings

I have been collecting recordings since my student days and I have built up quite a number of *Winterreises* over the years on LP, CD and DVD. While to some it might seem unnecessary to have over a dozen recordings of any one work, to me it seems just a modest fraction of its recorded legacy which, in turn, is a small part of its performance tradition. The work of course is not the score — it is so much more than just what Schubert wrote — but includes to all its realisations in sound where across time its potentialities are realised. And so one turns to performances and recordings to gain a reasonably rich concept of what the work can be.

To mention only a few of my personal highlights, the first recording which I got to know during my student days was that of the Hans

Hotter (1954/1999), which although underplaying the drama, will always be close to my heart. Then, like so many other music lovers, I recall finding the Fischer Dieskau recordings revelatory in their response to the text — the Deutsche Grammophon ones with Gerald Moore (1972) and Jörg Demus (1966/1996). His performance with Alfred Brendel from Berlin in 1979, now on DVD (1979/2005a), is a marvellous partnership. In the early 1980s I heard David Wilson-Johnson and David Owen Norris (on an 1824 Broadwood piano) perform the work live in England and it left an indelible impression. I bought the LP at the concert and later the CD (1995a). Theirs was clearly a refreshing and deliberately provocative approach (not only in adjusting the order of the songs back to Müller's original scheme) but moving nonetheless. Only later did I get to know the cycle sung by tenors, the voice-type for which Schubert originally conceived it. The extraordinarily intense live performance by Schreier with Richter (2002) is one I treasure though their approach is far removed from my own; a recording of an even more extraordinary live performance from Jon Vickers (1995b) defies description in a few words; Ian Bostridge on DVD (2007) brings a uniquely haunted quality to the work and the recording by Christoph Prégardien with Andreas Staier on a Fritz 1825 fortepiano (1998a) has many beauties. On DVD the live performance from Thomas Quastoff and Daniel Barenboim (2005b) is among the most moving of experiences. I also own three recordings of the cycle sung by women — Brigitte Fassbaender (2004, Mistuko Shirai (1991b), and Christine Schäfer (2006) not to mention one of a female viola player (Zimmermann, 1991). Of these, Schäfer's version with Eric Schneider (2006), which I have only come to know recently, stands apart (refreshing, deeply insightful, deeply responsive to the text … in a word, fabulous.) As I think back over all these recordings, I recognise how deeply my musical life has been enriched by them. That they colour my interpretation of the piece when I perform it is inevitable but, as a whole, they underline how many diverse approaches are possible. The potential of the work seems truly inexhaustible.

Some musicians claim not to listen to recordings of pieces they are playing and actively discourage their students from doing so. They believe that when preparing for a performance one should not risk even unconscious imitation but develop one's own interpretation directly from the score. But for me, recordings have become — perhaps more so in recent years — an important part of my interpretative process especially when I tackle large established works that have a rich performance tradition. Quite apart from the pleasures they offer, there is so much to learn from them. I should emphasise however that I listen to recordings only at certain stages of my preparation. Usually at early stages, I try to get an idea of the range of approaches that others have explored. Without consciously wanting to position myself in relation to them, it is inevitable that some will appeal and influence the way I play more strongly than others. I would certainly resist the temptation to consciously imitate any effect I'd heard but, as will be evident below, I will at times try to capture in my own terms feelings/moods/meanings that were revealed to me through particular interpretations. However, once I am working seriously on the music in private practice and rehearsal I set the recordings aside and search for my own voice.

When Greg and I were preparing our first *Winterreise* together we discussed many recordings but, of them all, the one that struck the deepest chord, I think for us both, was that by Peter Pears and Benjamin Britten (1965). As a student, Greg had studied singing with Pears (and met Britten) so there was a personal connection that attracted him to their interpretations. But for me it always seemed that the miracle of that recording was Britten's piano playing. One might say Britten's piano playing was beyond peer(s)! — if you excuse the pun. A DVD of them performing the work some years later in 1970 — regrettably with Pears in costume and Britten unseen — has been released by Decca (1970/2008). In both cases, this is music making of extraordinary vitality, subtlety and originality in its depth of musical insight. To me, Britten is incontestably one of the outstanding musicians of the 20th century and his recorded legacy with Pears is one to cherish. But, alas, not everybody values it that way.

I was appalled to read that Norman Lebrecht (2007) includes the Pears/Britten *Winterreise* among his list of the 20 worst recordings ever made. "Pears, in Lieder, hardly got through one sing unblemished ... Much of his Winterreise is frankly unpleasant, barely above amateurish" (pp. 289–290). Oh, please! While he concedes in passing that "Britten leaped in to save him with beautifully turned rubato" (p. 290), nevertheless I find the injustice of such criticism upsetting. Such cases remind me how deeply vulnerable we are as musicians as we lay bare our sense of beauty for public scrutiny. It is easy to say that one needs to develop a resilience, perhaps even indifference, to criticism especially when one knows it to be unjust. As I once heard a colleague put it many years ago, we need "the heart of a mouse, the hide of an elephant". But in truth many musicians feel deeply vulnerable to such attacks whether in the public press or whispered behind their backs. But it seems particularly unfair and ultimately damaging to the culture of classical music that a traditional, technically secure performance is much less likely to be criticised than one that takes risks in searching for new and original meanings. The vitriolic attack on Robert Levin's Schubert recording mentioned earlier (considered by Bilson, 1997) is another clear case in point. Back to the Britten recording, it seems to me that there is so much beauty, so much original insight and genuine depth of feeling here; it is remarkable that Lebrecht evidently does not hear, or value, any of that.

Pears and Britten give many of the *Winterreise* songs strikingly original interpretations but, of them all, to me their "Frühlingstraum" is among the most haunting. In those opening bars Britten seems to capture something impossibly poignant — his phrase is anything but cheerful but conveys a tenderness tinged with palpable sadness. And Pears follows it up beautifully. More so than any other recording I know, one imagines tears flowing behind that smile. I recall vividly that, when I first heard that recording, my concept of what the song could convey transformed profoundly.

One might ask whether such sadness was intended by the composer or whether a quality has been imposed beyond which the creator envisaged. But, while of course retaining respect for the composer and his work, the argument that a performer's responsibility is merely to realise the composer's intentions is a flawed one and the counter-argument has been made convincingly many times, most notably perhaps by Kivy (1995) and Taruskin (1995). One might go so far as to claim that the future health of classical music will require performers to further extend the potential meanings in the music, including ones unanticipated by the composer, if a vibrant performance tradition is to live on.

Evoking the Dream: A Personal Story

When Greg and I performed *Winterreise*, I was very conscious of trying to give the opening of "Frühlingstraum" a quality more complex than that of mere cheerfulness. While I did not play it as slowly as Britten I was certainly hoping to capture something of that wistful sadness. But on later performances I came to question that approach.

In 2007 I was asked to play a selection of songs from *Winterreise* for an ABCFM radio broadcast with a violist, Patricia Pollett, a fine musician with whom I've worked and performed on many occasions. It may seem strange to dispense with the words and transfer the vocal line to an instrument but in fact it can work surprisingly well, perhaps especially so, I expect, for those who already know the cycle and its imagery. The notes to Tabea Zimmerman's recording (Kohlhaas, 1991) claim that

> ... the viola is not inferior. In its timbre the bitter and the almost soothing, but often also the noisy, are united ... the immense modernity of this composition becomes apparent affecting and gripping the hearer ... One forgets the instrument and experiences the music. (p. 7)

I was delighted to be playing these songs in this form especially with a musician of Patricia's calibre. "Frühlingstraum" was (of course) among the selection but, when we came to rehearse that song, we had a rare disagreement, one which made me question my whole concept of the song and how I play it. Patricia was well aware of the imagery from the words and believed that, as a happy dream, the opening should be faster and more cheerful than I was playing it. To her, this glimpse of genuine happiness was a necessary relief amid the desolation of the surrounding songs. I replied trying to explain that there was another way of seeing it, and muttered something about nostalgia and about Britten — but felt I had been less than convincing. Different points of view went back and forth but it became clear we were not going to resolve the issue at that time. We decided to go away, think about it, and see how we felt about it at the next rehearsal.

I was quite concerned about the disagreement as this was one of those places where I had become very attached to a certain way of playing it, of hearing it, of feeling it. Such things can be very difficult to give up and it is all too easy to become defensive. When alternative ways are suggested in rehearsal I frequently tell myself: "Keep an open mind. Give it a proper go and then decide. One's interpretation must not stay static or habitual" or words to that effect. It is of course why one keeps playing music with different people to get fresh perspectives and hopefully assimilate new ideas and meanings. But although I told myself this, I found it much more difficult than usual on this occasion. I had become very attached to my way of feeling it and that was hard to let go of. I had told Patricia that I would reconsider it but, if I am honest, I would have to admit that I went away from the rehearsal trying to build in my mind a stronger case for why it should be the way I wanted. But I do not like confrontation and I recall that I had some anxiety about how we would resolve this at our next rehearsal.

I had been playing from the Dover edition on which I'd worked with Greg and which had my fingerings and other markings on it. Scribbled in pencil above the top lines of this song was "Not too fast" and "Still sad" and I was reticent to rub those out. Then I recalled that I'd bought a new edition of the work — what should be the most reliable modern Urtext edition, the combined Bärenreiter/Henle (1998b) and resolved to play from that, as from a clean slate as it were. But I also examined it closely to see if any further evidence for my case could be found there. What I did find in the appendix of that edition was the composer's earlier version of the song. There were some notable differences right from the opening bars where the left hand articulation had dots on each of the quavers. But of particular note was a different tempo marking. The familiar marking of *Etwas bewegt* (Always moving) was originally *Etwas geschwind* (Always swiftly/fleetly). So Schubert's original concept was evidently of a pretty fast tempo and, together with the detached notes in the left hand, this source was suggesting something quite removed from the rather melancholy concept I had formed. I revisited in my mind all those arguments about not having to necessarily obey the composer's performance directions.

> It is not illegal to play a piece of tempo at the wrong tempo: we risk neither a jail sentence nor even a fine. A certain school of aesthetics considers it immoral to contravene the composer's intentions, but sometimes it may even be a good idea. We have all heard performances at clearly inauthentic and even absurd tempos which turn out to be revealing, instructive, moving or brilliantly effective. The wrong tempo might still be more effective than the right one. (Rosen, 2002, p. 43)

I thought of Richter's performance of Schubert's B flat Sonata in Aldeburgh 1964 (recorded Music and Arts, 1990) where his slow tempo in first movement draws it out to over 25 minutes but is sublime music-making. Rosen's words above can always be a comforting thought but I also noted within myself a certain mounting defensiveness.

Back to Schubert's original version of "Frühlingstraum" (see Table 1), it was interesting also to note the tempo markings for the other two sections in the song. The familiar published version has three distinct tempi — *Etwas bewegt, Schnell, Langsam* — but in his first version there were only two with the opening stanzas both marked *Etwas geschwind*. I returned to listen to the Britten recording and was struck with how slow the opening tempo was. (My memory of it had recalled the affect of sadness rather than the way it was achieved.) In fact the slowness of his opening tempo changes the tempi relationships across the song. When the opening section returns in the fourth stanza the change of pace was negligible and it is evident that the opening tempo is actually that of the *Langsam*. (Moreover the middle sections are hardly *Schnell*.)

Table 1

Tempi Relationships Between the Sections of Frühlingstraum

Section	Published version	Original version	Britten/Pears
A Stanzas 1 & 4	Etwas bewegt	Etwas geschwind	(Langsam)
B Stanzas 2 & 5	Schnell	Etwas geschwind	(Moderato)
C Stanzas 3 & 6	Langsam	Langsam	Langsam

One had to concede that Britten's approach was clearly departing significantly from intentions of Schubert's initial version. While I was not inclined to aim for *geschwind,* I wondered if one could get that affect of sadness while still retaining Schubert's basic tempo relationships.

Then I noted a similarity with "Die Post" ("The Post") which comes two songs later in the cycle. This song starts the second half of the cycle and its unbridled jauntiness has always seemed to me worlds away from "Frühlingstraum". But, as I observed, here again is a song in a major key, in 6/8 and with an accompaniment pattern very close to an inversion of that which opens "Frühlingstraum", again articulated with dots on each quaver. And then to seal it all — oh dear! —I noticed "Die Post" was given the tempo indication of *Etwas geschwind* and my heart sank. Admittedly, Schubert later changed the marking of "Frühlingstraum" to the slower *Etwas bewegt* (and changed the dynamic marking from *piano* to *pianissimo*), but I reeled from the suggestion that Schubert had at one time conceived the tempo, dynamic and possibly affect at the beginning of "Frühlingstraum" to be in a similar ballpark to that of "Die Post". To me, "Frühlingstraum" had always seemed closer to "Tauschung" ("Illusion", no. 19), another of the songs in a major key — in fact the same key of A major — where again the simple musical materials can convey a similar heart-breaking nostalgia. But again, as I checked its tempo marking, I was taken aback to find again the instruction *Etwas geschwind* on that song as well. There, too, I had come to feel it should be played considerably slower than that tempo indication implies. As I note now, so did Britten.

I turned to my two "historically-informed" recordings on original instruments (2005a; 1995a) and then I listened to Tabea Zimmerman on viola (1991) and they all evoked the dream in a sprightly manner. With all this evidence building it was becoming evident my approach needed to be rethought. Was I becoming too indulgent, "sentimental" even? — heaven forbid! — and too far removed from what the composer had originally envisioned? Certainly Schubert had held back the tempi in his later version but was I still too far from what his markings imply? In my mind, the answer "perhaps" gradually turned to "probably" over the next few days. So, I resolved to explore the opening of "Frühlingstraum" differently — faster, more bouncy, perhaps more innocent, less precious though still a tad sentimental. And so, in the days before the next rehearsal with Patricia, I came to feel convinced by a new way of portraying it.

My anxiety about the next rehearsal had dissipated. But, when it came, Patricia announced immediately she that had been thinking about the opening of "Frühlingstraum" and now agreed it should be more nostalgic and slower than she had been advocating last time. It was ironic that now, after my change of direction, she was now closer to what I had been arguing for at the previous rehearsal. So we worked on it and in the end, neither viewpoint won over — ultimately we were both happy to meet somewhere near the middle. As I listen back to the recording of the broadcast now, it is clear that we are not nearly as slow as Britten's tempo but faster than I had played it with Greg. While attaining a certain simplicity, it still retained something nonetheless of that sense of nostalgia that, to me at least, still remains an important element. Moreover, across the song there were definitely three distinct tempi. In fact the desired effect may be closer to what Goethe's Werther describes in the quotation at the top of this chapter, in particular those words: "The darkness and madness of my soul are dispelled, and I breathe more freely again". That is certainly an outcome I am happy to aim for.

I am pleased to tell this story, first, because it was a successful resolution of an artistic difference of opinion. Although such disagreements are rarely resolved so easily or to the equal satisfaction of all involved, it has frequently been my experience of ensemble playing that individuals tug for a while in different directions before finding some common ground. This happens all the time, even if a compromise is not articulated in words — in fact it usually is not. Second, and most importantly, this story exemplifies how a conflict led to a reappraisal and resulted in a new concept and fresh way of feeling it. I don't believe any similarities with the Britten recording would be discernable on the surface — there never was a question of imitation despite its influence on the underlying concept. As I have tried to show, although that recording and a range of other factors fed into it, such influences were ultimately transcended as a new personal vision of the song emerged.

As the wonderful Graham Johnson (2004) reminds us (not specifically of *Winterreise*), the great thing about this repertory is that every time one approaches a great song, one can — indeed *must* — do so with a clean slate. It is impossible to erase the palimpsest of one's own experience hidden beneath the surface of each score, but this should be the most subtle and enlightened of background guides, not a blueprint for the future. (p. 326)

In practice and rehearsal, one plays with all sorts of variations — some obvious but many of them extremely subtle — and makes many conscious and unconscious decisions. But ultimately, most of these are in fact transcended in the act of music-making. At some point one hands the process over to the subconscious instincts to synthesise — to forge — all those details into a coherent form, inevitably one that is your own. There may be a period where things don't seem to fit or settle well together but bit by bit, or sometimes very suddenly, a clarity emerges. But, when it comes to performance, that whole process is left behind and remains invisible to the audience, as it must if they are to experience the work directly without any apparent interference from the performers. One wants the music-making to appear spontaneous, for the interpretation to "feel right", for the process to be so transparent — so far transcended — that no-one is aware that anything is in fact being "interpreted". It is an illusion certainly, but one that is deeply embedded in and essential to our musical culture.

In Performance

Und er lässt es gehen alles, wie es will,
Dreht und seine Leier steht ihm nimmer still.

And he just lets it happen, as it will,
Plays, and his hurdy-gurdy is never still.

("Der Leiermann"; "The Hurdy-Gurdy Man")

And then that moment arrives when one is performing the work in public and one comes to "Frühlingstraum". The previous song has finished — that silence between songs itself is precious and, from that, something magical must emerge. One knows deep inside that it is one of those decisive moments on which one's performance will be judged — by yourself as much as by others — but one cannot spare that thought even though the heart is likely to be beating faster. All the conscious ideas that have fed your preparation are dispelled. Nothing about notes or fingering or tempo or Britten must come to mind. One listens to the space, one takes a deep breath, one focuses on the image — evoking spring in winter — one gives oneself over to the moment in hope that some magic may be conjured. One must remain open to subtleties that may not have been planned or anticipated. Chances are that one is playing on an unfamiliar piano but, if it's a good one, that may also help. Such moments cannot be commanded. If we are lucky and open (hopefully, as they say, "in flow"), at such times grace may descend upon us.

I will perform *Winterreise* again next month with a German baritone, and so this extraordinary work is again in my fingers and on my mind. Having had some intensive rehearsal together I know this next performance will be significantly different from those I have done before. I will play excerpts from the cycle again in a concert with Patricia in June this year and look forward to that very much. Greg and I will be performing the cycle again next year when we will be unpacking our interpretative process in conjunction with the Queensland Conservatorium Research Centre as a case study examining Artistic Practice as Research. We will be exploring the work on a Dörr piano (c. 1820), and will be interested to observe how that different instrument transforms our interpretation, as it and the passage of time inevitably will. As Thomas Voight (as cited in Barenboim, 2005) observes "There are works of art with which one is never finished, either as a performer or as a listener" (p. 2), and for us this is clearly one of them. I hope and expect that I will continue to live with it as long as I am playing music. To quote Benjamin Britten:

> Though I have worked very hard at *Winterreise*, every time I come back to it I am amazed not only by the extraordinary mastery of it, but by the renewal of the magic: each time, the mystery remains. (As cited in Reed, 2008, p. 9)

This is why we return to experience some music many times, as it seems to be eternally regenerating. That it can, like the best art, continue to resonate with meaning, not only across successive generations, but across different stages of one's own life seems little short of miraculous. Perhaps Schubert's intentions in performance have continued to be modified ever since his friend Vogler sang them to Spaun and Schober. Perhaps such transformations need to keep occurring if such works are to remain more than historical curiosities but are to retain that intense, palpable sense of relevance to us today. Though alternative instrumental arrangements can reveal new perspectives — from playing it on a viola though to something like to Hans Zender's "Composed interpretation" (1994) — the work does not need such radical transformations to keep it modern. For performers and listeners it is mostly about the subtleties and nuances that can deliciously flavour the most intangible things and somehow reveal to us further layers of meaning. It is not that one aims specifically to be different or original. As Susan Tomes (2006) writes:

> We feel part of a continuum of music and musicians. I have no sense, when I play, that I am doing anything new. This is not to say that I don't have thoughts about the music, thoughts that make me play in a slightly different way from everybody else, and which make my style recognisable. But I don't regard newness as a particularly important aspect of my work, or a particularly meaningful one. It may be, indeed, that my most satisfying moments are when I have delved deep enough into something to make its oldness disappear. (p. 89)

References

Barenboim, D. (2005). Rehearsals and interviews with Thomas Quasthoff [DVD notes]. In F. Schubert, *Winterreise* [Performed by Thomas Quasthoff and Daniel Barenboim, piano] [DVD]. Hamburg: Deutsche Grammophon.

Bilson, M. (1997). The future of Schubert interpretation: What is really needed? *Early Music 25*(4), 715–722.

Capell, R. (1957). *Schubert's songs*. London: Duckworth.

Fisk, C. (2001). *Returning cycles: Contexts for the interpretation of Schubert's Impromptus and last sonatas*. Los Angeles: University of California Press.

Goethe, J. W. von. (1989). *The sorrows of young Werther*. (M. Hulse, Trans.). London: Penguin. (Original work published 1774)

Hudson, R. (1997). *Stolen time: The history of tempo rubato*. New York: Oxford University Press.

Johnson, G. (2004). The Lied in performance. In J. Parsons (Ed.), *The Cambridge companion to Lied* (pp. 315–333). Cambridge: Cambridge University Press.

Kivy, P. (1995). *Authenticities*. New York: Cornell University Press.

Kohlhaas, E. (1991). [CD notes]. In Schubert, F. (1991). *Winterreise* [Performed by Mitsuko Shirai, mezzo-soprano; Hartmut Höll, piano; and by Tabea Zimmerman, viola; Hartmut Höll, piano] [2-CD Set]. Germany: Capriccio.

Kramer, L. (2007). *Why classical music still matters*. Berkeley: University of California Press.

Landowska, W. (1969). *Landowska on music*. New York: Stein & Day.

Lebrecht, N. (2007). *The life and death of classical music featuring the 100 best and 20 worst recordings ever made*. New York: Anchor.

Lubin, S. (2000). The three styles of *Schwanengesang*: A pianist's perspective. In M. Chusid (Ed.), *A companion to Schubert's Schwanengesang: History, poets, analysis, performance* (pp. 191- 204). New Haven: Yale University Press.

Moore, G. (1975). *The Schubert song cycles with thoughts on performance*. London: Hamish Hamilton.

Reed, P. (2008). Mystery and magic. [DVD Notes]. In Schubert, F. (2008). *Winterreise* [Performed by Peter Pears, tenor; Benjamin Britten, piano] [DVD]. London: Decca. (Original recording 1970)

Rosen, C. (1996). *The romantic generation*. London: Harper Collins.

Rosen, C. (2002). *Beethoven's piano sonatas: A short companion*. New Haven: Yale University Press.

Schiff, A. (1998). Schubert's piano sonatas: Thoughts about interpretation and performance. In B. Newbould (Ed.), *Schubert studies* (pp. 191–208). Aldershot: Ashgate.

Schubert, F. (1965). *Winterreise* [Performed by Peter Pears, tenor; Benjamin Britten, piano] [CD]. London: Decca.

Schubert, F. (1970). "Frühlingstraum". In *Winterreise* [Score]. New York: Dover. (Reprint of Breitkopf & Härtel ed., Leipzig, 1895)

Schubert, F. (2008). *Winterreise* [Performed by Peter Pears, tenor; Benjamin Britten, piano] [DVD]. London: Decca. (Original recording 1970)

Schubert, F. (1972). *Winterreise* [Performed by Dietrich Fischer-Dieskau, baritone; Gerald Moore, piano] [CD]. Hamburg: Deutsche Grammophon.

Schubert, F. (1991a). *Winterreise* [Performed by Mitsuko Shirai, mezzo-soprano; Hartmut Höll, piano] [CD]. Germany: Capriccio.

Schubert, F. (1991b). *Winterreise* [Performed by Tabea Zimmerman, viola; Hartmut Höll, piano] [CD]. Germany: Capriccio.

Schubert, F. (1994). *Winterreise* [Performed by Hans Peter Blockwitz, tenor; Ensemble Modern: Zender] [CD]. New York: RCA.

Schubert, F. (1995a). *Winterreise* [Performed by David Wilson-Johnson, baritone; David Owen Norris, piano] [CD]. London: GMN.

Schubert, F. (1995b). *Winterreise* [Performed by Jon Vickers, tenor; Peter Schaaf, piano] [CD]. New York: Video Artists International.

Schubert, F. (1996). *Winterreise* [Performed by Dietrich Fischer-Dieskau, baritone; Jörg Demus, piano] [CD]. Hamburg: Deutsche Grammophon. (Original release 1966).

Schubert, F. (1998a). *Winterreise* [Performed by Christoph Prégardien, tenor; Andreas Staier, fortepiano] [CD]. New York: Elektra / Wea.

Schubert, F. (1998b). "Frühlingstraum". In *Winterreise* [Score]. Kassel: Bärenreiter/Henle.

Schubert, F. (1999). *Winterreise* [Performed by Hans Hotter, bass; Gerald Moore, piano] [CD]. London: EMI. (Original release 1954)

Schubert, F. (2002). *Winterreise* [Performed by Peter Schreier, tenor; Sviatoslav Richter, piano] [CD]. UK: Philips.

Schubert, F. (2004). *Winterreise* [Performed by Brigitte Fassbaender, mezzo-soprano; Aribert Riemann, piano] [CD]. London: EMI. (Original release 1988)

Schubert, F. (2005a). *Winterreise* [Performed by Dietrich Fischer-Dieskau, baritone; Alfred Brendel, piano] [DVD]. London: Teldec. (Original release 1979)

Schubert, F. (2005b). *Winterreise* [Performed by Thomas Quasthoff and Daniel Barenboim, piano] [DVD]. Hamburg: Deutsche Grammophon.

Schubert, F. (2006). *Winterreise* [Performed by Christine Schäfer, soprano; Eric Schneider, piano] [CD]. London: Onyx.

Schubert, F. (2007). *Winterreise* [Performed by Ian Bostridge, tenor; Julius Drake, piano] [DVD]. West Long Branch, NJ: Kultur.

Sgroi, C. (n.d.). Winterreise / Winter Journey. Retrieved 1 February, 2009, from http://www.mrichter.com/opera/files/winter.pdf

Taruskin, R. (1995). *Text and act: Essays on music and performance*. Oxford: Oxford University Press.

Tomes, S. (2006). *A musician's alphabet*. London: Faber.

Chapter 7

 # Letting it Go
An Autoethnographic Account of a Musician's Loss

Catherine Grant

January 2009. "Do you have any children?" I am with two friends of mine in a café, and they are meeting each other for the first time. I see the one hesitate. Her infant son died 12 months earlier. Instantly I perceive how this question could be one of the most difficult of all for my friend to answer. "No" leaves the life of her dead child unacknowledged. "Yes" will force her to qualify. Moreover, this skit will recur hundreds of times throughout her life, whenever she is asked this question; because whether that child died weeks ago or decades ago, the child is still her child, and still dead.

I don't know what it is like to have lost a child, and no doubt it is very different from the way I feel. But, sitting in the café, I identify immediately with the situation. When I first meet someone it's not long before they find out that I work at the conservatorium. "Ah!" they say, enthusiastically. "Do you play an instrument?" And even now I'm stumped, although my 'child' died 13 years ago. "No" is a lie; "yes" is a lie. Anything in between is more than a stranger bargains for, and often more than I care to enter into.

Following my debut concerto performance, an article was published in the local newspaper, complete with starry-eyed photo of my smiling teenage face. "Happiness, and a Bright Playing Future" ran the title (Cruise, 1996). During the interview, the reporter had asked me where I would like to be, professionally, in 10 years' time. My answer was honest, even if it didn't divulge my career aspirations as a pianist: "If I'm still playing the piano in 10 years and if people are still enjoying it, that's good enough for me". I look back on that article and the event it reviewed with fondness, and an acute awareness of its irony. Within a few months, I had developed a playing-related injury that led me into a prolonged depression, prohibited my playing the piano at all for many years, and put a firm end to any hopes I had of a career as a performing artist.

From the time my mother began teaching me at the age of three, the piano was central in my life. My most vivid childhood memories are musical ones: competitions and performances, rehearsing chamber music with my brothers, sight-singing Handel with my father, trying to catch out my mother's perfect pitch. I practised every day of the year. By my mid-teens, I was slipping off to dank music rooms at lunchtime. At first, my school friends merely tolerated this quirk; raised eyebrows soon grew into a certain respect, as I proudly reported back to them of my exam distinctions and competition wins.

The bilateral tenosynovitis (De Quervain's disease) I developed in my wrists and arms in my first year of conservatorium studies came on in a matter of days. An inflammation of the sheath surrounding the tendon in the wrists, I later learnt the condition often requires considerable time to heal, and that recurrence is a real risk. I was oblivious to that. Never having had any playing-related discomfort before, I was shocked to find I couldn't play the piano without pain. Nor could I turn a door handle, hold a book, or use a knife and fork. Typing an email or carrying the groceries home was agonizing, and falling asleep at night suddenly became a challenge, for the pain.

Statistically, I was among company. Figures citing the incidence of performance-related injury among musicians vary, but almost all the evidence points to worrying prevalence. In her practice as a teacher of the Alexander Technique, Shoebridge encountered playing-related pain in over half the students in a Victorian Certificate of Education (VCE) performance program, and in eight of nine participants in a high-level youth string fellowship program (personal communication, 26 May, 2008). In a recent study involving 87 student pianists at one major Australian tertiary institution, 59 of them (68%) reported a playing-related musculoskeletal disorder in the week preceding the survey (Bragge, 2008, p. 20). Yang, a tertiary music student herself, refers to a "near epidemic" of injury among conservatorium pianists (2001, p. 12).

The problem is not confined to student musicians, either. In 2008, the Australia Research Council committed $734,000 towards a five-year project (2009–2013) that aims to "establish the first injury surveillance system for musicians internationally and the first set of rigorous studies to evaluate the effectiveness of injury management interventions for orchestral musicians" (Ackermann, Kenny, &

Driscoll, 2008, Project Summary section) — a level of funding and scale of research that reflects the perceived magnitude of the problem.

Nothing and no-one had alerted me to the risk of serious injury from playing the piano, or prepared me for its onset. I desperately wanted to ignore the pain; an upcoming performance loomed, and conservatorium exams were not that far away. Fearful of doing further damage, though, I stopped playing the piano. It was an utterly foreign feeling, and I desperately missed the hours I spent alone with my instrument. I became anxious and aimless. Unable to fill the time constructively, my mind obsessed over my pain and my fear of the immediate future. Over and over again, countless times each day, one question played on my mind: How long until I can start playing again?

> **August 1996.** "How long until I can start playing again?" I ask my new physiotherapist. "I've got a performance in a couple of weeks and I really need to keep up the practice." She shakes her head a little. "This sort of injury can take a while, Catherine. At this stage I'd recommend cancelling the performance." Not wanting to believe it, I press further. Two weeks, then? A month? She avoids an answer, and my heart sinks. Longer than a month? How can I possibly not play the piano for a whole month?

> September 1996
> ... *love knows not its own depth until the hour of separation.*
> Kahil Gibran (1883–1930). The Prophet

Within weeks, initial shock developed into dejection, as I was required for the first time in my life to negotiate the maze of physical, mental and social challenges that accompany constant pain. Finding that using my hands even in the most basic of tasks not only caused pain but exacerbated it, I was increasingly forced to rely on other people. I quickly became tired of well-meaning advice — or worse, sympathy. More often than not, eighteen and proud, I would go out of my way to avoid the humiliation of asking for help. I began to hate telling people about my injury.

> **September 1996.** I am sitting attentively in a lecture on analysis. The lecturer knows me as a performer. He asks me to sight-read a score at the piano, by way of demonstration to the class. I am horrified. "Sorry, I can't ... It's ..." He looks at me, and I stutter something about not being able to play. He prods further. I am acutely aware of 30 or 40 pairs of eyes on me. The words stick in my throat. When the moment has passed, I slip out of the lecture and cry.

Reid, a pianist who has been managing a repetitive strain injury herself over the past 14 years, suggests that feelings of failure are common among injured students (2008, p. 29). Within the institutional environment especially, I felt this acutely. I felt as though the ability to play one's instrument well was what my teachers and fellow students valued and revered above all. It was what *I* valued above all. It was the reason I was admitted to conservatorium studies, the reason I was awarded a university scholarship, the reason people took notice of me, and I could no longer play at all. I began to feel like an imposter; I shouldn't have been in the building.

My experience of playing-related injury was not made easier by the culture of silence that I encountered in the tertiary music environment. Pain is culturally embedded: "The culture we live in and our deepest personal beliefs subtly or massively recast our experience" of it (Morris, 1991, p. 2). In a cruel loop that served to magnify the psychological and emotional impact of my physical condition, my beliefs were constantly shaped and reshaped by the conservatorium environment in which I was situated, an environment that by its heavy silence implicitly propagated a sense of shame and dishonour around injury. Feeling abandoned by my own culture, I will later sense some irony in the reality that injured musicians "desperately need emotional support and understanding from friends … colleagues, and teachers" (Mark, 2003, p. 149).

I don't underestimate the role I myself played in my isolation. As the weeks passed, I became less and less inclined to accept any support that was offered me. My friends found me taciturn and aloof. I had lost interest in their company; I did not want to hear their chatter about lessons, repertoire, and performances, and nor did I feel like discussing with them my predicament. I did my utmost to avoid my piano teacher, hating to have to report — again and again — no improvement in my condition. My family was interstate, and I didn't worry them with my troubles. Increasingly left to my physical and emotional pain, I began to withdraw. I recognised this happening, and I let it happen.

> October 1996
> *First the frog climbs into the hole, then the hole climbs into the frog.*
> Pak Sree

I tried to find ways to cope with my isolation. When I was desperate to play, I slipped into a practice room, locking the door behind me, and sat at my instrument in silence, with the lid closed. I prayed endlessly, though to whom, I didn't know. One thing I longed to do was to write a diary. I longed to get *out* of me what was *in* me. But holding a pen hurt, and more than a minute or two of writing or typing caused lasting pain. Instead, I decided to keep a note of any poems or texts I encountered that resonated with me in some way. I still do this to this day, and they number in the hundreds. I share a handful of them with you throughout this story.

Time passed. I took sum of the situation. I was in constant pain, and unable to perform the most basic of daily tasks without exacerbating my condition. I had lost my ability to play the piano, which had been my main source of joy and means of expression. With the loss of my principal talent also went my self-esteem and self-identity. Who was I, if not a pianist? My social and support network of friends and teachers had dissolved, and my career hopes were fading fast. First hand, I was experiencing that

> ... becoming injured can be emotionally devastating for a pianist. If a person's thoughts, aspirations, and, perhaps, very livelihood center around the piano, then to be unable to play one's best, unable to play without pain, perhaps unable to play at all, is a dreadful experience. (Mark, 2003, p. 149)

My feelings paralleled those of pianist Leon Fleisher at the onset of his focal dystonia: "If you spend your life training to do a certain kind of activity and suddenly it is no longer available to you, your life seems to come to an end" (as cited in Montparker, 1986, p. 9).

Among prominent performing musicians, Fleisher is one of the few to have spoken out about the psychological impact of injury. He reports a period of deep depression soon after the onset of his disorder, and attributes the break-up of his marriage to the strain (as cited in Tarchalski, 2008, p. 10). In speaking with candour, Fleisher displays particular courage. Wynn Parry has noted that "the music profession is quite naturally secretive about ailments" (2004, p. 42): Even revealing the existence of an injury holds possible repercussions for an active performer's career (Alford & Szanto, 1996; Grant, 2007; Weltz, 2003). Doubts about a musician's dependability, especially, may lead to agents or administrators thinking twice about making performance engagements. It is surely no coincidence that personal narratives are so rarely found among performing arts healthcare research. In the highly competitive world of the professional musician, where admitting to pain may lead to loss of a "gig", and losing one gig may mean losing more, revealing a "vulnerable, suffering, and searching self" (Ellis, 2009, p. 147) is a perilous undertaking.

Although data on the psychological impact of performance-related injury is scant, some researchers have at least suspected a significant prevalence of depression among injured musicians (Fry, 1987; Mark, 2003). I fitted the bill. Four or five months into my injury, the physical pain and its consequences were taking their full toll on my whole being. I had lost appetite and was unhealthily underweight, and felt constantly and deeply tired. One day, when a well-meaning friend (a medical student) began describing to me the anatomy of my injury, I fainted. I slept as much and as often as I could, to attempt some respite from the physical pain and general misery of waking life. The company of other people held no interest for me. Having lost sight of recovery, and finding my future impossible to imagine, I entertained notions of suicide.

I struggled on. The months dragged, one endless day at a time.

December 1996

Dear God,
These circumstances will change. This situation shall pass.
Amen

Michael Leunig (1945–)

In my wretchedness, I found the prolonged process of exploring treatments for my condition a tremendously arduous one. Other musicians with performance-related injury report similar sentiments (Milanovic, 2005; Fleisher, in Tarchalski, 2008; Walker, 2006). Over a period of many months, from the very onset of my injury, I pursued courses of physiotherapy, cortisone, medications, chiropractic treatment, acupuncture, pain management, Alexander Technique, Feldenkrais, meditation, homeopathy, kinesiology, Bowen therapy, neurolinguistic programming, and hypnotherapy. As my pain persisted with temporary or minimal improvement, I became increasingly discouraged. Not making things any easier was the lack of understanding I frequently encountered from healthcare professionals, clearly unused to dealing with the "relatively esoteric tribulations of pain-ridden performing artists" (Alford & Szanto, 1996, p. 44).

> **March 1997.** I am sitting in a sports medicine clinic with a physician of national repute. I've travelled here from interstate, on recommendation, to see him. I tell him the history of my injury, and he gives me the usual advice: no playing, good diet, exercise, patience.
>
> At one point during the consultation, obviously irritated by my desperate questioning, he frowns: "Look, Catherine, I see a lot of people with conditions that are life-threatening. Tendonitis won't kill you". Instantly, in my mind, I retort, "Not directly". Suicide kills. But I keep my mouth shut. This man doesn't understand me. He doesn't understand how much playing the piano means to me.

I'm tired of this, I think to myself. I'm tired of other people, of pain, of me.
I'm tired of life.

April 1997

Non senza fatiga si giunge al fine
(Not without effort does one reach the end)

Frescobaldi (1583–1643)

As I write these words, I wonder whether autoethnography as mode of enquiry lends itself exclusively to a more open personality type than mine. I'm not known for an inclination to divulge myself to others. To be frank, if I *must* tell my story, right now I rather fancy Ellis and Bochner's paradoxical notion of an "aloof autoethnography" (2006, p. 436). Earlier today, a colleague dubbed me "Miss-Anthropy," a good-humoured reference to my propensity to keep my self to myself. And yet here I sit, revealing to you, an unknown reader, my thoughts of suicide. I'm not sure I'll leave that bit in.

Then again, autoethnography "was designed to be unruly, dangerous, vulnerable, rebellious" (Ellis & Bochner, 2006, p. 433).

~~~

One evening, about a year after I had first stopped playing the piano, something shifted in me. The inner experience was completely concrete, yet language will not come close to expressing it, and I don't want to try. I will only describe it as an epiphany that "left its mark" on me (Denzin, 1989).

> **July 1997.** Late evening. In some remote part of my mind, I register the sounds of possums rustling in the palm trees; the neighbour's barking terrier; my housemate arriving home. A minute later, he comes out to the back deck, where I am doubled over the railing, sobbing. I feel a hand on my shoulder. "There are easier ways to water the plants, Cath," he says gently.
>
> I don't know what just took place within me. But in this moment, for the first time since I stopped playing the piano, my grief is not mixed with desperation, or denial, or despair. What I feel now is pure sadness. It's deep, and it's so sore. But I also recognise it as beautiful. It makes me curious. Grief is a complex thing, I think to myself, but maybe it's not impossible to cope with. In fact, I think I can cope with it. I think I can get through this.
>
> I look at my housemate, and manage a smile through my tears.

> August 1997
>
> *... To live in this world*
> *you must be able*
> *to do three things:*
> *to love what is mortal;*
> *to hold it*
>
> *against your bones knowing*
> *your own life depends on it;*
> *and, when the time comes to let it go,*
> *to let it go.*
>
> Mary Oliver (1935–). In Blackwater Woods

In the weeks that followed, I finally began to acknowledge and accept that my recovery from injury might take some time. I withdrew my enrolment at the conservatorium. Intensely inquisitive about my new world, my new understanding of pain and loss, I took some university subjects in philosophy and religion. I researched the effect of meditation on pain, and the treatment of grief through music therapy. I devoured literature about grief. I felt like Oscar Wilde, revelling in his new habitat.

> October 1997
>
> *I long to live so that I can explore what is no less than a new world*
> *to me. Do you want to know what this new world is? I think you*
> *can guess what it is. It is the world in which I have been living.*
> *Sorrow, then, and all that it teaches one, is my new world.*
>
> Oscar Wilde (1854–1900). De Profundis

While I gradually began to function again, the physical pain continued, and with it, its impact on my life. My studies were impeded by my limitations in writing and using a computer. I was under significant financial pressure, due to the loss of both my previous sources of income: piano accompanying work, and my conservatorium scholarship. Adding to the stress was the substantial cost of pursuing avenues of medical treatment for my condition. I began a sales position, and just as soon, felt forced to resign due to increased pain from the constant use of my hands. Any job that was available to me worsened my condition, and eventually, unable to support myself, I saw no option but to withdraw from university altogether and return to my parents' home interstate. I spent a long 18 months there, waiting, hoping, for a way out from limbo.

> May 1999
>
> *All things must pass.*
>
> Stephen Cassettari. *Reflections on the River*

Like much autoethnographic enquiry, this chronicle of my experiences embodies an effort to make sense of a situation in which I was forced to cope with loss of meaning (Ellis, 2004, p. 19). In my aimless existence, I decided to head overseas for a time; I ended up spending over three years abroad, travelling, teaching English for a living, meeting new people, acquainting myself with new cultures and languages. In these surrounds, I found I was quickly able to form a new identity. The challenges of living in foreign lands brought renewed self-esteem and sense of independence. Gradually, my injury and my inability to play the piano ceased to be the most important things in my life. I began to be "on speaking terms" with my body again (Pelias, 2004, p. 37), and to have days, weeks even, when I would forget about my loss. It was a welcome relief.

Sometimes the old grief surfaced when I least expected; occasionally it took a sharp edge, such as when a flippant comment stung my pride.

> **August 2002.** A gathering of friends. I'm making small talk with a guy I haven't met before. He chats about his studies, and asks me if I'm at uni. I reply that I'd started two degrees, but hadn't finished either yet. He smiles wryly. "One of those, are you?"
>
> I'm suddenly angry. When I developed my injury six years earlier, there was nothing else and nothing more I wanted in the world than to learn play the piano well. What made me defer both my degrees was not indecision, or incompetence, or lack of commitment, but physical pain and its impact on my life. Instantly, I don't feel like talking to this guy any more. "No, actually, I'm not 'one of those!'", I snap. He looks taken aback. I excuse myself and walk away, leaving him (unfairly) to wonder what provoked such a reaction.

> August 2002
>
> *If you seek to criticise me, you need to be inside me.*
>
> Adam Mickiewicz (1798–1855)

After a couple of years back in Australia, it was time to reassess my life direction. Music had been my childhood; I wanted it to be my life. I resigned from my English teaching job and enrolled in a non-practical honours year in music. Ever curious about grief, I wrote my dissertation on its representation in the music of Bach, and upon completion I began work as a research assistant at the conservatorium. So it was that I found myself again in my old haunt, around many of my old lecturers and teachers, around the pianos I'd once sat at in silence and tears, around the familiar strains of music seeping out of the practice rooms. It all felt like a quiet homecoming. I was more content than I had been since the onset of my injury, over a decade earlier.

> March 2007
> *It's the great mystery of human life that old grief passes gradually into quiet tender joy.*
> Fyodor Dostoyevsky (1821–1881). Brothers Karamazov

Autoethnography is a journey, not a destination (Ellis & Bochner, 2006, p. 431). My narrative explores rather than explains one thread of my life, perhaps raising more questions in the reader's mind about my experiences and the experiences of others than I could hope to address now, or maybe ever. No matter how comprehensive I try to be, in one chapter, or in ten, I will not be able to share with you all the ebbs and flows of my experience of injury. Maybe another time I will recount the trials of my encounters with healthcare practitioners, or what it felt like to be living with two conservatorium pianists — and two grand pianos — as I grappled with my loss, or my feelings of guilt surrounding my injury. Indeed, some things may be better left unsaid. For ethical reasons, I have chosen not to describe in detail the role of my teachers or fellow students in my experiences. I have not attempted to convey the sensations of my physical pain, because words will not make it real (Payne, 1996). And I am not yet ready to explore my sometimes overwhelming sense of shame at the period of my life when suicide was my fixation.

My experience of injury, like my effort to make sense of it, is not a closed chapter. I still live with pain. Like the weather, it comes and goes — and like the weather, I sometimes have to concede to it. At times I do this graciously; other times, I fight. My body and I are "cautious friends": "We do not have much trust between us, afraid the other will become a betrayer, if not today, then tomorrow. We stand guard, watching for signs" (Pelias, 2004, p. 37). When my body allows me, I play my instrument a little. I play Bach. It is my favourite thing in the world to do. Yet I do still feel confused when someone asks me whether

I play the piano: I certainly can't play nearly as much as I once could, or nearly as well, and there are times when I can't play at all.

I trust and believe I have not grown bitter from any adversity I have faced through my injury. For many things, I am grateful. My experiences have developed in me a far greater understanding of others, and of the world. I am less judgemental, more compassionate. I have formed a sturdier identity, based not on my talents, but on my self. I treasure grief, and all it has taught me. Most importantly of all, I have learnt what I value in life, and learned to value life. I am a novice at it no longer.

November 2007

Be like the bird who, pausing in her flight awhile on branches too slight, feels them give way beneath her, and yet sings, knowing that she hath wings.

Victor Hugo (1802–1885)

Despite these boons, like Jago (2002), who traces the complex course of her illness and recovery from an "academic depression", not everything I have garnered from my experiences has been affirming. If my outlook on life is at times pessimistic, that is the residue of grief. Emotionally, I sometimes feel old, worn. Most disquieting of all, I have developed a wary distrust of the power of my mind. "Time has become both friend and enemy, a paradox", Jago writes:

> Depression begets depression, my brain chemistry forever altered by past occurrences, an open invitation to repeat episodes. Then the reclamation process will begin again. Perhaps I will be better at it next time, more aware of the signs, the resources, the process, my ability to come out the other side. I see the future as perpetual efforts to keep disintegration at bay, a blend of success and failure. Hope and fear coexist. (2002, p. 743)

I do what I can, with what I have learnt. Since finding myself again in the conservatorium environment, I have campaigned a little for issues of Australian tertiary musicians' health. In 2008, on my initiative and with the support of its Research Centre, Queensland Conservatorium piloted strategies to increase student awareness of issues surrounding health and wellbeing (see Grant, 2008). Healthcare professionals were engaged to deliver a series of workshops; commencing students received information on optimising their health as musicians; a national web discussion forum on the topic was launched ("Health and Wellbeing for Musicians", 2008). At the time of writing (February 2009), a Queensland Conservatorium Research Centre proposal to encourage standardised healthcare strategies in institutions across the country sits with the board of the National Council of Tertiary Music Schools.

Like Alford and Szento (1996), I muse over what might be achieved if the three interlocking realms of performance, pedagogy, and medicine were to join forces in addressing the "pervasive experience of pain" in musicians (p. 44). Probing the potential for change, I continue to dip into the world of musicians' health, researching, agitating, constantly negotiating the delicate balance between subjective insider on the one hand, and impartial advocate on the other. It's a difficult equilibrium to establish: More than once I've felt like abandoning the cause, disinclined to talk about matters relating to pain, especially when I am in it. For now — for as long as I am able — I will do what I can, in the hope that my modest efforts may make a difference to someone's life.

December 2008

You are never asked to do more than you are able without being given the strength and ability to do it.

Eileen Caddy (1917–2006). *The Dawn of Change*

In more ways than one, this narrative "concentrat[es] on the body as the site from which the story is generated" (Spry, 2001, p. 708). My body, central to this story, has also been central in writing it. Typing these pages, perched at my computer, some days my body has given me pain, as normal, and sometimes it has been pain-free, also as normal. In both cases, in writing this narrative, in a way I have acted for you my life. The boundaries between text and body blur (Conquergood, 1991; Spry, 2001). Quietly, from my desk, I have been performing for you my autobiography.

> In autobiographical narrative performances, the performer often speaks about acts of social transgression. In doing so, the telling of the story itself becomes a transgressive act — a revealing of what has been kept hidden, a speaking of what has been silenced — an act of reverse discourse that struggles with the preconceptions borne in the air of dominant politics. (Park-Fuller, 2000, p. 26)

Thanks to the concerted dedication of a small group of academics, teachers, and healthcare professionals (Ackermann, Bragge, Shoebridge, and Wijsmann, among others), the long-standing and oft-noted taboo surrounding performance-related injury in the Australian environment (e.g., Fry, 1987; Yang, 2001; Bragge, Bialocerkowski, & McMeeken, 2006; Grant, 2007) is finally beginning to erode. Progress is slow but steady. The recently-founded national peak body for performing arts healthcare is gaining prominence (ASPAH, 2006), and carries significant potential to address issues of major concern, including the taboo.

Even so, I feel vulnerable in offering you, the reader, this personal chronicle of the impact of injury on my physical, emotional, social, and psychological self. Firstly, it is intimate, and you are an unknown. I am anxious about trusting you to be curator of my story. Secondly, I am apprehensive about entering unfamiliar territory. Autoethnographic accounts of injury in musicians are few, and I am aware that I transgress unspoken rules by writing one. And finally, the words that you have just read are inadequate. They don't convey the nuances of my lived experience. They contradict themselves at times, as life does. They do not fully describe, let alone explain, the chaotic mesh of my emotions, thoughts, and experiences. I am afraid that I may have done you — or me — an injustice in writing them.

At the same time, this account is the best I can do to help you understand something of me, and by so doing, it might help you understand the potential impact of performance-related injury on a musician's life. It might help you understand the weight of those "relatively esoteric tribulations" of performing artists. That is one reason I am writing this paper, despite my ambivalence and misgivings. But equally, I am writing in the hope that perhaps you might identify with my story in some small way. If so, I am happy, on two counts: It means *you* are not alone, and *I* am not alone. After all, we will not know "if others' intimate experiences are similar or different until we offer our own stories" (Ellis, 1993, p. 725). With those things to encourage me, then, I offer you these words, written with as much sincerity and integrity as I have. Maybe eventually, as performers, pedagogues, and healthcare professionals come to better understand the impact of injury, other musicians will feel encouraged to tell their stories too.

Acknowledgments

I would like to thank my anonymous reviewer for his/her helpful comments in the preparation of this chapter.

References

Ackermann, B., Kenny, D. & Driscoll, T. (2008). *Sound practice: Supporting sustainable careers in orchestral musicians through occupational health and safety initiatives.* Australia Research Council Linkage Project LP0989486. Retrieved 20 January, 2009, from ARC website.

Alford, R. R., & Szanto, A. (1996). Orpheus wounded: The experience of pain in professional worlds of the piano. *Theory and Society* 25(1), 1–44. Retrieved 15 January, 2009, from http://www.springerlink.com/content/u28114572012r882/.

ASPAH [Australian Society for Performing Arts Healthcare]. (2006). Australian Society for Performing Arts Healthcare [website]. Retrieved 20 January, 2009, from http://www. aspah.org.au/.

Bragge, P., Bialocerkowski, A., & McMeeken, J. (2006). Understanding playing-related musculoskeletal disorders in elite pianists: A grounded theory study. *Medical Problems of Performing Artists, 21*(2), 71–79. Retrieved 20 January, 2009, from http://www. sciandmed.com/mppa/.

Bragge, P., Bialocerkowski, A., & McMeeken, J. (2008). Musculoskeletal injuries in elite pianists: Prevalence and associated risk factors. *Australian Journal of Music Education, 2008*(1), 18–31.

Clandinin, J. D., & Connelly, F. M. (2000). *Narrative enquiry: Experience and story in qualitative research*. San Francisco: Jossey-Bass.

Conquergood, D. (1991). Rethinking ethnography: Towards a critical cultural politics. *Communication Monographs, 58*, 179–194.

Cruise, B. (1996, May 29). Happiness, and a bright playing future. *The Canberra Times*, p. 14.

Denzin, N. (1989). *Interpretive interactionism*. Newbury Park, CA: Sage.

Ellis, C. (1993). "There are survivors": Telling a story of sudden death. *Sociological Quarterly, 34*, 711–730.

Ellis, C. (2004). *The ethnographic I: A methodological novel about autoethnography*. Walnut Creek, CA: AltaMira Press.

Ellis, C. (2009). *Revision: Autoethnographic reflections on life and work*. Walnut Creek, CA: Left Coast Press.

Ellis, C., & Bochner, A. P. (2000). Autoethnography, personal narrative, reflexivity: Researcher as subject. In N. K. Denzin & Y. S. Lincoln (Eds.), *Handbook of qualitative research* (2nd ed., pp. 733–768). Thousand Oaks, CA: Sage.

Ellis, C. & Bochner, A. P. (2006). Analysing analytic autoethnography: An autopsy. *Journal of Contemporary Ethnography 35*(4), 429–449.

Fry, H. J. H. (1987). Prevalence of overuse (injury) syndrome in Australian Music Schools. *British Journal of Industrial Medicine, 44*, 35–40.

Grant, C. (2007). Beyond prevention: Addressing the needs of tertiary music students with playing-related injury. *Music in Australian Tertiary Institutions: Issues for the 21st Century*. [Conference proceedings of NACTMUS national conference, Griffith University, Brisbane, July 2007]. Retrieved 18 January, 2009, from www.nactmus.org .au/NACTMUS/.

Grant, C. (2008). Taking pains: Addressing issues of musicians' health in tertiary music students. In *Music Forum. Journal of the Music Council of Australia. 14*(3), 34–35.

Health and wellbeing for musicians: A network for Australian music students. (2008, August). Website. Retrieved 15 January, 2009, from http://www.musicianshealth. ning.com.

Jago, B. J. (2002). Chronicling an academic depression. *Journal of Contemporary Ethnography, 31*(6), 729–757. Retrieved 14 December, 2008, from Sage database.

Mark, T. (2003). *What every pianist needs to know about the body*. Chicago: GIA.

Milanovic, T. (2005). *To play or not to play: An exploration of students' experiences of the Taubman approach to piano*. Unpublished masters dissertation, Griffith University, Brisbane.

Montparker, C. (1986, October). The indomitable Leon Fleisher. *Clavier, Oct 1986*, 6–11.

Morris, D. B. (1991). *The culture of pain*. Berkeley: University of California Press.

Park-Fuller, L. (2000). Performing absence: The staged personal narrative as testimony. *Text and Performance Quarterly, 20*, 20–42.

Payne, D. (1996). Autobiology. In C. Ellis & A. P. Bochner (Eds.), *Composing ethnography: Alternative forms of qualitative writing* (pp. 49–75). Walnut Creek, CA: AltaMira Press.

Pelias, R. J. (2004). *A methodology of the heart: Evoking academic and daily life.* Walnut Creek, CA: AltaMira Press.

Reid, H. (2008, April 26). The pain shame. In K. Clarke (Ed.), *Classical music, 864,* 29. London: Rhinegold.

Ronai, C. R. (1992). The reflexive self through narrative: A night in the life of an erotic dancer/researcher. In C. Ellis & M. G. Flaherty (Eds.), *Investigating subjectivity: Research on lived experience* (pp. 102–124). Newbury Park, CA: Sage.

Spry, T. (2001). Performing autoethnography: An embodied methodological praxis. *Qualitative Inquiry, 7*(6), 706–732.

Tarchalski, H. S. (2008). Happy 80th birthday, Leon Fleisher! Nearly four score of legendary music-making: Part one. In *Keyboard Companion, 19*(3), 6–11.

Weltz, K. (2003). Health Education. *The Strad, 48*(2), 250–253.

Wynn Parry, C. (2004). Managing the physical demands of musical performance. In A. Williamon (Ed.), *Musical excellence: Strategies and techniques to enhance performance* (pp. 41–60). Oxford: Oxford University Press.

Yang, K. C.-H. (2001). *Pianists' physical injuries: Strategies of treatment and prevention.* Unpublished masters dissertation, Griffith University, Brisbane.

Chapter 8

Becoming a Bass Player
Embodiment in Music Performance

Chris McRae

As a trumpet player, now learning to play the bass guitar, I notice changes happening to my body that I was unaware of as I learned to play the trumpet. Specifically I notice the changes that are happening to my fingers. These changes that are happening as I learn to play the bass, as well as the relationship I have with the instrument, are physical and embodied. They are specific to my experience, and they are layered with cultural and social meanings. In this chapter, I consider how learning to play the bass alters my experience of the world both on and off stage. Technologies, such as musical instruments, are connected to and with our experience of the world at an embodied level, and these connections shape the ways in which we know the world and are in the world. As I learn to become a bass player, I am changing even at the level of my body, and therefore changing both who I am and how I come to know myself.

The strings of the bass guitar dig into my fingertips as I move my left hand across the fret board and use the index and middle fingers on my right hand to pick the strings. In my second week playing this new instrument my fingers are still sensitive to the thickness of the steel string, and they slice through the calluses I developed on my fingertips from playing the guitar for six years, and push against the nerves creating sensations of pain with every note I play. My left hand moves awkwardly along the fret board, and my right hand struggles to pick each individual note. I tap my toe, and try to keep time because I am still not completely sure of myself when it comes to rhythm, even though as the drum major of my high school marching band I was somehow able to conduct 150 musicians. I listen for the chord changes so I know when to play new notes, and my ability to hear the changes is pretty good, having played the trumpet for 15 years. I am training my hands and fingers to play the bass, and in so doing I am again changing the physical makeup of my body for my practice as a musician. Now the pain I feel in my fingertips from learning to play the bass is evident to me even as I type these words on the keyboard of my computer.

My sensation of touch has changed from learning to play the bass, but the changes my fingertips are undergoing do not only impact my ability to play music, these changes impact the way I move through the world. I now know differently about my body and about performance as a result of learning to play this new instrument. Performance changes bodies and changes how we know about the world and are known as performers in the world. In this story of music and performance I consider the physical relationship between my body and technology (the bass guitar), and the ways in which this relationship necessitates change. This change is realised for me, both in playing music and in the performances of everyday life. The performance also works within and can work against cultural and social expectations. My story of playing the bass is a story of embodied ways of knowing the self and others through performance.

Instrumental Changes

Playing music is exciting; and I especially enjoy the challenge of learning to play a new instrument. When I was 10 years old, my parents presented me with an old cornet they had purchased at a pawn shop, and when I tried to play my new horn for the first time nothing happened. I was devastated, but slowly I began to learn how to play the trumpet, and over time I improved. I played trumpet throughout high school, I played for two years in the university marching band, and then I joined an eight piece swing band playing various gigs including private parties and weddings.

When I started college, I began teaching myself how to play the guitar. A friend of mine had given me his beaten-up old acoustic guitar before he moved west to Los Angeles to try and make it big with his band. I spent hours in my room learning how to play chords, and I tried to learn simple songs that I could play and sing. Eventually I began to write my own songs, and started to hear new ways of combining melodies and chord progressions. Playing the trumpet helped me play the guitar because I was able to hear melodies that would fit over certain chord progressions. Playing the guitar helped me play the trumpet, especially when it came to improvising. I could hear chord progressions better when I was improvising as a result of learning to play chords on the guitar.

The process of learning to play both of these instruments continues today. Every time I pick up either the trumpet or the guitar to practise I am learning. I am adding to and changing my ability to play. Each repetition of a song, scale, or technique improves or adds to what I know, but each repetition also changes the foundation from where I will start the next time I practise or play. Similarly, each time I learn to play a new instrument I am adding to what I know, but I am also changing who I am in relation to what I know. New technologies, like the various musical instruments I play, change not only how I play as a musician, but they change my body, and these changes impact all aspects of my life from my interpersonal relationships to my scholarly practices. As I learn to play the bass I am particularly drawn to and aware of the changes I am undergoing especially because I notice the changes happening to my fingers. Reflecting on these changes helps me to understand how my practice as a musician extends into my practice as a student.

Bass Strings

Playing music requires and redirects my energy and focus from work and school to the pleasures of creativity and sound. The performance of playing music gives me the opportunity to put my work in a new perspective, and so I am constantly searching for this opportunity. I practise trumpet or guitar every day even when I am not playing with any bands. But I am also always looking for the chance to play with others. At the beginning of my first semester as a PhD student at Southern Illinois University I found myself in conversation with a local musician and faculty member at the university who was looking for a bass player.

"Our last bass player graduated and lives too far away to play with the band anymore. You don't happen to play the bass, do you?"

"Actually no I don't. But I have been playing the trumpet for 15 years now. And I play some guitar too."

"Well, would you be interested in learning?"

"The bass? Sure, why not? I guess I could try."

"Well, why don't you come over on Monday night to rehearsal and I'll show you some things on the bass? It's actually my primary instrument and so I have one you could use. I think you'd be able to pick it up pretty easily, especially since you've been playing music for so long."

The conversation ends with me agreeing to come to band practice for my first attempt at playing the bass guitar. It is the first band practice I have ever shown up to without an instrument. It feels kind of like going to class without a pen or a notebook, but as promised I am equipped with a bass as soon as I walked through the door. I am also shown some basic scales and patterns. I am easily able to translate my knowledge of music theory from playing trumpet and my knowledge of stringed instruments from playing guitar to playing the bass, but I am not fully prepared for how thick the strings of this instrument are. I notice this immediately because as soon as I start to play I find my fingertips hurting.

My threshold for pain is normal, I suppose; however, I generally avoid putting myself in situations where my body will necessarily be subject to physical pain. And the pain from applying repeated pressure to four stainless steel wound strings with diameters of less than a tenth of an inch thick is not in any way excruciating. It is however, enough to change the tips of my fingers in such a way, that even after the calluses have formed and broken open and formed again, I am aware of the difference of my fingertips. During the first night of playing the bass the pain is noticeable. It is also enough to split open the tip of my index finger on my right hand. This hurts, and I'm not sure I'll be able to take notes in class tomorrow.

"G" String (0.05" diameter)

I want to extend what I know from my own experience performing music to performance studies because playing music is an embodied practice. I learn to play music through and with my body, and through music performance I am constantly changing as a musician and as a performer. There are conversations happening in performance studies about musicians; for example, Auslander (2004) calls for research in performance studies that focuses on and analyses performers specifically in popular music. He expands on Frith's (1996) explanation of the performers of popular music to create a model for critique of these performances. In discussing the popular music performer, Frith describes a process of "double enactment" in which the musician enacts "both a star personality (their image) and a song personality, the role that each lyric requires" (Frith, p. 212). Auslander then identifies three layers of performance to be used in the analysis of performers of popular music. These are the real person, the performance persona, and character (p. 6). For Auslander this typology is a useful form of criticism of the popular music performer, and although he recognises the potential for the simultaneous presence of these three signified aspects of the performer, he places the most emphasis on the persona in thinking about the relationship between audience, performance and performer.

This is similar to Graver's (1997) list of eight different typologies for analysing actor's bodies on stage, including what he terms "personage". Auslander (2006) also expands on Graver's discussion of personage in his own development of the idea of musical personae. For Auslander, musical personae are the primary performance of musicians: "What musicians perform first and foremost is not music, but their own identities as musicians, their musical personae" (p. 102). In expanding his idea of musical personae to all musicians, Auslander locates the creation of personae with the audience, saying: "It is the audience that produces the final construction of an identity from the impressions created by the performer" (p. 114). Auslander considers musical performance in terms of the relationship between musician and audience instead of thinking about the relationship between musical works and performance as a way of thinking about performances of identity (p. 117). My interest in the musician as performer is in line with Auslander's call for studying music in performance studies, but I am less interested in his typologies and more interested in what this performance means for the performer. How does playing music shape the embodied experiences of the musician?

In my performance as a novice bass player, I cannot clearly locate myself in one of Auslander's typologies. Even at my first gig with the band I am unaware of my persona. Do I even have one? My initiation process into the band has involved two practice sessions where I learned not only how to play the bass but also how to play about 10 songs. Standing on the stage, I feel as if everyone in the smoke-filled dive bar can tell that I am new at this. I am wearing jeans, a T-shirt, and a corduroy fedora pulled down low over my eyes. I stand in the back corner of the stage, and try not to draw attention to myself. It's all I can do to keep up with the songs we are playing. My body is tense and I never really feel comfortable until a break is called. Is this nervous, tense, fedora-wearing musician my persona?

The typologies Auslander and Graver provide form a useful frame for analysing performance from an outside perspective; however, I am not looking on and criticising a performance or a performer, instead I am locating myself in the centre of the performance, and trying to understand what it means for me to be the performer. What does it mean to be the bass player? The typologies of performers do not fit with my experience or with my thinking about my experience. I may have a persona, and I may never be aware of this persona. But in thinking about what performers know through performance, a heuristic approach to analysing experience seems to be a useful method for answering questions about knowledge in performance.

"D" String (0.07" diameter)

Other performance studies scholars are also interested in questions of identity, music, and the relationship between performer and audience especially in terms of culture. Delgado (2000), in his analysis of Chicano rapper Kid Frost, looks to the construction and performance of a necessarily political, cultural, and masculine identity by the performer. Lengel (2004) considers the performance of music by Muslim women as a practice and performance of resistance to hegemonic power structures that creates an opportunity and space for "understanding women's agency, power, and ability to engage in *nushuz* (rebellion)" (p. 218). By looking at lyrics and performance to unpack possible meanings about identity, the work of Delgado and Lengel cause me to question the cultural impact of my own performances as a musician. Not all musical performances are overtly political or resistant, but the possibility for change exists in the close relationship between music performance and culture. How does my particular experience of learning to play the bass function culturally? Likewise, how does culture impact my experience of learning the bass?

Each week I practise with the band and learn new songs. As my repertoire grows, I start playing more songs during the gigs. I still feel tension in my shoulders and legs as I play, but instead of retreating to the back corner of the stage, I start purposefully standing in the back corner next to the drummer. This is where I belong, even if I am still hiding. As a graduate student, learning to play the bass starts to change my approach to both music and school. In class on mornings after playing with the band until 2 a.m. I am exhausted, and my shoulders and back are sore. But I am particularly aware of the pain in my fingertips. As I participate in class discussions I develop the habit of feeling my fingertips. Other students tap their legs, or twirl their pens, but my new nervous habit is an increased awareness of my fingers. I feel the calloused and blistered tips of my fingers with my still unchanged thumbs. Some mornings the blisters on my fingers are so bad that I cannot hold my pen in order to take notes.

This physical consequence of learning to the play bass becomes apparent to me because of my particular cultural experience as a graduate student with an interest in theorising about the body. That my fingertips are changing is exciting, because this is a material effect of my performance. But it also draws my attention away from other ways my body may be changing as a result of my performance. Do I move differently? Do I dress differently? Do I talk differently? That my fingertips are sensitive to the strings of the bass is also related to my decision to stay in school where the kind of work I do would not result in my hands developing calluses. My performance as a musician is inseparable from my practices as a student. I am also starting to hear the music I listen to differently. Bass lines that were once easy to ignore become increasingly apparent to me. And as the underlying structure in music becomes clearer, the underlying structure or metaphorical bass line becomes clearer to me in class discussions. I literally and figuratively hear structures and rhythms of arguments in conversations and texts.

Another way to consider the impact of music performance is in looking to the audience, and analysing and interpreting their responses. Davidson (2002) points to the importance of the audience in the performance of music, particularly in regards to solo performances of classical music. She argues performers communicate expressive meanings through their bodies with their audiences. This is a "two-way communication" between audience and performer as there is a constant exchange of visual and aural information (p. 149). Davidson is less interested in performance of identity than Auslander; however, she is similarly interested in the relationship between performers and audiences as a location for the co-creation of communicative meanings. It is in these communicative meanings that I locate the possibility for change made by and in performance.

You and I impact each other. Our relationship shapes the possible meanings of this performance, this writing. What I say shapes what you will read, but you bring your experience to this piece as well. Similarly, my performance as a bass player is impacted by the audience. In this band we cover songs by the Grateful Dead, Rolling Stones, Credence Clearwater Revival, and other music from the same genres and generation. The rhythm guitarist counts us off quickly, "One, two, three, four", and the staccato notes of the opening riff to "Proud Mary" catches the attention of some of the bar patrons. There is a cheer of recognition from a woman sitting at the bar. A young couple makes their way to the space in front of the stage, creating a temporary dance floor. The audience's familiarity with the music creates an expectation of my performance and the performance of the band. My own performance then is one of not only trying to play the bass correctly, but also of trying to meet the cultural expectations of what a cover band should do. That is, to play music in a given context that is recognisable and enjoyable to a certain audience.

I may not implicate myself or my audience in my performance in resistant ways, but my performance does create and perpetuate a certain aesthetic: the aesthetic of the unified band working to create a musical experience for an audience. I stand in the corner listening carefully to the drums and to the chords. My fingers slide across the strings, and I tap my foot to keep time. We repeat the opening riff to end the song, and I turn to face the guitarists as we all slow and end the song together. This is a performance that suggests musical expression as a moment of hope and joy or release. This is a moment when sounds come together and evoke memories and feelings for an audience.

"A" String (0.085" diameter)

Reflecting on the embodied experience of performing provides me with the most productive understandings of how learning a new instrument, a new technology, changes the way I move through the world. DeChaine (2002) argues the embodied experience of music is a way of understanding and explaining identity from his perspectives as both musician and audience member. He locates the body *in* and not merely next to music. He says, "The body offers itself up in *collaboration* with sound in the production of the musical text. In this way, it functions as both performer and instrument" (p. 83). Music as embodied experience for DeChaine suggests that the body is never separate from the music, the performance, or meaning (p. 86). My body is in collaboration with the sound of the bass guitar. My fingertips are forever changed in this collaboration, and through my performance my body is marked.

DeChaine's embodied approach to understanding music perform-ance moves away from Auslander's typologies and into an experiential analysis of performance, and is similar to Stephenson's (1998) decon-structive analysis of how her performance of Mickey Mouse, as a summer job, implied various social and cultural meanings especially regarding gender, power, and identity in relationship to herself. This raises epistemological questions. If music is an embodied experience, and performance can imply different cultural meanings, then what do I know from my embodied experience of playing the bass guitar? The changes are slowly happening. Physically the changes are in my finger-tips. The changes are in my posture, both on and off the stage. Hearing and listening for bass lines changes, the way I talk, the way I walk, and the way I argue. This embodied knowledge is about feelings and grooves, about structures and rhythms, about constraint and restraint.

It is knowledge that could, like the bass line, easily go unnoticed. However, this knowledge, like the bass, is foundational.

I am tangled in webs of meanings and histories that I am connected to and that I am creating as a performer. These layers of meanings are not exclusive to performers or musicians; audience members also have embodied experiences of performances that change and shape their bodies. Holman Jones (1999) presents an embodied understanding of the relationship between music and audience. She sees women's music as gesture or a fleeting moment of "experience-in-creation" created by music, and speaks from her position as an audience member experiencing this gesture (p. 217). Holman Jones argues that in her writing about music she is enacting her own gesture, "a reaction to the musician's gesture in all of its force, insistence, excess, and pleasure" (p. 217). Listening to music, like performing music, also changes bodies. It changes how we hear the world, and therefore it changes how we move through the world.

Focusing on how the bass changes my body also reveals the ways my body is always being altered and shaped by the various technologies I encounter. For example, writing has material consequences. The physical relationship of my hands to the instruments I use (computer keyboard, bass guitar, and so on) is different, but also the ways in which I negotiate the world as a result of using this instruments changes. How I feel and feel about myself and the performances around me as a result of writing or playing the bass is different from how I might have felt if I had not written or played the instrument. The only times I notice the change in my fingertips is when I use them, and the only times I use my fingertips are in the intimate moments of touching, typing, and playing music. The physical difference in my body gives me an understanding of how my body is dependent on certain technologies, and it also gives me insight into the power of difference. The slightest change in a body creates a new perspective, and it is through performance that these new perspectives become possible.

"E" String (0.105" diameter)

These discussions of performers' and audience members' physical and embodied reactions to music ultimately work to address and resolve a tension between the mind/body split. The performance studies perspectives towards music, in which the mind and body are not seen as separate, echo a similar call by some musicologists for a return to the body in music. For instance, Cusick (1994) argues for a return to the body in musicology as the body is central to the performance of music.

Cusick wants to move beyond the mind/body split in thinking and theorising about music, and wants to pay close attention to the performing body as a location for the performance of gender and identity within certain systems of music.

When I stand on stage playing the bass, my primary concern is with playing the right notes. I strain to see the fingers of the guitar players so that I can figure out what chords they are playing. I occasionally will ask for clarification before the song starts, but once I figure out the pattern or the progression I look down at the bass and focus on my fingers. My fingers are still sore, and each note that I play comes with a matching pain in my body. I cannot keep playing. I cannot make it tonight. My fingers hurt too much. I must keep playing. I must finish the song. I will deal with the pain later. I want to sound good at all costs. I am constrained by my sense of pride, but I am also constrained by the system of music in which I am performing.

Walser (1991) argues the body informs our experience of music much in the same way the body informs our use of language. He states: "By focusing our attention on the role of culturally-specific preconceptual experience in creating discursive meanings, we can avoid the search for inherent universals while preserving a means of accounting for cross-cultural similarities of structure and interpretation" (p. 126). For Walser, music is a site for cultural meaning in its material reception and production. As an example he unpacks meanings surrounding the use of distorted electric guitar as a culturally produced discourse (pp. 121–25). Music performance in this way works to impact listening bodies through performances. Not only then does music performance have impact and meaning on a performing body, but it also has impact and meaning for listening bodies.

This return to the body in musicology brings forth questions of social and cultural meanings in the bodily experience and production of music, but it also raises questions relating specifically to the experience and knowledge of the performer. What do I come to know about myself from playing the bass? What does this teach me about the relationship between bodies and various technologies? For example, what do I learn about my body in terms of gender or race through playing the bass guitar? Clarke (2002) considers the psychological aspects of music performance and talks about skills, expressions, and movements of the musician. He notes that "playing music is a concrete form of musical thinking, and the body is as much a part of finding out about music as it is a means for its actualisation" (p. 68). Clearly the body knows about music through playing music. There are physical manifestations of musical ideas produced from the body of the musician. How this musical thinking impacts a body becomes a question of the relationships between bodies and language, and bodies and performance.

Similar to Clarke, Dunsby (2002) is interested in how performers speak about their performances. In asking how it *feels* to perform music, Dunsby describes feeling as "an amalgam of being and doing" (p. 226). This complex understanding of feeling offers an explanation for why it is so difficult to describe what it feels like to perform, and many performers according to Dunsby can describe the final musical product, but he makes a call for understanding the process of performance (p. 234). Dunsby (1995) also recognises a lack of a unified 'disciplinary' conception of musical performance studies, and in questioning reasons for this lack he emphasises the importance of and need for the perspective of the performer located in musical performance. If Clarke is interested in musical thinking, then Dunsby is interested in musical feeling. These feelings associated and created with performance are situated in a performer's body and subjective experience. Not only does the body of the performer know musically, the body of the performer also feels musically. The more I play the bass, the more I know about the bass, but I also am learning how to feel the structuring rhythms of the bass in music, in teaching, and in conversation. Together, knowing and feeling create and are created by the performer in performance.

Bass Line

The move to locating the body at the centre of musical performance functions in four distinct ways. First there are the meanings created by the body in performance. My body interacts with the bass guitar, and makes the instrument meaningful in performance. Second, there are the meanings created on the body in performance. The strings of the bass guitar literally mark my body as a bass player. Third, the performance of the body has an impact on culture. My performance creates and re-creates what it means to be a bass player. Finally there is the impact of culture on the body. Playing the bass, or any musical instrument, is always connected to other cultural meanings. Becoming a bass player is not only a question of personal identity formation; it is a question of a cultural identity. For me, learning to play the bass exemplifies the four ways in which the body functions in musical performance. I am impacted by and have an impact on the performance and cultural meanings.

Through the use of performative writing in *Torch Singing*, Holman Jones (2007) uses language to write the experience of listening to performances of torch songs. She also imagines (and allows the reader to imagine) her own musical performance of torch singing in her writing. This text is a performance of music and musical interpretations. As a writer, Holman Jones performs and sings her own torch song, and in so doing creates a story of what it means to sing torch as "an everyday form of resistance" (p. 13). Her use of citations throughout the text tells a story of theory and philosophy that accompanies and supplements her performance. There is always one more layer to the story of the musician's performance (and to the listener's experience). The layers of meanings that exist in the performance of audience members, musicians, writers, and readers are many. The possibilities for connections and meanings are endless, and they are always embodied.

With Holman Jones I see these multiple layers of meaning functioning in similar ways as the body in music performance. I feel a connection between writing and performing as a musician. Both of these experiences change who I am and who I can be. The bodily performance of writing is a performance of meaning creation for the reader, but it also creates meanings for the author. The text gives the reader insight into the possibilities of torch singing (the performer's impact on a performance); and the writing gives the author new understanding of what it might mean to sing torch songs (the performance's impact on a performer). This text also takes cultural meanings about torch singing and torch singers and performs the meanings and re-performs the meanings.

(Not) A Bass Player

The relationship between my body and the technologies I interact with is an active interaction, in which my body is changing because of the technology (the bass), and it is changing the technology. Because I interact with the bass, how I know the world changes, but I am also changed. Barad (2003) argues for an understanding of performativity that does more than offer a critique of how language constitutes bodies, and she argues against representational epistemologies which suggest representations (words) and things represented (matter) are ontologically separate (p. 804). Instead language and matter are always interrelated and therefore ontologically inseparable (p. 813). She calls for a performativity that "incorporates important material and discursive, social and scientific, human and nonhuman, and natural and cultural factors" (p. 808). She argues: "It is vitally important that we understand how matter matters" (p. 803). Barad's argument calls for a posthuman-ist performativity, or a performativity that considers the complex rela-tionship between language and all matter (human and nonhuman). This posthumanist perspective seeks to disrupt notions of "human" and "non-human" by arguing that boundaries between language and matter are never fixed. Similarly, there is no clear distinction between myself and the bass guitar, or any technology. It is in my relationship with the bass guitar that the instrument comes to matter, but it is also in this rela-tionship, this interacting, that I come to matter.

From a posthumanist perspective it is impossible to distinguish between human and nonhuman because "matter is always already an ongoing historicity" (Barad, 2003, p. 821). For Barad, "*matter comes to matter* through the iterative intra-activity of the world in its becoming" (p. 823). Systems of language, material practices, and the languages of and about material practices work to produce (not con-struct) matter. In other words, language and material practices cannot be thought of as separate because they are always already intertwined. Lastly, Barad argues for a connection of ontology and epistemology, an "onto-epistem-ology," or a "study of practices of knowing in being" (p. 829). This is necessary because "the separation of epistemology from ontology is a reverberation of a metaphysics that assumes an inherent difference between human and nonhuman, subject and object, mind and body, matter and discourse" (p. 829). Onto-epistem-ology therefore offers a useful way for considering how bodies come to know in and through performance.

Week after week, the sores on my fingertips become less and less sensitive. The texture of the skin on the tips of my fingers is changing and becoming callused and hardened. There is less sensitivity in the tips of the fingers I use when playing the bass. This is functional. Now when I play the bass it does not hurt as much as before. However I am always a bass player. I do not mourn the loss of sensitivity in my fin-gertips because I can still use the pads of my finger for touching and feeling, but I am aware that my practice has changed who I am in the world and how I move through the world.

My fingertips may have changed in learning to play the bass, but the impact of this performance on my body and my body's impact on this performance (or any performance) operate ontoepistemologically in that I come to know through my body's performance. Playing the bass offers a clear physical mark of performance on my body in that my body has changed by playing the bass, and by changing, my body is now able to better play the bass. In other words we come to know through per-formance and this knowledge enables us to continue performing.

Bass Player

After playing this new instrument with this new band for about three months I am already aware of the ways in which the performance of playing bass has had an impact on my body (see my fingertips). I can also begin to see how my own body impacts the performance. For one, without my body the performance of playing the bass could not happen. But I also bring to the performance my own understandings of music and musicianship, and now that my fingertips have started to change I can perform with greater ease.

It is the impact of culture and social meaning on my performance, and my own impact on these meanings with which I still struggle. At a recent gig while waiting for the final set to start a man enters the bar and approaches me and one of the guitar players. We are standing around by the stage, but we are not near our instruments.

"Are you guys with the band?"

"Yeah."

"Are you gonna play soon?"

"In a few minutes. We have one last set."

He turns to me and asks, "Are you the bass player? You *look* like the bass player. You *must* be the bass player."

"Yeah, I'm playing the bass tonight."

At this point I have been playing the bass for almost three months. I do not feel like a bass player. I feel like I can play the bass well enough to get through about thirty songs, but only because I have learned to memorise certain patterns. I do not feel like I can claim myself to be a bass player even though I do play the bass. And yet for some reason I look like a bass player to this man. He can't see my fingertips, and I'm not holding the bass guitar, but something about my body reads "bass player". The social and cultural meanings that inform and are informed by my performance even beyond the moment when I am on the stage playing the bass may or may not be visible to everyone including myself, but these meanings are connected to my performance. My body is connected with meanings that are both physically apparent in performance and in relation to the technology or instrument I use, but I am also connected with the historical, social, and cultural meanings that are layered on and in the bass guitar. The relationship between our bodies, technology, and identities are always connected with multiple layers of meanings, and we carry these meanings with us always as part of our bodies.

References

Auslander, P. (2004). Performance analysis and popular music: A manifesto. *Contemporary Theatre Review*, 14, 1–13.

Auslander, P. (2006). Musical personae. *The Drama Review*, 50, 100–118.

Barad, K. (2003). Posthumanist performativity: Toward an understanding of how matter comes to matter. *Signs: Journal of Women in Culture and Society*, 28(3), 801–831.

Clarke, E. (2002). Understanding the psychology of performance. In J. Rink (Ed.), *Musical performance: A guide to understanding* (pp. 59–72). Cambridge: Cambridge University Press.

Cusick, S. G. (1994). Feminist theory, music theory, and the mind/body problem. *Perspectives of New Music*, 32, 8–27.

Davidson, J. (2002). Communicating with the body in performance. In J. Rink (Ed.), *Musical performance: A guide to understanding* (pp. 144–152). Cambridge: Cambridge University Press.

DeChaine, D. R. (2002). Affect and embodied understanding in musical experience. *Text and Performance Quarterly*, 22, 79–98.

Delgado, F. (2000). All along the border: Kid Frost and the performance of brown masculinity. *Text and Performance Quarterly*, 20, 388–401.

Dunsby, J. (1995). *Performing music: Shared concerns*. Oxford: Clarendon.

Dunsby, J. (2002). Performers on performance. In J. Rink (Ed.), *Musical performance: A guide to understanding* (pp. 225–236). Cambridge: Cambridge University Press.

Frith, S. (1996). *Performing rites: On the value of popular music*. Cambridge: Harvard University Press.

Graver, D. (1997). The actor's bodies. *Text and Performance Quarterly*, 17, 221–235.

Holman Jones, S. (1999). Women, musics, bodies, and texts: The gesture of women's music. *Text and Performance Quarterly*, 19, 217–235.

Holman Jones, S. (2007). *Torch singing: Performing resistance and desire from Billie Holiday to Edith Piaf*. Lanham: AltaMira.

Lengel, L. (2004). Performing in/outside Islam: Music and gendered cultural politics in the Middle East and North Africa. *Text and Performance Quarterly*, 24, 212–232.

Stephenson, T. (1998). My silence speaks volumes: Mickey Mouse and the ideology of an icon. *Theatre Annual: A Journal of Performance Studies*, 51, 54–70.

Walser, R. (1991). The body in the music: Epistemology and musical semiotics. *College Music Symposium*, 31, 117–126.

Section Three
Learning and Teaching

Chapter **9**

Studying Music, Studying the Self
Reflections on Learning Music in Bali

Peter Dunbar-Hall

In explanation of her fieldwork in India, Ganguly-Scrase (1993) notes how since the mid-1960s anthropological research has included levels of reflexivity through which researchers analyse and discuss their own positions as researchers in the field. This is alongside the usual interpretation of findings about the contexts they set out to study, and leads to consideration of how a researcher's persona and activity not only influences the conduct of fieldwork but affects the writing of research outcomes. This reflexivity has the potential to change ways a researcher perceives her/himself and her/his professional profile. Therefore, as Ganguly-Scrase goes on to explain, this development in research focus and outcomes moves beyond "merely … observing and recording 'facts'; it is also a highly intricate interpretative process" (p. 37). Through this development in research practice and concentration on the roles and responsibilities of researchers, greater consideration of cultures of knowledge, epistemologies, methodologies, and power relationships in the sites of knowledge has become a topic of study. At the basis of this is awareness of one's self as a researcher, an area of study that has acquired its own label — autoethnography.

Despite recognition of this development, definitions of the term "autoethnography" and the types of writing that are classified as autoethnographic remain diverse. For example, Reed-Danahay (1997) lists three main types of autoethnographic writing: that in which those formerly the subjects of writing become authors about their own cultures; personal reflections by members of minorities; and that in which anthropologists include discussion of themselves in their writings (p. 2). Consequently, agreement over what constitutes autoethnography, its range of applications in researchers' work, theorisations about its contribution to academic discourse, its place in post-modern views of research, and the ways in which it is practised are areas of debate. There is agreement among writers, however, that autoethnography challenges received conceptualisations of the sites of research, the work of researchers, and the influences research can exert, especially on the researcher (van Manen, 1990; Crick & Geddes, 1993; Perry, 1993; Hammersley & Atkinson, 1995; Barz & Cooley, 1997; Ellis & Bochner, 2000; Tedlock, 2000; Hill, 2006; Stephens & Delamont, 2006).

For my purposes, autoethnography is defined as deconstruction by the researcher of the relationships between the researcher and his (in my case) research, its aims and objectives, locations, processes, personnel, and outcomes. In this view, the researcher becomes a text for analysis alongside his original research topic, often adding a completely new research area to his profile. This is not a complacent position for a researcher. As my experiences discussed below indicate, it exposes one's insecurities, forces questioning of assumptions, and requires re-assessment of ways of thinking and believing. For me it created large amounts of knowledge to be learnt and assimilated, not only about music, but about pedagogy, music as cultural practice, research, and personal interaction. As Ellis and Bochner (2000) note, it exposes the researcher as "a vulnerable self" (p. 739). In this autoethnographic view, a researcher has roles beyond those assumed of an objective investigator. He acquires responsibilities, gains the power to influence, and is affected by his research. Among the responsibilities that emerge through ethnographic consideration of one's research are that of implementing ideas that are encountered, and that of representing the people collaborated with in the field.

In the following chapter I explain my position on autoethnography through description of a decade of study of Balinese gamelan music with Balinese teachers in Bali, and the effects of this on myself. As this case study demonstrates, realisation that my research into Balinese music was also research into my own learning and teaching processes led to refashioning of my ideas on music as a pedagogic undertaking, subsequently influencing my professional role as a university teacher in both ideological and practical ways. Once the experience of working with Balinese musicians had become a facet of my musical persona, complacency and the status quo in music education as a discourse were not options, therefore autoethnography became a means of redefining my professional identity, of outlining directions my professional position needed to follow, and of emphasising the responsibilities inherent in the preparation of music educators.

Experience

I began learning to play Balinese gamelan music in 1999 in response to one event: hearing a Balinese gamelan perform live while I was a tourist on a short stopover in Bali. I draw attention to "live" as this had an effect that no amount of undergraduate study of Balinese music (from recordings) or listening to recordings since being a student had had. The attraction to the sound of Balinese gamelan music in live performance was immediate and cognitively acknowledged — itself something worthy of investigation. In addition to my sensuous response to the sound of the instruments, my initial reaction to watching the performers was to marvel at how they played a long program of complex pieces of music without notation. My music educator background led me to wonder how this could be, what sort of learning and teaching could lead to this, and how I could investigate the pedagogy that produced such results. Clearly, there was a highly successful form of music education at work here from which I could benefit. The ten years since that event have consisted of regular periods of learning from various teachers in Bali. This has been supported by membership of an Australian group in Sydney that learns and performs Balinese music.

Once I became a learner, for Balinese musicians my position immediately typified me as one of many Westerners who had studied/study Balinese music. On reflection, this led me to historicise myself and my learning. My first teacher, Wayan, could immediately place me in a line of non-Balinese students he had taught. Other Balinese musicians asked me whether I owned a copy of McPhee's book on Balinese music that had resulted from his time in Bali in the 1930s (McPhee, 1966). As they explained, this was a book they relied on for information about many theoretical aspects of Balinese music, such as its tuning systems and repertoires. Others asked whether I was writing a book about Balinese music myself, or if I knew other non-Balinese writers about Balinese music — Michael Tenzer was mentioned, probably because his first book on Balinese music was available in local bookshops (Tenzer, 1991). For these musicians I belonged to a succession of people stretching back to the 1930s and from outside Bali who had wanted to study Balinese music.

That Balinese musicians placed me in this category warned me that just as researchers often categorise their subjects for the purpose of understanding them or fitting them into their worldview, I too could be categorised and made to fit a pre-existing mould. This situation had advantages. Identification of me as one of a line of learners meant that any study I would undertake did not require high levels of explanation. This was not only the result of the existence of a strong history of the study of Balinese music in general, but also to the fact that Ubud, the village where I spend my time, is a regular tourist destination for Western people, a centre of strong arts activity (including music, dance, painting and carving), a place where nightly performances of music and dance are staged for tourists, and an active centre of music and dance learning and teaching, both for Balinese people and for students from outside Bali. Wanting to learn Balinese music was not considered unusual in this village; I was simply another non-Balinese person who was learning to perform.

The initial focus of learning was to be able to perform. As Balinese music is not notated for teaching or performance, the only way to become a proficient player is to learn large amounts of repertoire. Alongside this was the necessity to learn performance technique, repertoire-specific styles of playing, the contexts that pieces of music could be used for, and various other features of the music, such as the need to respond to drum signals and the gong patterns that underpin the structures of the music. This was not yet research, it was beginner lessons. Not only was I a beginner, but research on Balinese music as an object of both analysis and socio-cultural investigation well beyond my limited knowledge of it already existed (e.g., de Zoete & Spies, 1931; McPhee, 1966; Tenzer, 1991).

As learning pieces of music proceeded, a number of research agendas began to develop, and it was my awareness of this that first alerted me to a nascent autoethnographic identity. Four research areas began to coalesce around my times in Bali: (1) As I was resident in a village where performances were staged for tourists, investigation of the effects of tourism on Balinese performing arts became a topic of interest, especially as I was learning some of the repertoire performed for tourists (Dunbar-Hall, 2003, 2006a); (2) From an interest in reading what past researchers had written about Balinese performing arts, study of and historicisation of non-Balinese research into Balinese music, dance and drama developed as a topic I could undertake when I was not in Bali (Dunbar-Hall, 2008); (3) Analysis of Balinese aesthetic positions on music in relation to contemporary events in Balinese life emerged as a way of understanding contemporary Balinese uses and significances of music (Dunbar-Hall, 2007a); and (4) In depth study of Balinese pedagogy, from observation of teaching/learning situations and from personal experience, linked my learning with my academic position in music teacher preparation (Dunbar-Hall, 2000, 2001, 2002, 2003, 2005a, 2005b, 2006b, 2007b, 2007c). It is this last area of research that best demonstrates my autoethnographic persona.

Learning

As a learner, it did not take long to reveal to myself my problems in learning to play Balinese music. Memorising pieces was the first hurdle. Coping with the music's rhythmic complexity, playing my part against my teacher's contrasting (and rhythmically off-putting) part, and the slowness with which I acquired pieces all surprised me. Working without notation was at first unsettling. The teacher's stance (repeat, repeat, repeat without any verbal direction) was unusual. That my initial pieces were not simplified or simple indicated that grading of pieces from those suitable for beginners, through stages of moderate difficulty to pieces for expert players, was not a way of teaching. Technique was learnt as necessary, and was not learnt for its own sake, an intriguing and novel practice. Like other researchers into cross-cultural music learning who have written about problems that arise from different expectations of teaching and learning in foreign contexts (e.g., Rice, 1994; Stephens & Delamont, 2006; Mackinlay, 2007), I confronted many issues. Those with backgrounds in learning music in Western based systems (from notation, with verbal instruction/explanation, through canonic graded repertoire, and using contrived technical exercises) will understand the situation. I was being asked to learn in a way I had not experienced, and it seemed as if through years of learning music in Western ways I had unlearnt a raft of learning strategies. It became an objective to re-establish these in my learning; along the way I learnt to analyse my own learning and observe how I solved problems.

I sensed that my initial attempts to learn a simple piece of Balinese music were frustrating to Wayan. The lack of notation and my growing awareness that many years of playing instruments from notation had allowed my ability to memorise music and subsequently perform it to deteriorate led me to notate sections of the pieces I was learning. I used these not to perform from, but as a way of memorising. This was based on my belief that repeated listening to and aural analysis of music is a productive way to learn music. As the tuning of the instruments we were using did not equate to that of Western music, I needed to invent my own form of notation to show what I was playing. The disparity between Wayan's teaching style and my learning strategies became obvious in the way that I was keen to ask questions about the music, while he, as is usual among Balinese music teachers, was not used to explaining but to playing and having me copy what he played until I could perform it automatically. I slavishly recorded my lessons and would listen to them later each day and try to work out the rhythms that presented so much difficulty. Learning proceeded like this over a number of lessons until we began a new piece of music. This piece used some of the same repetitive rhythms as the first piece (that had presented so many problems). I immediately commented to Wayan, "*Sama dengan lagu yang lain!*" ("It's the same as the other piece!") — and he agreed. This was a large step forward for both of us: Wayan could see that some verbal explanation based on theoretical aspects of the music would help me, and I realised that different pieces of music drew on a set of rhythmic and melodic patterns — that once one piece of music had been learnt, others similar to it could be learnt quite quickly.

Here autoethnography began to play a role as I realised that I had become an observer of myself, and that I could draw on multiple identities to study the teaching/learning process. I thought of this in terms of what I called musical schizophrenia, and discovered later that this, using other terminology, was an aspect of autoethnography. For example, Reed-Danahay (1997) refers to "ideas of 'double consciousness'" (p. 3); Ellis and Bochner (2000) explain autoethnography as "an autobiographical genre of writing and research that displays multiple layers of consciousness" (p. 739); and Hill (2006) discusses what he calls his "multiple roles and identities" as a teacher–researcher (p. 926). I simultaneously occupied at least four positions related to pedagogy. First, I was a beginner trying to learn as much as I could about Balinese music. Second, I had been a long-time music learner, having been the recipient of lessons (piano and viola) since the age of seven. Thus I had a background of learning to compare to my Balinese lessons. Third, for some years I had been a secondary school music teacher used to planning, delivering and assessing instruction. Fourth, I was currently a member of a university teaching team that prepared music students as music educators. This last identity meant that I was used to identifying, analysing, theorising and critiquing pedagogy.

Acknowledgement of these multiple identities became the impetus for my research into Balinese pedagogy, as it provided me with a series of research lenses through which to understand my learning. This proceeded through questions. What were my problems? How did I internalise them? How did I solve them? What learning strategies did I consciously construct, trial, assess, and reject or retain? How did I become a different learner? Which of my abilities had been neglected? How did my experience differ from that of my past? What typified Balinese music teaching practices? Most importantly, how could what I was experiencing benefit my professional responsibilities in the preparation of music educators?

Thinking

These questions led me to the area of meta-learning, assisting me both to learn and to comprehend how I learnt. They also began to influence my work with pre-service teachers. I began to expect my students to work increasingly without notation, to engage in teaching/learning activities that required little or no verbal interaction but much sound, to memorise repertoire, and to locate and utilise forms of learning that had, to that time, been left untapped. Understanding their own learning, as I had found for myself, was intended to make my students better teachers.

As learning in Bali became more developed, these objectifiable aspects of my teaching led to changes in ways of thinking. From researching links between cultural expectations of music and profiles of teachers and teaching contexts, a picture of music's roles, meanings and significances in Balinese culture emerged. This picture justified the learning and teaching of music in cultural terms as a strong expectation of Balinese Hinduism, a religion in which artistic endeavour is considered a personal offering and means to *taksu* (spiritual fulfillment; see Harnish, 1991). To many Balinese there is no question about learning to play an instrument or dance: It is expected, commonplace almost. Coming from a culture where justification of music as a subject in schools occupies large amounts of time and effort, to learn in a situation where this was not questioned revealed deep cultural beliefs in the power of music. Alongside this, questions about why and how different cultures develop different ways of teaching and learning music, and how the cultural applicability of different teaching/learning styles could be studied to advantage music education in general began to emerge. This led to formalisation in my thinking of the music pedagogy ideology increasingly known as the cultural aesthetics of teaching.

The cultural aesthetics of teaching links teaching practice to culture. It is based on the belief that just as music differs from culture to culture, so too does the teaching by which it is transmitted. Further, that teaching practices reflect culturally shaped ways of interacting. To understand this, it became necessary to study Balinese culture in depth, which confirmed that, in this case, music pedagogy is more than a set of instructional principles; it is a reflection of culturally held values and ways of behaving. To demonstrate this it is necessary to explain an aspect of Balinese life known as *gotong royong*.

Much of Balinese life revolves around the concept and automatic practice of *gotong royong* — collaborative effort through which individual participation results in group outcomes. In line with this social way of behaving, it would be rare in Bali for a Balinese person to learn an instrument by her/himself. Rather, learning is done by a whole group. Teaching practice (and consequently learning) is governed by this way of people working together, even if this is non-verbalised. As an extension of this, it is also common for teaching to be delivered by a group of instructors simultaneously. Not only is teaching aimed at a group of learners, teaching is also a form of *gotong royong* on a smaller level.

Observing this proceeding around me contributed to my growing understanding of culturally influenced music pedagogy. At the same time, it demonstrated a way in which my learning contravened an accepted Balinese way of teaching, thus emphasised how the presence and agendas of a researcher change the contexts of fieldwork. Instead of learning in a group, my learning was in a Western, one-to-one manner. What I found interesting about this was that for my teachers this was normal for teaching non-Balinese learners, alerting me to the fact that these teachers had learnt a means of coping with non-Balinese students, and had taken on Western ways of instructing them. This became a topic Wayan and I regularly discussed, so that my learning and research were matched by his questioning about how music was taught *di barat* ("in the West"). I interpreted this as a collaboration growing out of my desire to learn — one that became comfortable and beneficial to both of us. Discussions with other teachers confirmed regular inquisitiveness about how music was taught in other contexts. Researching teaching thus was not a one-way direction in these transactions, with Balinese teachers as keen to understand teaching and learning from my perspective as I was to understand theirs. In a similar way to my realisation that I would be typified as a non-Balinese learner, this indicated that in research there are reciprocal agendas at work at the same time.

Consideration of my learning revealed another aspect of pedagogy — that learning is often a case of confirming what a learner already "knows" from her/his surrounding culture. This idea was proven for me by my lack of surrounding Balinese culture on which to draw for clues in my learning. I had to learn Balinese music as an adult "from scratch", without the benefit of knowing how it should sound or be played, what its embedded stylistic traits were, or what its predictability consisted of. As I was a *tabula rasa* as far as enculturated knowledge of Balinese music was concerned, autoethnography became a way to study this aspect of music learning. As a logical step in my learning (as after my first periods of learning in Bali I had reached the realisation that I was engaged on a long-term enterprise) was development of a simple way to overcome my lack of a surrounding Balinese soundscape from which I could learn subliminally: I began listening extensively to Balinese music so that its rhythms and tuning systems, its nuances of interpretation, its various stylistic repertoires, and the differences between gamelan groups began to become natural to me.

Doing

Beyond altering my work with my students, understanding of my experience helped fashion changes in my work place. Balinese gamelan lessons (from a local Australian specialist and using a gamelan hired from a museum) were written into both the undergraduate and graduate music education degree programs I work in. After some years of this, purchase of a Balinese gamelan by my university seemed logical. This opened other possibilities for students, for example, use of the instruments by students in their own compositions, sampling of the sounds of the instruments for technology based work, and conduct of research experiments into Balinese pitch and tuning systems. My understanding of how a Balinese gamelan was tuned was enhanced by spending two weeks with a gamelan maker as he tuned and repaired two Balinese sets of instruments in Australia. Taking all of these aspects of Balinese music into consideration, and based on my belief that learning in Bali from Balinese teachers had been influential on me, establishment of student fieldwork in Bali for the purposes of learning music and dance became an imperative — another example of how my experience as a learner was mandating how my university teaching should continue. Beginning to teach Balinese gamelan pieces was another step in the ongoing process of converting experience and belief into action, and an opportunity to analyse myself in another Balinese music context — a chance to add another identity to my musical schizophrenia. Significantly for me, this was reification of my Balinese teachers' comments that I should teach gamelan to my students, and a means of acting out my responsibilities to those teachers.

Teaching gamelan pieces allowed me to create a discursive site (Brogden, 2008) in which my students could theorise about the cultural aesthetics of pedagogy by extrapolation from experience. This involved analysis of teaching and learning practices, understanding of the roles and expectations of learners and teachers in different music education contexts, and consideration of how cultural context implied forms of music transmission. Students provided these comments on the teaching they experienced in my gamelan classes:

- students were expected to imitate the teacher
- there was no notation
- teaching proceeded by rote
- there was much repetition
- the teacher modelled technique
- sometimes the teacher taught "backwards" sitting in front of a student's instrument, reversing pitch to hand address
- the teacher rarely talked about what was being learnt
- the teacher addressed the group, not individuals
- there were times of noisiness when students were engaged on separate, uncoordinated tasks at the same time
- the music was conveyed at the speed at which it would be performed
- Western teaching dissects and breaks down separate elements of music, while Balinese teaching allows students to launch straight into practical work without unnecessary analysis
- teaching is practical with information provided only when necessary
- the instruments (and therefore the players) were set up in a square so everyone could see everyone else in the group.

To help them see more clearly the relationship between teaching strategies and learning, they were asked to reflect on how they had adapted their learning in response to this type of teaching. They listed the following ways they had done this:

- watching the teacher and other players to visually identify what notes to play
- memorising patterns
- singing the parts internally
- visualising the patterns of the notes
- concentrating on the rhythms
- identifying the repetitive patterns from which pieces of music were constructed

- learning to work without notation
- relying on repetition
- realisation that parts were to be learnt relatively quickly so movement to the whole piece could occur
- adjustment to the non-verbal style of teaching.

Through these discussions, my experience of learning had been transformed into teaching that could influence how students thought about pedagogy.

Responsibility to my teachers was made in other ways — in what is sometimes called reflexive ethnomusicology, I returned research outcomes to those who had assisted in carrying it out. This grows out of awareness that a researcher owes his knowledge to those who have given it to him. To do this, teachers were listed as co-authors of research material (e.g., Dunbar-Hall & Adnyana, 2004); copies of photographs and recordings I had made were sent to those who had let me film them; I learnt Indonesian so I could interact in a language spoken by my teachers, giving away cultural dominance and yielding this to my teachers. In published materials, these people's responses are given in Indonesian and then translated, so that their words acquire primacy and their voices can be "heard". In these ways subversion of my identity as the controller of the fieldwork, resulting from analysis of the levels of power implied by fieldwork, became a standard aspect of my work, and continuing attempts were made to acknowledge and contradict "the role language plays in the researching and writing process" (Subedi & Rhee, 2008, p. 1071).

Conclusion: Autoethnography as Life Style

From my experiences of learning Balinese music in Bali, consideration of how I was conducting research, of my reactions to events, of my relationships with people, of my awareness of the culturally influenced ways I was taught (and expected to learn), and of the effects of the experience on my identity as a learner and a teacher, autoethnography became an element of my persona. By this I mean that I consciously adopted an analytical stance to my actions, and proactively used the outcomes of this analysis to guide my thinking and actions across a range of areas, not only my teaching or my music performance. Principally, the experience worked in the reformulation of my "scholarly identity", as Potgieter and Smit (2009) define the site of investigation of a researcher's background and work. In their view, and similarly in explanation of my experiences, "the central conundrum or the academic puzzle ... is that (we) receive mixed messages" about knowledge when our past and the ideas that grow from it differ from the realities uncovered during research (p. 214). By selectively combining aspects of my background in learning music, performing music and teaching music, and contrasting these with learning to do them through the (new) medium of Balinese gamelan, I reshaped both my thinking and my teaching. The advantage for me, perhaps more so than for researchers in other fields, is that my professional position in music teacher preparation allows me to apply the outcomes of my experience to my daily responsibilities. This provides me with ongoing opportunities to alter practicalities of university teaching, to expose students to new ways of thinking about music pedagogy, to formalise ideas about the cultural aesthetics of teaching, and above all to carry the input of my Balinese teachers across a cultural and geographic gap into a quintessentially Western educational setting, a university. Definitions of autoethnography might remain diverse, but the individuality of each researcher's understanding of it, and the ways in which s/he takes up the challenge to apply and interpret the "auto" part of the term allows autoethnography advantages that other forms of research do not have access to.

Acknowledgements

My understanding of Balinese music and of my attempts to perform it would not have occurred without the assistance and personal support of I Wayan Tusti Adnyana, I Ketut Cater, Cokorda Raka Swastika, Cokorda Sri Agung, Agus Teja Sentosa, I Nyoman Parman, I Dewa Berata, and Emiko Susilo.

References

Barz, G., & Cooley, T. (Eds.). (1997). *Shadows in the field: New perspectives for fieldwork in ethnomusicology*. New York: Oxford University Press.

Brogden, L. (2008). Art-I/f/act-ology: Curricular artefacts in autoethnographic research. *Qualitative Inquiry*, 14(6), 851–864.

Clifford, J., & Marcus, G. (Eds.). (1986). *Writing culture: The poetics and politics of ethnography*. Berkeley; University of California Press.

Crick, M. (1989). Shifting identities in the research process: An essay in personal anthropology. In J. Perry (Ed.), *Doing fieldwork: Eight personal accounts of social research* (pp. 24–40). Geelong, Australia: Deakin University Press.

Crick, M., & Geddes, B. (Eds.). (1993). *Research methods in the field: Ten anthropological accounts*. Geelong: Deakin University Press.

de Zoete, B., & Spies, W. (1931). *Dance and drama in Bali*. London: Faber.

Dunbar-Hall, P. (2000). Concept or context: Teaching and learning Balinese gamelan and the universalist-pluralist debate. *Music Education Research*, 2(2), 127–139.

Dunbar-Hall, P. (2001). Diversifying music education through Balinese gamelan teaching strategies. *Proceedings of the XIIIth National Conference of the Australian Society for Music Education, Adelaide*, pp. 75–80.

Dunbar-Hall, P. (2002). Developing culturally aware music education through ethnomusicological activities: Pre-service students' reactions to *gamelan* experiences. *Proceedings of the 7th International Conference on Music Perception and Cognition*, pp. 253–256.

Dunbar-Hall, P. (2003a). Musical objectivity and cultural knowledge in music learning: Reflections by a non-native student. *Proceedings o f the 14th National Conference of the Australian Society for Music Education*, pp. 46–49.

Dunbar-Hall, P. (2003b). *Tradisi* and *turisme*: Music, dance, and cultural transformation at the Ubud Palace, Bali, Indonesia. *Australian Geographical Studies, 41*(1), 3–16.

Dunbar-Hall, P. (2005a). Music education as translation: Reflections on the experience of learning music in Bali. *Proceedings of the XXVIIth Annual Conference of the Australian Association for Research in Music Education*, pp. 61–66.

Dunbar-Hall, P. (2005b). Training, community and systemic music education: The aesthetics of Balinese music in different pedagogic settings. In P. Shehan Campbell, J. Drummond, P. Dunbar-Hall, K. Howard, H. Schippers & T. Wiggins (Eds.), *Cultural diversity in music education: Directions and challenges for the 21st century* (pp. 125-132). Brisbane: Australian Academic Press.

Dunbar-Hall, P. (2006a). Culture, tourism, and cultural tourism: Boundaries and frontiers in performances of Balinese music and dance. In J. Post (Ed.), *Ethnomusicology: A contemporary reader* (pp. 55–66). London: Routledge.

Dunbar-Hall, P. (2006b). An investigation of strategies developed by music learners in a cross-cultural setting. *Research Studies in Music Education, 26*, 63–70.

Dunbar-Hall, P. (2007a). '*Apa salah Baliku?*' ('What did my Bali do wrong?'): Popular music and the 2002 Bali bombings. *Popular Music and Society, 30* (4), 533–548.

Dunbar-Hall, P. (2007b). Research enhanced teaching: Lived research experience in Bali as the basis of teacher preparation in Australia. *Synergy, 26*, 7–12.

Dunbar-Hall, P. (2007c). The world music ensemble as pedagogic tool: The teaching of Balinese gamelan to music education students in a university setting. *Proceedings of the XXIXth Annual Conference of the Australian Association for Music Education Research*, Perth, July, 47–55.

Dunbar-Hall, P. (2008). "Good legong dancers were given an arduous program of training": Music education in Bali in the 1930s. *Journal of Historical Research in Music Education, 30*(1), 50–63.

Dunbar-Hall, P. & Adnyana, W. (2004). Expectations and outcomes of inter-cultural music education: A case study of teaching and learning a Balinese *gamelan* instrument. *Proceedings of the XXVIth Annual Conference of the Australian Association for Research in Music Education*, 144–151.

Ellis, C., & Bochner, A. (2000). Autoethnography, personal narrative, reflexivity. In N. Denzin & Y. Lincoln (Eds.), *Handbook of qualitative research* (pp. 733–768). London: Sage.

Ganguly-Scrase, R. (1993). The self as research instrument. In M. Crick & B. Geddes (Eds.), *Research methods in the field: Ten anthropological accounts* (pp. 37–58). Geelong: Deakin University Press.

Hammersley, M., & Atkinson, P. (1995). *Ethnography: Principles in practice*. London: Routledge.

Harnish, D. (1991). Balinese performance as festival offering. *Asian Art, 4*(2), 9–27.

Hill, M. (2006) Representin(g): Negotiating multiple roles and identities in the field and behind the desk. *Qualitative Inquiry, 12*(5), 926–949.

Mackinlay, E. (2007). *Disturbances and dislocations: Understanding teaching and learning experiences in Indigenous Australian women's music and dance*. Bern: Peter Lang.

McPhee, C. (1966). *Music in Bali: A study in form and instrumental organization in Balinese orchestral music.* New Haven: Yale University Press.

Perry, J. (Ed.). (1993). *Doing fieldwork: Eight personal accounts of social research.* Geelong, Australia: Deakin University Press.

Potgieter, F., & Smit, B. (2009). Finding academic voice: A critical narrative of knowledge-making and discovery. *Qualitative Inquiry, 15*(1), 214–228.

Reed-Danahay, D. (Ed.). (1997) *Auto/ethnography: Rewriting the self and the social.* New York: Oxford.

Rice, T. (1994). *May it fill your soul: Experiencing Bulgarian music.* Chicago: University of Chicago Press.

Stephens, N., & Delamont, S. (2006). Balancing the *berimbau*: Embodied ethnographic understanding. *Qualitative Inquiry, 12*(2), 316–339.

Subedi, B., & Rhee, J. (2008). Negotiating collaboration across differences. *Qualitative Inquiry, 14* (6), 1070–1092.

Tedlock, B. (2000). Ethnography and ethnographic representation. In N. Denzin & Y. Lincoln (Eds.), *Handbook of qualitative research* (pp. 455–486). London: Sage.

Tenzer, M. (1991) *Balinese music.* Singapore: Periplus.

van Manen, M. (1990). *Researching lived experience: Human science for an action sensitive pedagogy.* London (Ontario): Althouse Press.

Chapter 10

The Road to Becoming a Musician
An Individual Chinese Story

Wang Yuyan

I don't remember when I started envying people who were forced to learn an instrument by their parents when they were very little. I guess it was when I started realising how much I had missed due to my "wasted years", the time I was not allowed to learn music. I have been in love with music ever since I can remember. When I was two years old, I would stop immediately whenever I heard music and become completely absorbed in the sound. This must have been strange for somebody only two years old, as I have been told, so friends and family suggested to my parents to give me a chance to learn an instrument.

Unfortunately, my father had different ideas. To him and his side of the family, who come from a rural, traditional Chinese background, a girl was, simply said, useless. Only boys could do great deeds when they were grown-ups, because only they would be able to take the responsibility for the family. It was unnecessary to invest in a girl's education, as sooner or later she would become somebody else's. So they thought, and many in China still do ...

In the following personal story I document the road I have travelled to become a musician, despite my father's initial apprehension. It is a story that reminds us of the extent to which societal and cultural structures and family pressures can affect a musician's life, and indeed, an individual's choice of career. It is a story that also reveals many social and cultural aspects of Western music pedagogy and performance practice in China in the 1980s to 1990s. While stories such as my own have scarcely been told, there have been other writers who have touched on a range of relevant issues relating to Chinese culture (e.g., Broaded, 1991; Lee, 2008; Ong, 1995), and learning in cross-cultural contexts (e.g., Schippers, in press; Hood, 1960).

To put my story in perspective, it is worth noting that it was only a decade before I was born that China began to open up to the modern world. The ramifications of this coupled with the long-lasting effects of the Cultural Revolution (1966–1976) were in full force by the time I was born in 1980, the very year that the one-child policy was implemented. At this point in time, the professional world of the classical Western musician in China was little over five decades old. While constantly adapting to contemporary world trends, a particular Chinese characteristic had already been established with a rigidly entrenched education and recruitment system for professional instrumentalists.

My story reveals a number of insights into this system, and touches on many of the social attitudes in the music industry at the time of my youth. Issues such as the expected height of percussionists, the decline of the Russian xylophone, gender stereotypes, and the importance of *guanxi* — extended family and community connections by which one may give, receive, and thereby function in the world — all played a role. Other cultural and social aspects of China revealed in my personal narrative include the scarcity of mobile phones and music technology, and the complicated (and inherently corrupt) admission process of music conservatories. These issues, and many others, played a significant role in the long and difficult journey I endured to study music at China's oldest conservatory, and paint a revealing picture of the road one has to travel to become a musician in my home country.

~

My father was born around the beginnings of Communist China, and his parents were fruit farmers. He is the fourth of six children and, as he would say, the one who got the least attention, not being the oldest. Due to a coincidence my father joined the military when he was 16 years old. In his opinion, being young and weak actually helped him, because only three months after he joined there was no other option for the officials than to transfer him. Rather than have him sick all the time, he was transferred to the cultural centre, in the department of movie projection. With the high ranking associated with this position, my father went from soldier to officer.

In retrospect, this position opened up a much broader range of possibilities for my future than if he had stayed in the fields with his family, like all his brothers and sisters. However, it did not diminish the influence of his traditional rural education, and the associated closed-mindedness. The older I grow, and the better our relationship becomes, the more I am convinced that the influence of this education, in the form of his family, has played the biggest role in our ongoing differences. It probably does not help that I adopted large parts of his stubborn character, but few of his ideas.

The day I was born must have come as a shock to him, just like much of what followed came as a shock to me. My mother told me she only saw him a couple of hours after my birth, because he could not accept the fact that I was a girl. He just hid in disappointment. To explain: I am part of the first generation of children born under the one-child policy. My birth meant that my father would never have the chance for a son to carry on his family name. I do not quite understand why my mother got the blame for it, but a scapegoat had to be found, and sadly she was the only option. Luckily my mother took the experience to form a special bond with me, and ever since has been an advocate for the equality of the genders with respect to ability and value. This is probably why I am sometimes overly sensitive to the many forms of discrimination as they are practised throughout the world, not just in China.

The Quest Begins

My mother has a very different family background. She is from Tianjing, and her parents were both university students from before New Communist China. They moved to Lanzhou after the Korean War, working in the Gansu province government. Like me, she loved music from when she was little, but in her case it was her mother who did not support her, and even discouraged it. After going through the regular school channels, my mother was sent to a village in the countryside to work under the Communist Party Knowledge Exchange Program, where young people underwent "re-education". After that, she worked in a factory for two years before becoming an elementary school teacher.

My mother was immediately supportive of my natural inclination for the arts. When, at three years old, I asked my parents whether I could learn to play the piano, and the drum kit, and the violin, and any other instrument I knew at the time, my mother tried everything she could, but the economic conditions did not allow her to buy me an instrument at her own expense. Also, with my father very much against it, I never had a real chance. That should have been the end of it, but I never gave up. Three years later — a long time now, and an eternity at that age — my mother's school introduced extra-curricular violin classes. As the teacher's child I was allowed to join, and got my first-ever instrument: a violin.

After a couple of lessons I had to start at a new primary school and could not continue with the violin classes. The reason was the distance between the schools, and my mother's unwillingness to accept any possibility of lower performance in the basic subjects. After that, I was once sent to dance school, but was discouraged to continue because the instructor anticipated I would never be tall enough for a lead role. Fortunately, at that point in time it did not occur to me that as a deeply music- and arts-loving girl I had wasted what the Chinese call the "golden years", all of early childhood when skills are acquired easily and playfully. Fortunately I say, because I probably would have given up had I known.

At 13, I finally was able to buy myself a Yamaha electronic keyboard. It had taken six years of saving, mainly the money given to me by relatives on Chinese New Year. In my linear world view at that time, the implications were clear: Having an instrument is the one condition that needed to be fulfilled to be able to demand a teacher, and now that I had an instrument, this is what I would do. I was backed up by my mother, who found me a teacher. The teacher was actually a cello player, so after the first lesson, she discreetly told my mother that I should change to piano because I learned too quickly. Five lessons later I had already finished a year's work compared to other students, and at that point, the teacher refused to teach me any longer and introduced me to a piano teacher. After all, an electronic keyboard had little to do with a real piano.

After six months of lessons without an appropriate instrument, my mother had no other option if she didn't want to destroy my potential, than to buy me a piano. She did this by borrowing money from friends and family and combining it with emergency money that she had saved for many years. In addition to the immense financial sacrifice, my mother was also faced with my father's strict opposition to my music learning. Her whole side of the family knew about it, but was very scared to let my father know.

We initially bought the piano in the summer. Every day after school, I went back to my grandmother's place, where we had hidden the piano, to practise from 6.00 to 7.30. My father was always angry because I would come home late. He assumed that I had a boyfriend. By Chinese New Year 1994, six months later, my family had been through very hard times. In the end, my grandma was nominated to talk to my father for the family. I still can remember how unusual a Chinese New Year's Eve it was, because nobody talked at the table and the atmosphere was very nervous and tense. When my father heard the news, he had to keep face and could not say anything at that moment. Then he sort of accepted his fate, and three days later, we finally moved my piano into my room at my home. After ten years of fighting, I finally was able to do what I always had wished for, to "sneak" onto the road of learning music.

In some people's life, one single step can sometimes decide their fate. Thinking back about my life, there were several times when I felt that I no longer had a chance to continue with music. Even though I then had a piano, and just when everything was going well for me, my parents started to have concerns about my middle school records. The class I was in was exclusive to the best students, but I was still only the twenty-first out of sixty-four people. In order to not fail in the all-decisive middle school test, my parents asked me to not only think of going to study in high school, but at the same time save a chance for vocational training. This I did by signing up for an audition in the provincial kindergarten teacher school.

There are many different kinds of exams in this audition, including calligraphy, singing, drawing, sports, piano playing, dance, mandarin reading and acting. The day of the first exam I was already sick and tired of that school, because even before the exams had started, I heard people competing about whose family background was better and who had the better connections. What I hated most, however, was the height requirement. Before the first exam they check how tall you are, and they still do. That time I was only 1.53 metres tall. Obviously that was way too far away from the required 1.65 metres, so I lost a lot of points. I still don't understand why an educator in a kindergarten has to be of a certain height. I don't think one needs to be a model, and when dealing with little kids, being shorter should not be a disadvantage. "Unfortunately", even with this handicap, I still got the fifteenth place out of five hundred, without any connections or special background.

I still remember the day my father took me to see the results on the wall. I had been praying for days that I would not get accepted into that school, as the teachers we met were quite unfriendly. It turns out I would have comfortably passed if I had been from a different district, but as it was, I had just missed a place by two points. There was the option of doing a preparatory course for 6,000 Yuan. Once in that course, I would be given consideration first if a place opened up. Now, if there was one fact I could trust at that time, it was that my father would never pay that amount of money for a school that only enabled me to go to the villages behind the mountains to teach kids. Also, in 1995, 6,000 Yuan was almost enough to complete a university degree. I had successfully avoided being ripped off.

Not long after that, one day in May 1995, I spent my last music lesson in middle school with Mr Zhou, my music subject teacher. He was teaching major and minor triads, pure fifths and chord inversions, even though I was the only person listening. All the other students were reviewing other subjects or talking about the upcoming high school test. It is a big deal for every Chinese person to choose the right high school and then university. I really cherish that last middle school class and treasure Mr. Zhou's efforts spent on me. Suddenly one of my classmates passed me a flyer and said, "Hurry up, you still have time, go now!"

I was really shocked and quickly looked at it. There was information about a No. 14 Middle School music course audition. In China the high schools are numbered by their academic standing, and No. 14 was the only one in the North-West that had an integral music curriculum. My first reaction was to forget about it. I hadn't prepared anything, and I also had never heard about this school. As my classmate did not stop trying to convince me, I had no other option than to raise my hand and ask Mr Zhou to come and have a look. He said, "Go now. Don't give up any chance in your life." Those words will be stuck in my head forever. He pushed me out from the classroom. "I will ask for your permission to leave. Go now and take the audition. Even just sing a song. If you ever become a musician, don't forget to come back and thank me." With Mr. Zhou's backing I ran to the North-West Music School and arrived there at four o'clock in the afternoon.

The auditions had just finished. The jury members from the Military Dance and Orchestra Company had left. I looked at the audition room in despair, and thought that if I went back to school now I could still catch the last lesson of the day. Then somebody asked me: "Are you here for an audition? What are you playing?" I told the teacher: "Oh, never mind, anyway it's already finished. I was going to take the vocal audition." The piano requirements in that school were very high, and I wouldn't have stood a chance. "Just wait here for me. I will go to talk to them." After five minutes he returned and told me to prepare a little bit, I would have an audition in the office. Having sung two pop songs, I was ready to dig a hole and disappear forever. It was really unacceptable. Somebody said, "You can go now, thank you."

Obviously the head of the music school had no interest in me. Just before I went out the door, I felt quite uncomfortable as I knew I could present myself much better. *Why had something like this happened?*

Would this be the end of me and my musical aspirations? I don't know where the courage came from, but I interrupted them:

"Oh, teacher, you are also getting piano students, right?"

"You can play piano? What is your level?"

I answered very clearly: "Very low." But he had a surprising reaction: "Never mind, just play." After I had played a piece called *The Wild Rose* by Schubert, I heard somebody say, "Nice, the technique from Czerny is fantastic." Then Mr Han, the Head of School, came to the piano and asked me to turn around and sing the pitches he was playing on the piano. I sang them all correctly with names. I could sing them because I still remembered the key from the piano piece I had just played. Then he started playing chords: the first one was major, the second one minor in first inversion, the third one minor in second inversion. Total silence. Somebody started speaking: "All right, you can leave now. And don't forget to pick your admission papers up tomorrow after school."

I loved the moment after I left that office. I saw the teacher who had asked for my audition and my mother who had come to pay for the audition. I hadn't even paid the registration fee. By that time I still had no idea what exactly was going on. I told them Mr Han asked me to pick up the papers the next day, and they started laughing. The teacher said: "See, I never make a mistake. I can always recognise the seed that is about to sprout". I had used the knowledge I had just learned from my middle school music teacher, Mr Zhou. The contents of that last lesson with him meant I was the last one who attended the audition, and the first one to have the result confirmed. In a sense, my newly acquired knowledge of chords and triads had helped me get a place in the school on the audition day, while all the other hopefuls had to wait for the results to be published on the next day. After so many years I still think back to that specific moment when I simply could have left the audition room, but decided not to.

From there on everything should have become considerably easier, but it didn't. As I had registered for both music and normal high school classes, both schools wanted me as a student. No. 14 Middle School and North-West Music School is a combination of two schools. When orientation day arrived, I realised I hadn't received my orientation pack. This meant that I had to decide right there, at the gate in front of the school, right that moment whether to go to the normal high school, where only if I was very lucky I could go to university later, or the music school, with slim chances of making it into any conservatory. Without exaggerating, it didn't feel like I actually decided myself. It was like having a ghost pushing me in the direction of the music classroom. I remember that in the first year of high school, all the normal high school teachers were trying to convince me to switch, and laughed about me because my exam score was about 200 points higher than anybody else's in the entire music school. Everybody thought I was wasting my life and burying my future in that music class. But I never changed my mind, because I had been fighting for so many years, and finally had the feeling I was taking my first steps towards a life as a professional musician.

In August 1995, just after starting high school, I was asked to change my major. I had started playing piano too late, so I was offered French horn. I hated that instrument at the time, because I could only think of French horn players with very round faces and bodies. Ironically, the French horn is translated as "around horn" in Chinese. I was worried that if I started playing the French horn, I would become just like that. To avoid this, I had to fake breathing problems. The next option was oboe, and I hated the oboe even more than the French horn. I always felt it was the nastiest sounding instrument in the world. The reason for this was that I had never heard anybody play the oboe properly. In my opinion, except for making a noise like a duck, there was nothing special about the oboe. By that time I had set my mind on percussion, and was eventually allowed to enter the course.

We had five percussion students in the class, and all the others were piano majors. They were all preparing for the conservatory piano auditions. I was the only beginner, and I was the shortest one. In those years, one of the first requirements for an orchestral percussionist was to be tall, as being tall meant looking cool. I worked very hard, maybe because it is in my character, or perhaps because playing percussion was one of my first dreams. At the beginning the teacher only paid attention to the only boy in class. He liked the boy, and the orchestra did, too. In China, whether it be orchestras or conservatories, all pay more attention to men, because they think all famous musicians in the world are men. This was still very common in the 1990s. You would often see a job description reading "only men required".

I was glad we had a boy in the group. He pushed me one step further. I was always the first to complete the set homework, was the best at it, and always did more exercises to make my teacher happy — just to get his attention. And very soon I did. He told everybody I was working hard and a smart girl. He even started teaching me timpani in the first semester instead of the second year. I also started with the xylophone in the second semester. The teacher was the principal percussionist of the Lanzhou Military Dance and Orchestra Company. He was also a famous soloist, called the "North-West Drum King". To be a military percussionist one has to be very versatile, as there is Western orchestral repertoire, Chinese folk music and military composition playing. All military-trained percussionists can play Western percussion, especially the snare drum, but then also play ethnic instruments.

The other students and I often went to see the teacher perform. He always played *paigu* (Chinese tom-toms). Seeing him stand behind those fantastic red instruments and creating that special atmosphere, I always felt he looked like a tiger. He was like a god. That was the first time I really felt like studying ethnic Chinese percussion playing, but every time I asked him, he refused to teach me.

"Why do you want to learn Chinese percussion? Loser. You are going to get into the Western orchestra department and you are going to get into some symphony orchestra in the future."

At that time I often thought to myself: *That makes sense. If I can play Western percussion it is already quite amazing.*

Learning to Persevere

In July 1997 I went to a conservatory looking for a professionally qualified teacher for the first time. In China, if you want to get into a conservatory, you have to see the teacher before and start taking lessons. You have to let the teacher know about you. This is a very common practice. Everybody who has ever studied in a conservatory has gone through this process more than once. There was no special treatment for me.

I had to see the teacher exactly one year before the audition. I remember it was a very hot day, and the percussion room was on the 14th floor. I don't know whether it was because I was nervous or because of the height of the building, which was mainly made of glass, but I couldn't stop shaking. It wasn't long before the playing in the practice room nearby stopped, and a young lady teacher emerged. Her first sentence was: "How long have you learned percussion?" That was the scariest question for me. As far as I knew, every other kid started learning their instrument at the age of three or four. I, on the other hand, still called the timpani a "bass drum" at 14.

As it turned out, this became the main reason why the teacher lost interest in me at first, but since I had found her through a family member who was the head of the orchestra department, she agreed to have a look. I went into the practice room. After a couple of minutes I finished, and the teacher said nothing, directly went to the other room and started talking to my mother:

"I am very surprised she can play at this level after only two years of study, but the speed of her doubles is not fast enough. I would like to give her a chance, but next year we have a very bad situation. Four more students are coming from Beijing, and we are only getting two, so it will be very competitive. And she has never played marimba. That means she has no chance against them. Nobody plays Russian xylophone any longer. You can think about it. She can stay here to study with me for one year. Two lessons per week until the following year, then she can try again."

At that moment, it seemed like everything I had tried so hard to achieve was wasted. I started feeling everything before had been a lie. I was truly very far away from the point of getting anywhere, and so I started thinking about my future. That night, when we got back to my grandmother's sister's home, I overheard the conversation between her and my mother: "Why doesn't she learn something else? Why does she have to learn music? This road is not clean." That comment seemed fair, considering that I had just been asked to spend a whole year there, give up all my regular subjects, pay 300 Yuan each lesson (my mother at the time earned 500 Yuan a month), and pay for accommodation and living. After we left my mother encouraged me to go to Beijing, to see another teacher.

Mr Yang was the principal percussionist of the China National Broadcasting Symphony Orchestra. I knew him from before, when his orchestra had toured my hometown in May 1997. I actually had a chance to talk to him before the concert, because the usher on duty backstage was our neighbour. Mr Yang asked me to play for him on the snare drum on stage, and after I finished the audience started clapping. Mr Yang immediately accepted me after this test. In Beijing, I told him why the previous teacher had refused me, and so he tested me with an electronic metronome he had bought from Hong Kong. That was the first time I had seen something like that. After I played the doubles he made me speed them up for two minutes. Then he screamed, excited, pointing out from his balcony: "You are right now playing much faster than anybody from that building." That was the Central Conservatory of Music. He lived directly opposite the conservatory. We could even hear the people practising. Obviously, the lady at the other conservatory needed to find some excuse to tell my mother to keep me there for another year. Mr Yang said: "Kid, I have to tell you. You have to try to make yourself feel better. Understand that in China, learning music is a life full of injustices and extortion. Especially in Beijing. Always remember that if you are gold, you are always going to shine, anywhere. You do not have to be in the supposedly best place to move towards the best future." He made me understand that when you take a step back, you can actually see the bigger picture.

As Mr Yang was not a teacher at any conservatory, I had to go on my next trip to see another teacher. Without the backing of an institutional degree, there is virtually no chance to get any job in China. So every weekend during the first semester of the last year of high school, I went to the closest city with a conservatory. I got on the train Friday night, arrived in the morning, went to the lesson, took the train in the afternoon, and arrived back home at four on Sunday morning. It was winter and nobody was on the street. It was a miserable situation, but I understood that it was something I had to do, even if only to keep my hopes up. The first time I went to see the new teacher my father came with me. It is customary in China to bring gifts with you when meeting a teacher for the first time. It was not so much the 500 Yuan my father paid to replace one pair of snare drum sticks and a pair of mallets for the Russian xylophone that apparently was not used any longer in any conservatories in China, according to the previous teacher. What got to my father was the teacher's constant pointing out of electrical appliances in his apartment that needed upgrading.

Even the teacher himself would say, "Learning music is like passing by the same pirate ship over and over again, especially for the parents. The payments never stop, and there is most likely nothing that comes from it. I suggest people do not study music at all!" This point of view is interesting, because contrary to what I have experienced abroad, musicians in China are relatively well respected and wealthy. That said, I guess some of the reasons for that have become apparent by now. To put those prices in perspective, I bought the exact same sticks in 2006 for one-third of the price. And strangely enough, the equipment kept needing upgrades over the years, as I was later told by the teacher's students. Fortunately my father could not be convinced to buy a Russian xylophone, the one nobody used any longer, for 8,000 Yuan, because I saw it the next day in a music store for 3,000 Yuan. For reasons that were never given to me, I was denied an audition spot for a place in the conservatory.

The refusal of this teacher hurt my father more than it did me. He just had started to warm to the idea of me becoming a musician, but this experience changed him back to his old views. His plan was to send me to the military arts school, even though that was the most difficult school to get into. There was a common sentence to describe it: "It costs 100,000 Yuan to touch the floor of that school once". From the end of January 1997 until March, my mother fought on my behalf to give me one last chance at attempting the Shanghai Conservatory of Music audition. On the fourth of March, my 18th birthday, I was allowed to leave for Shanghai, under the condition that if I failed, I would have to go to the military arts school auditions in Xi'an and Beijing. If I failed those, I would have to join the military. My mother secretly gave me a bankbook with 6,000 Yuan. "Do not come back until you get into the conservatory, and don't ever contact us to give your father a chance to get you back. If you have no chance this year, use the money and live by yourself for a year and try again the year after."

I got on the train on my 18th birthday, for the first time in my life all by myself. Just after the train left the station, I realised I had forgotten the letter my high school percussion teacher wrote to introduce me to a student he knew at the Shanghai Conservatory. That was it. There was no other contact option and not many mobile phones were around at that time. I managed to find a young businessman with a mobile phone and called my parents.

My mother was angry, very angry, but as always she thought practically and said she would fax the letter to my accommodation the next day. With thirty-six hours to pass on the train, I spent most of the time practising. Then I noticed a young boy staring at me from the next compartment. My parents had made me very aware of girls disappearing from trains to be sold on the black market, so I was a bit worried. In the evening I had to make space for some people having their dinner, and that was when the boy got his chance.

"Are you a percussionist? Are you studying with Mr. Jin?"

How did he know? Was he trying to kidnap me? How did he know all these details?

"Yeah, how do you know?"

"Oh, I am a percussionist, too!"

No way, I thought, another one! He was probably going to look for the same contact that I had, find the teacher, and that would mean my chance was gone. There was no way two percussionists from the same city would get accepted into the same school.

"Are ... you looking for Zhang Da Zhi as well ...?"

"I AM Zhang Da Zhi!"

I could not believe it. Of all the days, all the trains leaving my hometown, the tens of carriages, hundreds of compartments, the person I was looking for was right next to me. That must have been the biggest birthday present anyone had ever received! I borrowed the mobile phone again, and very briefly told my parents what had happened. The next day, I got off the train. When my father's colleagues picked me up they seemed strangely excited, like I was some pop music star. What I didn't know was that after I had called, my parents couldn't sleep the whole night. They had assumed the boy must be a criminal and were convinced that by the morning I surely would have disappeared from the face of the earth. Instead I was going directly to see the teacher.

It was a bit different from what I had expected. The greeting was very unfriendly, unlike all the other first meetings that I had had with percussion teachers. I was already prepared for that moment, however, as I knew there was no chance for me to get into what is considered the best conservatory in China.

"I can only have a look for you," the teacher said. "I do not think there is enough time for you to prepare for the audition at this point. There are already seven students who came here much earlier than you, and we only have one position this year. Should I have a look now or do you want to make an appointment?" I thought it would be easier to just get it over with and go back home. I could probably even save all of my mother's money. While playing the last section of the piece, I thought of a good exit line. "Thank you dear teacher, I am going back home now."

"Next week same time," he replied. He did not say anything else and let me out from the room.

Epilogue

Not long after, I was accepted into the Shanghai Conservatory of Music, the only percussionist that year. The only expenses I had were a pair of shoes seven centimetres high and long jeans to cover them, in order to make it to the required 1.65 metres. Reflecting on my story and its key moments, I can see the importance of all the encounters with people I have come to appreciate as real musicians on my journey. People who do music because it is a calling, not a profession; people who have overcome social and cultural, internal and external obstacles, with an unbound will to spend their lives with music; people who day by day reconcile the ideal with the real with skills of adaptation, perseverance, artistic integrity, and luck, if you choose to call it so. Sometimes these people are known as performers, other times as teachers, or students, or researchers, but they are really musicians, and they have all helped shaping my understanding of what it means to be a musician today.

On my road this far I feel I have achieved a lot of what I wanted, and I feel as though it is now the time to start giving something back. Through my practice and research, and the story told in this chapter, I hope to open eyes and doors for more people in China to pursue their musical dreams like I did. I also hope to open windows into China for people outside this culture, and show the interesting but challenging road one has to travel to become a musician in this country.

Acknowledgments

I would like to thank my anonymous reviewers for their ideas and advice in the editing of this chapter.

References

Broaded, C. M. (1991). China's lost generation: The status degradation of an educational cohort. Journal of Contemporary Ethnography, 20, 352–379.

Hood, K. M. (1960). The challenge of bi-musicality. *Ethnomusicology 4*, 55–59.

Lee, K. V. (2008). White Whispers. *Qualitative Inquiry, 14*(6), 896–900.

Ong, A. (1995). Women out of China: Traveling tales and traveling theories in postcolonial feminism. In R. Behar & D. A. Gordon (Eds.), *Women writing culture* (pp. 350–372). Berkeley: University of California Press.

Schippers, H. (in press). *Facing the music: Shaping music education from a global perspective*. New York: Oxford University Press.

Chapter **11**

⌒ "Where Was I When I Needed Me?"
The Role of Storytelling in Vocal Pedagogy

Margaret Schindler

The one-to-one teaching setting is a unique environment in which the teacher's knowledge, experience and persona converge to form a holistic pedagogical approach. The teaching profile of those working in these one-to-one settings is often that of "performer/teachers". This is very strongly the case in the area of classical voice. Despite its prevalence the pedagogical implications of this on student learning remains largely unexplored. The chapter aims to shed light on this situation, and identify the ways in which performer/teachers influence student learning in the one-to-one teaching studio. In light of the paucity of literature relating to this important aspect of vocal pedagogy, the storying of performer/teachers' professional journeys, through autoethnography allows us to use our professional profiles as an important resource. By telling stories, such as my own, we are able to reflect on those events and characteristics which have shaped our professional identities as well as our pedagogical culture and teaching strategies.

As Clandinin and Connelly (2000) remind us, "in ethnography, people are viewed as embodiments of their own lived stories" (p. 43). My story, which I share in this chapter, is an "audit" of myself as a performer, teacher and continuous learner. It sheds light on aspects of personal experience that form an important part of the tacit exchange in my music teaching and learning practice. In much the same way that the autoethnographic author builds a relationship with the reader, the relationship between the voice teacher and singing student also develops through an incremental layering of trust in the teaching and learning exchange. This is subtly illustrated in the following personal narrative and critical reflections that follow, as I trace my journey as a singer from early beginnings to the present day. My narrative and reflections show how my own journey has deeply and positively impacted upon my relationships with my students and my pedagogical approaches to studio teaching practice.

~

> There must be at least one note in my range that belonged to my grandmother, and certainly my mother's soprano and my father's deep love for new music have given much of the color and depth to my sound. Their voices are our inheritance, part of the amalgamation of who we are and what we have learned. We are unique, each human voice, not because we are completely self-generated but because of how we choose to assemble the countless factors that made us. (Fleming, 2005, p. 222)

I was born the youngest of four daughters into a middle-class family in Washington DC, United States. My mother, an Australian, was a gifted pianist and church organist who in her capacity as church musician for our local Christian Science church selected the repertoire required for weekly services, rehearsed the soloists in our home and accompanied the congregation. Additionally, she maintained a modest piano teaching practice in our family home. My father was an attorney who had no musical background or experience whatsoever. He was a Jewish man, and our household was a vibrant mix of spiritual beliefs and tradition. The practice of music was a fairly normal and integral part of family life. Two of my mother's brothers had been gifted classical singers and would sometimes give impromptu performances at family gatherings, much to our great embarrassment.

When my father died suddenly in 1968, the family moved to Australia where we were given the opportunity to study music more formally. I sang in a community children's choir from age 11 to 16, but received no formal vocal training until I was 16. My exposure to operatic singing was limited to an obsession with Janette McDonald and Nelson Eddy films. My mother had remarried when I was 10 years old. Unfortunately, my stepfather and I had a somewhat hostile relationship and in a bid to avoid the tension in the house, I spent many weekends and holidays in the company of my mother's only sister, Joyce. My aunt was a cultured woman whom I adored and who had an enormous influence on my upbringing. Aunty Joyce had worked for the United Nations and had lived in numerous exotic countries and exciting locations. At one stage during a seven year posting in New York City, she dated a principal tenor from the Metropolitan Opera. It was through him that she acquired a love of opera and established a large collection of opera recordings. My first real exposure to operatic singing was through listening to some of these recordings plus a life altering performance by Joan Sutherland of *Norma,* which I witnessed, aged 16. That experience was pivotal in cementing my desire to become a singer.

My formal musical education began at the Queensland Conservatorium, where my training followed a strong practical performance emphasis. On reflection, I realise that my early voice teachers were working models of performer/teachers. They maintained profiles as concert singers, albeit modest, performing chamber music, oratorio and song repertoire. The opportunity to hear my teacher in performance was not frequent; however, I still recall the impact it had on me to be present in the audience on those occasions.

My experience of music study was a happy and relatively carefree one. The joy and sense of wholeness that accompanied my performances was powerful and life-affirming. I had a natural voice, not without its faults; however, I managed to negotiate these shortcomings through other musical attributes. Some of my peers went on to have major international careers. Even as students they were outstanding, although my teacher never made me feel less than worthy. I was a competent musician, quicker than most singers, and my teacher instilled in me a musical integrity and intelligence that gave me a sense of individual merit. I sensed recognition of herself in me; our voice types, musical and intellectual styles were similar. It was a safe environment; in many ways I did not want to leave ...

My teacher's vocal pedagogy was based largely on imitation and mental imagery, a traditional and empirical teaching method which has its roots in the *bel canto* style. There was little technical emphasis; rather this was approached via repertoire. This provided me with some sound aural and musical models; however, this did little to foster my independent learning and understanding. I loved my teacher and wanted very much to please her. I felt that my failure to succeed technically was a reflection on myself, and not her.

Although my teacher was a progressive and intelligent pedagogue, the sophisticated level of knowledge and understanding available to voice teachers today simply did not exist at the time I was studying. I graduated a musically intelligent singer but with limited technique or understanding of how my instrument worked.

I enjoyed numerous early successes as a young singer, winning national competitions and awards and scholarships for overseas study. I was not especially competitive but had no real problem with nerves or anxiety. My established faith and belief in God allowed me to fully assume the role of musical conduit rather than personally shouldering the responsibility for my ability. It was tremendously liberating in one way; however, I was aware even then, that I was technically insecure and it slowly began to unnerve my performance in spite of my reliance on God.

After completing my studies at the Queensland Conservatorium, I was accepted as a founding member of the Song Company, a professional eight-voice ensemble based in Sydney. This innovative group performed a range of vocal repertoire from Renaissance music to new Australian works and collaborated regularly with Australia's eminent musical organisations. This was largely a positive experience; however, I still had Joan Sutherland's singing in my ear and so I auditioned for the chorus of Opera Australia. I was accepted, aged 24, and remained there for approximately two years.

This was a stimulating but exhausting work environment. In two years, I learned 40 operas and took part in over 300 performances. Owing to my musical proficiency and eagerness to get on, I was given opportunities to understudy roles and perform minor solos. I learned an enormous amount, both good and bad, through participation and also through observation of eminent singers, producers, and conductors. I found this environment to be inspirational on many levels, but began to realise that I lacked the technical and psychological armour to cope with the more challenging aspects of the job. I left the chorus after two years, to take up study opportunities that awaited me through several prizes and scholarships I had won, including the ABC Instrumental and Vocal Competition, the Britten-Pears Scholarship for Advanced Musical Study, and an Australia Council Grant for Overseas Study.

In 1988, I left for overseas. My first experience was a summer school in Belgium which was a pivotal in terms of meeting a teacher who would have a major influence on my singing. The summer school brought together several renowned teachers from the Curtis Institute Philadelphia, and the Guildhall School of Music and Drama, London, as well as internationally acclaimed singers and pianists. In a masterclass for Marlena Malas, I sang better than I had ever done in my entire life. The feeling of exhilaration that accompanied that performance was addictive. I was convinced that Ms Malas was the teacher to help me become the singer I wanted to be. When she agreed to teach me in New York I felt as though I had been admitted to an exclusive club. However, I had already committed myself to studying in London with another eminent voice teacher. Strangely, I went ahead with this plan and endured about two months of somewhat limited instruction before moving to New York.

Marlena was a guru in teaching style. One didn't ask questions, in fact there was very little exchange of any type. I found her immensely charismatic, with crystals draped around her neck. She was direct and to the point; this was a pedagogical tone I had never before encountered.

Marlena Malas was not a performer and had had a very short singing career. She once told me, in a rare moment of candour, that her career had lasted nine months owing to her inability to audition. It didn't seem to matter. Her "students" routinely included big name performers appearing at the Metropolitan Opera, who would drop by for a check up. I hoped she would address issues of breathing and support, which I had struggled with for years. However, her approach to this area seemed to me rather circuitous at the time, although now I think it was absolutely right. My time and money ran out and I returned to Australia with a determination to go back overseas as quickly as possible. Six months later I won the German Operatic Award and received a posting in the Cologne Opera Studio attached to the Cologne State Opera.

Winning the scholarship, which provided engagement within the opera studio at the Cologne State Opera, would prove a profound experience on a number of levels. It was my first experience of an international opera house and I was overwhelmed by the calibre of singing and productions that took place there. My colleagues were mostly American singers, very friendly and supportive. They were very together: iron-clad techniques, strong musical and linguistic proficiency and a positivism that wouldn't quit.

However, instead of feeling excited and inspired, I was consumed by a rapidly growing sense of inadequacy. Being limited in the German language only added to my shyness. I struggled with daily tasks and found myself becoming sick more often, which was out of character for me. I quickly learned that to gain respect I needed to show assertiveness and that was probably the one quality that was impossible for me to demonstrate! I felt totally out of my depth, vocally, although not musically. While I sustained the roles I was assigned, I was certain that people were criticising me and that I simply didn't have what it took to be there.

I was singing the role of *Fiordiligi* in *Cosi fan Tutte*. This role is not suitable for my voice and I knew that, so entered into the project with fear and negativity. My previous ability to negotiate and "fake" my way through roles that were too demanding would no longer support me. I was 27 and could not wing my way through something as lengthy and exposed as this role. During the rehearsal period I noticed my voice diminishing in volume. The tone remained clear but became very restricted. A visit to the throat specialist confirmed that I had strained my strap muscles or sterno-clydomastoids. These are large muscles; it takes a considerable amount of exertion to strain them. I was given muscle relaxants to take and limped through the performances. This was a final wake-up call for me. I realised that unless I learned how to sing properly, I would lose my voice. Although professional offers continued in Germany, and in the midst of separating from my husband, I returned to Australia to re-group.

This was a dark, albeit short, period of my life when I faced for the first time the prospect of not making a living out of singing and perhaps of not singing at all. I had a hundred dollars to my name, had no job and a broken relationship. I managed to pick up a small amount of freelance work with Opera Australia and in concerts, but was basically unemployed.

When voice teacher Janice Chapman visited Brisbane in 1992 I went to see her, in considerable vocal and psychological disarray. She was able to identify quickly the fundamental areas lacking in my technique such as breathing, support and freedom of articulators. For the first time in a few years, I was able to begin to make some free sounds. I felt instantly buoyed by that experience and arranged to study with her in London later that year. Janice, a singer who suffered a vocal crisis early in her career and spent many years after that rebuilding her voice and acquiring sound pedagogical knowledge, implicitly understood my state of mind and believed that the key to getting a singer feeling better lies in getting them singing better.

I spent three months in London, where I worked twice weekly with Dinah Harris, a voice teacher specialising in Accent Method Breathing, had a weekly lesson with Janice Chapman, and a weekly coaching with David Harper. I also received regular treatment from an osteopath named Jacob Lieberman who specialised in laryngeal manipulation to assist in releasing the recalcitrant tension, which had built up in my neck, throat and jaw through years of poor vocal function and emotional/psychological stress. Although the consolidation of this work did not really begin until I was back in Australia, I felt, for the first time, that I was being taught how to play my instrument and that I understood the process. There was a sense of elation and empowerment, accompanied by a terrible sense of grief at lost opportunities and time and money wasted; also for the psychological battering that the struggling singer endures when the teacher or vocal coach or conductor who cannot identify or assist in correcting their faults, affixes blame either tacitly or explicitly, onto the performer. On my return to Australia, I attended a series of courses run by voice teacher and researcher, Jo Estill, and later, courses on voice science, some of which were facilitated by Janice Chapman. I began to acquire a secure understanding of how the voice worked and I became eager to learn more.

When I accepted some part-time teaching of voice at the Queensland Conservatorium Griffith University, Queensland University of Technology, and University of Queensland, I knew there were still huge gaps in my understanding; however, I felt sufficiently equipped and experienced, to begin some teaching. There was a strong sense of mourning which accompanied my move into teaching. Teaching singing had not been part of my "greater plan". A big part of my identity was changing, and it took some years to feel comfortable with the notion of a dual career path. However, it became a type of mission to inform students in the way I had not been informed, in a bid to give them a better footing than the one I had.

Although there were regular opportunities for me to perform in concert throughout Australia and New Zealand and in opera with Opera Queensland particularly, the formation of Southern Cross Soloists in 1995 afforded me the opportunity to enhance the profile of my professional singing while maintaining my teaching work. The dual career paths of teaching and performing have proved to be an enriching combination and a process that is self-generating: Teaching informs my performance practice and vice versa. My growth as a professional singer, both technically and artistically, maintained through regular performance, tuition, coaching, and professional development, as well as the learning which one experiences through teaching, has brought me to that place which so many performer/teachers find themselves: wishing that they could now, as more knowledgeable, proficient, "together" singers, be given those original opportunities over again.

As I mark my 15th year of full-time voice teaching at the tertiary level, I note that my life has actually led me back to the environment where I experienced some of my most joyous music making and formed some enduring partnerships. Perhaps I have retreated to the environment in which I felt safe, successful and approved of in earlier times. I'm sure that there is more than a little truth to that. Remaining a performer has allowed me to remain a student in many ways and to perpetuate some of the joy that I experienced in my earliest years of singing. Only now it has the added dimensions of experience, knowledge, understanding, and love.

Critical Reflections: Implications for Vocal Pedagogy

The experiences, struggles and successes described in this personal narrative are I believe commonplace among professional singers, though not routinely documented. I wrote this narrative in one continuous sitting. It was as though, having relived its contents many times in my head, the words simply tumbled out onto the page. It still rings very true, although I am acutely aware of the risk of it becoming a type of self-help fable; a tale of self-discovery through vocal discovery. It has, however, served me well as a resource from which I can reinforce certain principles to my students. Having said this, as I reflect on this personal account, it also concerns me that it may not be an exact representation of the "truth" that, perhaps with the passage of time, I have romanticised certain aspects of my life or conversely, catastrophised those experiences that were less than positive. However, as Ellis and Bochner (2000) state, the accuracy of storytelling is not the main objective with autoethnography. "The question is not, 'Does my story reflect my past accurately?' as if I were holding a mirror to my past. Rather I must ask, 'What are the consequences my story produces? What kind of a person does it shape me into?'"(p. 756). Phillip Adams (2007) concurs, saying, "Memory, like all forms of autobiography, is a work of fiction … our lives, even our past lives remain works in progress, subject to the editorial process" (p. 42).

In terms of vocal pedagogy, this story highlights a number of areas of key concern. The first of which is the absolute imperative for singers to acquire, at the beginning of their learning experience, solid vocal technique plus a secure psychological foundation for singing. One of the overriding messages from this narrative is the inextricable link between technical proficiency and a balanced psychological and emotional operative state. Renowned baritone Håkan Hagegård (as cited in Brandfonbrener, 2000) agrees, "I miss not having had psychology, mental training, and training in handling the profession" (p. 3). The absence of psychology in training performers at tertiary level does nothing to address this gap in performer knowledge. A period of psychotherapy in my mid-30s assisted me in gaining a better perspective on my singing and my life generally, a process which also facilitated the broadening of my approach to teaching.

The performer–teacher then, runs the risk of bringing not just their experience and knowledge to the teaching and learning environment, but their "baggage" too. Identifying the *con*structive and potentially *de*structive elements that accompany performance knowledge and experience are a pedagogical concern. Susan Lee (1997) identifies similarities with the field of dance education: "The most insidious of the problems are the ways in which unresolved personal issues with a career transition are communicated to the next generation" (p. 39).

In reflecting on the early successes I enjoyed as a performer and the safe, nurturing environment of my student days, it is not surprising that I had few coping mechanisms for dealing with criticism. The way in which I idolised my early voice teachers and placed complete trust in them is testament to the power and influence these individuals often have not just over our voices but our entire lives. Renowned soprano Grace Bumbry (as cited in Matheopoulos, 1991) speaking about her voice teacher, performer Lotte Lehmann, explains, "I always say my mother gave me my first birth and Madame Lehmann gave me my second. She opened me to the world" (p. 258). Furthermore Kiri Te Kanawa (ibid) comments, "My rule is never to listen to anybody except for myself and my teacher, Vera Rosza" (p. 217).

My experience in Germany also taught me the empowerment that comes with knowledge. This was possibly the most important period in my life in terms of gaining real perspective on international standards. My admiration for my colleagues with their technical proficiency and total assurance as singers fuelled my quest for greater understanding. This quest for further knowledge is something I try to instil in my own students too.

The concluding section of my narrative reveals a process of healing that has served to ease the pain of early career disappointments. I feel comfortable with who I am and with what my voice is. This has also come about through the process of teaching. Performer/teacher Laura Brooks-Rice (as cited in Blades-Zeller, 2002) agrees: "Voice teaching often becomes a matter of convincing people that, yes this is your voice. It's no smaller than this, it's no bigger than this, it's no more beautiful than this — this is your voice" (p. 143). It is also debatable as to whether the technical issues I had as a young singer would have responded to appropriate technical instruction even if it had been offered me, owing to my profound emotional issues. As Brooks-Rice reminds us, "Half of voice teaching is psychotherapy. You deal with reasons why you can't release your breath or reasons why you can't release your jaw. Your own personality traits are reflected in your voice" (as cited in Blades-Zeller, 2002, p. 143).

My narrative also gives rise to a further pedagogical concern: There remains a lack of understanding or support for "failure" within the performance culture, in spite of an increase in the number of highflying professional singers who admit to vocal pathologies or vocal crises, such as Natalie Dessay (Canning, 2007) and Renee Fleming (2004). Wounded singers are not supported in the way that injured athletes are sidelined and rehabilitated. As Dosher argues, "Too many people are using phrases like 'get out of the kitchen if you can't stand the heat.' I don't believe in that, either at the training level or at the professional level. I don't that's the way human beings behave and I think encouragement and support is the best thing you can do" (as cited in Blades-Zeller, 2002, p. 221).

As Ellis and Bocher (2000) explain, the "work of self-narration is to produce this sense of continuity: to make a life that sometimes seems to be falling apart come together again, by retelling and restorying the events of one's life" (p. 746). In the case of my own storytelling, this process was extremely useful and even necessary in enabling me to fully reflect on the experiences and influences that have played a key role in determining the nature of my work today both as teacher and performer. Chapman concurs, "My own story is an integral part of the journey to my current philosophy and methodology" (2006, p. xvii).

This narrative also highlights the changes that have come about in my attitude to performance and teaching. Before I commenced teaching I was one of those people who secretly viewed teaching as the "refuge of the failed performer" (Durrant, 1992, cited in Persson, 1996b, p. 45). Although there has been considerable examination of identity shifts in performers who make a move to education, the perception of singers who are engaged as teachers retains a tacit stigma of compromise. Callaghan (2000) attributes this prevalent view to the fact that "performing is valued above teaching" (p.112); that teaching is the "consolation prize for not finding work as a performer" (Lee, 1997, p. 9). Perhaps this has been my greatest lesson of all. In light of the change in pedagogical profile referred to by prominent American voice teacher, Swank (as cited in Blades-Zeller 2002), there is no longer any room for that type of arrogant and simplistic view: "This is the period when, for the first time, voice teaching has become a professional entity in itself; not a lot of performers start teaching because they quit performing. There is now a different direction" (p. 231).

As my research in this area has progressed, I have reflected on video footage of my teaching to see how the issues I have described in the narrative above have been playing out in my own teaching studio. Some of my observations resonate strongly with the journey I have just described. For example:

> Teaching style is direct, almost businesslike. I note a personalised approach with appropriate adjustment according to individual students; however, the general efficacy and content of the lessons strikes me as being structured and containing clear objectives. I wouldn't mind having me as a teacher! It's almost as if I've invented my own teacher having struggled for so many years to find one. I appear to be a type of amalgamation of all those people with whom I have studied. I perceive an almost driven desire to get the student functioning freely and on the right path. (Personal observations of video footage, October 2005)

On closer reflection, my teaching persona also appeared to incorporate those elements which I regard as missing from my persona as a singer. The teacher I viewed was confident, assured, competent and personally engaged with the student. The performer I am "performs" confidence and assurance, but is vulnerable and insecure and simulates a "shared" experience with an audience. This leads to areas of investigation regarding the link between persona and psychological armour.

In my role as a teacher, I have invented someone I would like to learn from, someone to look after my "inner singer." Similarly, in an interview with voice teacher Janice Chapman, she commented that often when reflecting on the deficits of her early experiences as a voice student and the status she enjoys today as a renowned voice teacher, she finds herself saying, "Where was I when I needed me?" (personal interview, October 9, 2006).

> I am aware that although I am talking to the student observing the student, listening, there is another agenda going on. I can see that I am thinking 'around' the student, choosing to direct the lesson in a particular way while making notes to myself of how next to proceed or what to keep in my head. There is a strong sense of control over the exchange between the student and myself; at times a conscious withholding of thought combined with information that is deemed appropriate and timely. (Personal observations of video footage, October 2005)

This footage proved very revealing in terms of persona. I witnessed for the first time the way in which I had constructed a professional persona as a type of amalgamation of former teachers, conductors, coaches, colleagues, mentors, rivals, and so on. I was curious to see if this construction of my artistic environment resonated with Anais

Nin's sentiments (Oakley, 1984 as cited in Ellis and Bochner, 2000): "I could not live in any of the worlds offered to me ... I believe one writes because one has to create a world in which to live" (p. 746). I suspect the same was possibly true for the environment that I had constructed for myself and the persona I had assumed within it.

Conclusion

Singers are not strangers to storytelling; the act of creating the world that their characters inhabit is inherent to their craft. As a teacher of one-to-one voice, the opportunity to examine my own story truthfully has produced some key pedagogical insights as well as some profound observations about myself. Many seemingly insignificant episodes in my life have taken on greater meaning when viewed through such a narrative lens.

The teaching imperatives to emerge from this chapter centre on the importance of providing students in formative years with a strong, balanced skill base and awareness of themselves as members of a wider musical world. This chapter has also served to highlight the diverse facets of being a performer and the numerous ways, both tacit and explicit, in which these elements shape a teaching strategy and philosophy. My pedagogical content is comprised of those technical skills that were absent from my own training, as well as a balanced and informed perspective on professional practice borne of longstanding activity, previous and current, within the profession. In serving voice students in this way, I assume the role of teacher as experienced colleague rather than a distant authority.

There is a certain vulnerability that accompanies the telling of one's story, especially those episodes of perceived failure. Yet these experiences are the ones that in my case proved ultimately most empowering. As Beck (2007) wisely states, "If you see failure as a monster stalking you, or one that has already ruined your life, take another look. That monster can become a benevolent teacher" (p. 92). Performers are familiar with vulnerability: It lies at the heart of meaningful communication in performance and so too, at the heart of meaningful one-to-one teaching. It is hoped that this chapter will serve to illustrate the potency of our individual stories in enriching pedagogical practice and to illuminate the significance of formative learning experiences and professional journeying in shaping the creative performer/teacher identity.

References

Adams, P. (2007, Apr 7–8). [Column]. *The weekend Australian magazine*, 42.

Beck, M. (2007, November). The woman who fell to earth. *Oprah Magazine*, 92.

Blades-Zeller, E. (2002). *A spectrum of voices: Prominent American voice teachers ciscuss the teaching of singing.* Lanham, MD; Oxford: Scarecrow Press.

Brandfonbrener, A. G. (2000). Performer's Perspective: Interview with Håkan Hagegård. *Medical Problems of Performing Artists, 15*(1), 3–5.

Broom, S. (2008, October). Second thoughts on love: The voyage out. *Oprah Magazine.*

Callaghan, J. (1999). *Singing and voice science.* San Diego: Singular Publishing.

Canning, H. (2007, Jan 15). On song at the front line. *The Australian,*14.

Chapman, J. L. (2006). *Singing and teaching singing: A holistic approach to classical voice.* San Diego: Plural Publishing.

Clandinin, D. J., & Connelly, F. M. (2000). *Narrative inquiry: Experience and story in qualitative research* (1st ed.). San Francisco: Jossey-Bass.

Ellis, C., & Bochner, A. (2000). Autoethnography, personal narrative, reflexivity. In N. K. Denzin & Y. S. Lincoln (Eds.), *Handbook of qualitative research* (2nd ed.) (pp. 733–763).

Fleming, R. (2004). *The inner voice: The making of a singer.* New York: Viking Penguin.

Lee, S. A. (1997). The artist as teacher: A psychological perspective. *Medical Problems of Performing Artists, 12*(2), 38–40.

Matheopoulos, H. (1991). *Diva: Great sopranos and mezzos discuss their art.* London: Victor Gollancz.

Persson, R. (1994). Concert musicians as teachers: On good intentions falling short. *European Journal for Higher Ability, 5*(1), 79–91.

Persson, R. (1996a). Brilliant performers as teachers: A case study of commonsense teaching in a conservatoire setting. *International Journal of Music Education 28*, 25–36.

Persson, R. (1996b). Studying with a musical maestro: A case study of commonsense teaching in artistic training. *Creativity Research Journal, 9*, 33–46.

Winfrey, O. (2008, December). Oprah talks to Daniel Pink. *Oprah Magazine*, 278.

Section Four
Researching Identity and Cross-Cultural Contexts

Chapter 12

From *Ca Tru* to the World
Understanding and Facilitating Musical Sustainability[1]

Huib Schippers

In the morning coffee break, I turn to a group of three young staff from the conservatorium hosting a conference in Hanoi on the training of professional musicians. During the presentations and discussions, they have been sitting almost motionless on chairs against the wall, strikingly quiet while their superiors were at the meeting table. However, during short conversations between sessions, I have delighted in their insightful and sometimes irreverent comments on specific presentations and the idiosyncrasies of various participants — including myself. Behind their demure manner hides a resolve to do things their way once their time comes; I sense the promise of a major generational shift from the old socialist order to a new Vietnam.

Expressing less than complete enthusiasm at the prospect of the obligatory group excursion to a temple or a silk village looming on the conference program, I ask whether it is possible to visit a place *unlikely* to attract any tourists, in order to get some impression of what this country means for its people rather than for its visitors. The young teachers are a little taken aback, but during lunch one of them, Pham Thi Hue, asks whether I would be interested to visit a village some 20 kilometres from the capital, where she has been studying music with an 80-year-old master musician of *ca tru*, an ancient genre of sung poetry. I confess I am more than a little interested. These are the opportunities I have always sought out while exploring the musics of the world over the past three decades. Sometimes they lead to nothing remarkable, but more often they at least delight, or — even better — challenge my pre-conceptions about practices of music from a global perspective, nurturing new insights and often inspiring new projects and collaborations.

A taxi is arranged, and while I watch my colleagues climbing into their buses we take off through the busy streets of central Hanoi, make our way across the suburbs, and drive into the countryside. Rice paddies and vegetable gardens, dotted with characterless concrete buildings with corrugated iron roofs, line the road. Halfway, as Hue points out, there is the village famous for canine meat. That does not need much pointing: The road is lined with uncompromising "hot dog stands": hairless fried animals ranging in size from Pekinese to Great Danes grace simple wooden tables along the wayside.

Arriving in the unassuming Ngãi Cầu Village in Hoài Đức district (not the faintest threat of tourism here), we walk through a narrow alley where a small gate gives access to a little compound harbouring a vegetable patch and a simple house with a front porch. Hue eloquently, and I at least reverently, greet our host, Nguyễn Thị Chúc. Being used to the etiquette surrounding visiting Indian gurus, I had asked Hue what I should bring. From a plastic bag, she produces the combination of ceremonial fruit and flowers offerings on our behalf, as well as more mundane soft drinks and processed cookies, overly sweet and artificially fruit-flavoured beyond recognition. They are accepted with grace, and we are invited in for tea. Inside, the house is dark. As my eyes adjust, I see a single room with a large Buddhist altar around the central wooden pillar, from which emanates an indeterminate number of beds for the master and her relatives, some of whom pass through unannounced during our visit as we exchange polite nods and smiles.

Such settings have all the characteristics to make me feel profoundly ill at ease. I am literally and metaphorically thousands of miles away from my comfort zone: I am used to being reasonably in control of matters, working in cultures where I know the music, the conventions, the people. I am clearly not in control here. I don't know the language, and have no clue of the decorum in this culture, of appropriate ways of dealing with elders, relatives or women in these settings. To be honest, I did not even know *ca tru* existed until a few days before.

Yet somehow, I feel surprisingly comfortable surrendering to this position of vulnerability. I have been in a similar situation several times before: nervously sipping tea with the Maharaja and Maharani of Jodhpur while researching the biography of my Indian music master who used to be employed as a court musician in their palace in the 1940s; travelling up the Gambia River in a small boat with *kora* player Alagi Mbye recording songs on the heroic deeds of Mandinke kings as we passed places of historical significance; squashed in a Turkish stadium in Bodrum to hear *saz* virtuoso Arif Sağ play live for an all-Turkish audience; arriving in the remote Indigenous community of Borroloola, where my whiteness emphatically and understandably was not a guarantee that I would be embraced by the local Yanyuwa people; and — perhaps most strikingly — finding myself alone with two hundred urns containing ashes of the dead as the "live audience" at a Balinese *gamelan* performance during a ceremony for the deceased in a small village in the mountains near Singaraja.

These are situations where my academic status, my relative affluence, my five languages and my culture-specific social skills have no currency. It is not only humbling; it is also refreshing to be removed from even the potential of pretence. It inspires alertness and receptiveness to engage with whatever occurs, without bias or preconceptions.

A long introductory dialogue in Vietnamese between Hue and master Chúc ensues; I switch off language recognition (nothing to latch on to for me in this foreign tonal tongue) and try to gauge vocal timbre, body language and facial expressions. These women seem to have negotiated a solid relationship: the master revered as an embodiment of traditional knowledge, but the student far from completely subservient, and respected for her understanding of the world. After about ten minutes of animated conversation, some of which obviously refers to me, Hue starts drawing me into the conversation: "Master Chúc says she is worried about the future of *ca tru* music. There used to be many musicians singing this style, now there are only a few old masters left. And the young people, they are not learning; this style is not taught at the Conservatorium. Only I am learning here" (personal communication, January 2007).

I have a strong passion for — and concern with — the rich variety of systems of music transmission across the world, which in many ways are the lifeline of aural traditions: one generation dropping out of the chain can mean the end of a musical style or genre. As the discussion develops, I ask whether I can get an idea of how *ca tru* is learned and taught. When I return later, a lesson is arranged for Hue on the porch in front of the little house. Soft sunlight across the courtyard; the women singing the poetry and marking its elusive rhythms on the *phách*, dressed in elegant black Vietnamese dress contrasting with whitewashed walls; cocks crowing in the background: The video turns out to be an ethnographer's dream.

The process that unfolds largely answers my expectations of an aural tradition that has successfully been handed down for centuries: the master sings a line, the student copies, gradually refining the words, melody, rhythm, timing, timbre and intonation over many repetitions. Both are sipping tea as text, rhythm and ornamentation are leisurely discussed. Even so, contemporary learning aids have entered into the system of this aural tradition: Hue uses written text to remember the poetry, and her minidisk recorder is on the tea cosy, so she can continue absorbing the subtleties of the music by playing it back time and again while she is cleaning the house or taking care of her daughter, whom she has since started teaching as well.

The mood, pace and depth of this transmission process contrast with what I have seen in the teaching studios at the Hanoi Conservatorium during the days before. While Vietnam has a strong commitment to "preserving and developing" traditional music — particularly of the Viet majority (many of the 53 ethnic minorities are in acute danger of musical extinction) — it has transformed once-vibrant living traditions into static repertoires: improvisation, fluid tempi and even instrument-specific tunings have largely been ironed out in institutional settings, which emulate the emphasis on efficiency in terms of learning technique and repertoire found in most Western conservatoires.

To me, this crude canonisation seems like a "slow puncture" approach to sustainability: while it is officially being supported, the music is robbed of some of its most attractive features, so it runs the risk of being met with apathy by the next generation. But then again, the barely hidden agenda of the director of the institute is more the "development" than the "preservation" of Viet music: rather than focusing on the subtleties of music for soloists or small ensembles, he dreams of large orchestras of traditional instruments, modelled on Chinese examples. He seems ready to sacrifice timbre, improvisation and even distinctive tuning systems in the process. Meanwhile, some of the students who have graduated in traditional musics venture outside and work with surviving old masters to breathe life into the music they have learned. I find it striking that they feel this need after a 15-year association with the conservatorium (from selection at age eight until their final degree at 23); in fact a perfect length of time to master complex oral traditions if the curriculum is developed and delivered with sensitivity to the specific qualities of the music culture rather than a carbon copy from Western classical music.

As the afternoon passes in the little village, I gradually get a more comprehensive picture of the rise and fall of an elegant sung poetry, accompanied by the long-necked lute Đàn đáy and *phách*, a wood-block beaten with two bamboo sticks. *Ca tru* developed as ritual music in village and neighbourhood temples, and as entertainment in private houses where people would gather to enjoy singers render romantic poetry, sipping tea and drinking wine at low tables. Over time, the secular tradition moved to the city and gained considerable popularity, while its ritual counterpart all but disappeared. Dedicated *ca tru* houses were established. During the 1950s, there were ten of these houses in Khâm Thiên Street in Hanoi (Nguyễn Thị Chúc, personal communication, January 2007). However, some of these houses began to offer less widely accepted forms of entertainment as well; *ca tru* became yet another music that blossomed in the context of houses of ill repute, like geisha culture in Japan, tango in Argentine, *raï* in Algeria and *thumri* in India.

In the eyes of the communist government, however, this connection proved to be almost lethal for *ca tru*. The immoral places were outlawed, and the musicians tainted by association were sent back to villages to work in the fields. *Ca tru* had no prestige, no money, no infrastructure, no training, no audience. This was not caused by a lack of creative appeal; non-musical factors prevented this music from continuing to flourish for over 30 years. Now a small number of people are trying to revive the tradition. The music is being documented (most notably by the Musicological Institute in Hanoi which, thanks to fortuitous political connections, has recently moved to an enviable, purpose-built building in one of the best suburbs of Hanoi). Small-scale performances can be seen on occasion. I found one in a small record shop where the displays were covered with black cloth to create the atmosphere of a performance space, with low tables and cushions for the audience to evoke traditional settings. Some teaching is being organised informally, as well as a "*ca tru* club" in a suburban communal temple; much of it by the indefatigable Hue, who has also managed to reach the national press on several occasions with her heroic battle for the preservation of this music.

In the evening, back in the Hanoi Prince Hotel (I never got around to asking what in this pleasantly unassuming but utterly graceless concrete building inspired its royal name), I reflect on what I have just witnessed and learned. It resonates strongly with other experiences from the past two decades. I think of sitting inside the office of Mr Kofi, the Head of the Music Department at the University of Cape Coast in Ghana. While he entertained my colleague Trevor Wiggins and me, outside his office I heard a student playing Bach's *Well-tempered*

Clavier on a piano that was seriously out of tune — a wonderfully ironic experience given the title of the piece. Like much of the music of Bach, it survived this butchering, and even gained an unintended but fascinating twenty-first century "global edge". Our host assured us that, besides his serious classes on Bach and Wagner (he had spent a little time studying in Germany), he also left some room for African music: some of the cleaners on the campus were Ewe, and they occasionally were given an afternoon off to work with the students on their percussion music.

I was shocked: I had heard the music of this particular ethnic group before. It entails some of the most intricate rhythmic patterns in African music: elusive, subtly shifting, almost melodic, like fugues in percussion. At CalArts, one of the more prestigious liberal arts colleges in United States (established by Walt Disney and funded by the Disney Corporation), it has featured in the world music degree course since the 1970s. It is hard to understand how it can have such low status in Ghana itself; 50 years after independence, colonial preconceptions of superiority and the association with economic and military power still seem to define the musical hierarchy (cf. Schippers, in press).

I cynically — or maybe just strategically — think that increasing local awareness of the status of Ewe percussion in the United States might make a difference. In India I have witnessed this in action. There has been a major revival of the ancient but almost extinct style known as *dhrupad* after French scholar Alain Daniélou "revealed" this as the "true" tradition of Indian music, and started inviting its aged masters to perform in Paris. Before long, there were *dhrupad* festivals in India: If the French like it, it must be something worth preserving. When I asked famous sitarist Ravi Shankar about this, he ridiculed this process: "The French thought they 'discovered' *dhrupad. Ah, le dhrupad, c'est magnifique! Dhrupad* used to be great, but it is not any more. They are holding up a skeleton and saying 'look what a beautiful woman'" (Schippers, 1983). To him, some European fancies seemed to be *The Emperor's Clothes* in world music.

I think of other forms of music that have profited from popularity in the West and a strong basis back home: tango, djembe, gamelan, samba, flamenco. These are music genres that have not only weathered globalisation, but profited from it in expanding markets. In spite of the pervasive ethnomusicological conviction that music can only be really understood in its original context, I have been amazed at how most music appears to travel remarkably well. Hardly any music has an identifiable "original context"; repeated recontextualisation is the rule rather than an exception. This goes for Western classical music (from church to court to upper middle-class audiences), for jazz, for rock, for pop, and for most forms of world music. Other music has come into being because of globalisation, from the delightfully sweet film songs of Bollywood to salsa, and the exotic mix of samba and Indian *bhangra* to *sambhangra* in London (Higgins, 2000).

Yet I see other music that seems to be at risk of disappearing in this environment of rapid change, often for extra-musical reasons: the effects of colonisation, migration, and rapid technological development have put a major strain on the capacity of most music to gradually evolve with social and cultural changes. In other cases, the threat is more active, including forcible displacement of people, war or genocide, religious prejudice, or adverse laws and regulations. I am not the preservationist type. Musical instruments, styles and genres have been emerging and disappearing throughout history; I see this as a natural process driven by inevitably changing tastes and contexts. But over the past five decades, it has intensified exponentially with drastic political, social, technological and economic change. The reality that music once constrained to a single locale is now available across the planet (and the underlying issues of markets, power and perceptions of prestige) has created shifts in musical dynamics that led to opportunities for some, but threatened the futures of many other forms of musical expression, well beyond the evolutionary processes that have governed musical diversity in earlier periods.

When I discussed this phenomenon with leading ethnomusicologist Anthony Seeger, who has worked extensively with UNESCO and with the Suyá in the Amazon, he expressed it succinctly and eloquently:

> The problem is it's not really an even playing field: it's not as though these are just disappearing, they're 'being disappeared'; there's an active process in the disappearance of many traditions around the world. Some of them are being disappeared by majority groups that want to eliminate the differences of their minority groups within their nations, others are being disappeared by missionaries or religious groups of various kinds who find music offensive and want to eliminate it. Others are being disappeared by copyright legislation. (QCRC, 2008, §11)

Technological developments, infrastructural challenges, socioeconomic change, failing educational systems and loss of prestige constitute additional reasons for the decline of many musics I have found in fieldwork and discussions with colleagues.

I am aware these threats to global musical diversity are hardly a secret. In the past few years, UNESCO has adopted a Universal Declaration on

Cultural Diversity (2001) and a Convention for the Safeguarding of Intangible Cultural Heritage (2003). For several decades now, governments, NGOs and development agencies have provided support for specific music cultures over a defined period of time, ranging from a single event or festival to projects running for a number of years. I have seen these function as a highly positive impulse for the cultures supported. Another way to counteract decline in musical diversity has been the documentation of traditions in danger of disappearing. This is occurring on a considerable scale across cultures and continents. Through these initiatives, the sound of many traditions is being preserved for posterity, allowing future generations to reconstruct, at least to some extent, musical styles and genres that may have since disappeared.

Valuable as they are, I do not think these efforts provide sufficient basis for the actual survival of musical styles as part of an unbroken, living tradition, which many will argue is a key condition for maintaining the essence (explicit and tacit, tangible and intangible) of specific styles and genres. I start conceiving ways to work in close collaboration with communities themselves; not only for their histories and "authentic" practices, but also for their dynamics and potential for recontextualisation in contemporary settings, which includes considering new musical realities, changing values and attitudes, as well as political and market forces.

This shift from historical preservation from a Eurocentric perspective to sustainability from the perspective of the stakeholders themselves resonates with the work of "applied" ethnomusicologists, who denounce the illusion of objectivity and detachment, and are committed to "giving back" to the cultures and communities that inform their work. From my work and experiences over the past 30 years, I strongly identify with such an approach, which acknowledges recontextualisation of performance practices, institutionalising transmission processes, changing audiences and markets in terms of business models and technology, as well as increasingly fluid relationships between ethnic background and musical tastes/activities, particularly in relation to youth culture.

As the idea for a global project to promote musical sustainability from this perspective emerged, I discussed it with Deborah Wong, the President of the Society for Ethnomusicology. She applauded the fact that it "is not romanticised. It's so easy to talk about musics that are in danger of disappearing ... This is looking at music as something that is already mediatised, already globalised" (QCRC, 2008, § 3). In a later conversation, Anthony Seeger was enthused about the idea of a "systematic study of musical traditions to see how they are sustained and what makes the successful ones successful, and how the other ones are being affected by some of these causes of 'disappearing' ... and also how they're being affected simply by changes in musical taste musical interest that have nothing to do with oppression or power". He said he believes that

> if we understood those better ... communities would probably be able to better defend the things that they think need to be defended and preserved, and safeguard those traditions they think they'd like to safeguard, and change the ones they want to change. Instead we are reinventing the wheel every time we face a community that's trying to preserve its own traditions. (QCRC, 2008, § 11)

After a round of discussions with a number of other colleagues around the world, I came to distinguish five major domains that appear to influence the sustainability of any music culture beyond musical structure and content itself. As is evident from the story of *ca tru*, the realities of being a musician and one's relationship to the community (for instance, in terms of careers and esteem) are of great importance for the future of any tradition. Second, systems of education and training, or how people learn music (formally or informally) will determine whether there will be competent performers in the next generation. For many musics, the music industry (media and markets) is crucial, whether who pays is an audience, a government, a corporation, or philanthropy.

Infrastructure and regulations are often taken for granted and underestimated, yet there is music that owes its existence to leniency in enforcing sound restrictions, protection of copyright, and international trade agreements, while other musics have virtually been regulated or taxed out of existence. The final domain, contexts and constructs, may be the key to sustainability for much music: how it relates to its stakeholders, how it functions in traditional and new contexts, and especially how it is regarded in its community in terms of cosmologies, aesthetics and prestige, which has always been a crucial trigger for musical sustainability.

I fully realise that these domains are far from straightforward. Each of the domains overlaps and interrelates in how it affects music cultures. For example, change can be driven by shifts in values and attitudes, technological developments and/or audience behaviour. The manner of musical transmission is strongly determined by the regulations governing its (institutional) environment; while media attention, markets and audiences can often be linked to issues of public perception and prestige.

The power and potential of such a template is easily illustrated by not only applying it to some ailing music "out in the jungle", but to Western classical opera in the 21st century. At first glance, this music would seem to have insurmountable obstacles in terms of required infrastructure — a theatre with excellent acoustics, a large stage, and a fly tower; extended and expensive training to a high-level for the participants — director, conductor, soloists, orchestra, and chorus; and finally an audience sufficiently enculturated to appreciate the event, and sufficiently affluent to be able to afford tickets. For all my belief in impossible projects, if anyone came to me and said they wanted to start a new genre of music that had all these requirements I would have told them it would never get up. In spite of this, I observe that by and large, opera survives quite well on its carefully constructed prestige as one of the highest and most complete forms of art of European culture, which inspires the governments, corporate sponsors and philanthropists to support it to a level incomparable to any other art form.

While opera played its cards right in the area of constructs (values and attitudes), much commercial popular music did so with audiences, media and markets; and country music or brass bands in engaging communities. Indian classical music developed a change-resistant system of learning music through close association with gurus, which has outlasted court patronage by almost a century now. Most of these "successful" musics also braved major changes in context, while other musics continue to struggle. Why is that? What are the underlying forces? And if properly understood, can they be influenced?

As I combine and order the reflections triggered by a seemingly random taxi ride out of Hanoi, the picture of a global project to identify mechanisms for musical survival emerges. I believe these mechanisms, once identified, can inform and empower communities to forge their own musical futures, if made available freely through an accessible web-interface which will make it possible for people across the world to access advanced tools for analysis and practical case studies to inform forward planning across cultures and communities, on their own terminals and on their own terms. This will eliminate the need for me (or any other middle-aged white ethnomusicologist) to decide what is worth preserving and how.

What can that mean for *ca tru*? Hue shares with me her dreams about reinstating a *ca tru* house where these refined songs will be sung again in an intimate music room for interested listeners. In contemporary Hanoi, such a dream may well become a reality by linking it to a steady stream of culture-oriented tourists, who, by paying $25 for an evening of traditional entertainment (not watered down for hotels), can help support a number of talented and dedicated musicians, who can in turn link to a local school and the conservatorium to train a next generation. Sometimes, the insights and connections that come with the privilege of having seen and experienced music across several cultures can help making such dreams a reality. I cannot think of a more valuable way to apply my research (and myself!) to giving back to the musics and people that have taught and delighted me so much over the years.

Endnote

1   This article constitutes a reworking of the (non-refereed) essay "Ecologies of Creative Diversity," which appeared in Essentially Creative (*Griffith Review*, Autumn 2009). It draws on fieldwork conducted in Vietnam during July 2006, January 2007 and March 2009, and earlier experiences by the author described in his forthcoming monograph *Facing the Music: Shaping Music Education from a Global Perspective*, which is scheduled to appear with Oxford University Press later in 2009.

References

Higgins, L. (2000). "ConCussion, a synthesis of old and new technologies." *Music Education Research*, 2(1), 87–93.

Queensland Conservatorium Research Centre. (2008). *Twelve voices on sustainable futures*. [Video recording.] Brisbane: QCRC.

Schippers, H. (1983). Interview with Ravi Shankar. *Indian Music Newsletter*, 6, 3.

Schippers, H. (in press). *Facing the music: Shaping music education from a global perspective*. New York: Oxford University Press.

UNESCO. (2001). *Declaration on the promotion of cultural diversity*. Retrieved March 1, 2008, from www.unesco.org/education/imld_2002/unversal_decla.shtml.

UNESCO. (2003). *Declaration on Intangible Cultural Heritage*. Retrieved March 1, 2008, from www.unesco.org/culture/ich/.

Chapter 13

Looking into the Trochus Shell
Autoethnographic Reflections on a Cross-Cultural Collaborative Music Research Project

Katelyn Barney and Lexine Solomon

Lexine and Katelyn are standing ready at the front of the seminar room at Griffith University. Katelyn glances over at Lexine and waits for her to start. Lexine clears her voice and begins:

"Good evening. I'd like to acknowledge the traditional owners of the land on which we meet tonight. My name is Lexine Solomon and I'm a Torres Strait Islander woman. My father, who raised me, is from Badu Island in the Torres Strait. This is Katelyn Barney and we're going to present on our research project 'Performing on the Margins: Torres Strait Islander Women Contemporary Performers'. I'd like to welcome you all here today". Lexine then pauses, swallows, smiles at Katelyn, and looks back at the audience. She thinks to herself, what am I doing here? I am an Indigenous Australian woman presenting in this "white" place. I don't "get" this academic scene. Katelyn smiles at Lexine and nods encouragingly to continue. "I'd like to welcome you all," Lexine continues, "by singing a Torres Strait Islander welcome song. The language was recently given to me by Aunty Bonnie Robin. The language is Torres Strait language Kala Lagaw Ya and the words say 'we extend our hands and welcome you'". Lexine begins to sing, her strong smooth voice fills the room. Katelyn closes her eyes briefly and listens to Lexine. Not for the first time, Katelyn wonders what does the audience think when they see these two women standing together: a non-Indigenous music researcher and an Indigenous performer and researcher. Do they wonder how they ended up working together? Who is benefitting? Is Katelyn viewed as just another non-Indigenous researcher "writing off the backs of blacks"?[1]

꙳

This chapter is an autoethnographic reflection on our research experiences together undertaking the project *Performing on the Margins: Torres Strait Islander Women Contemporary Performers*. We draw on narrative "vignettes" (Ellis, 1998; Humphreys, 2005) and our journal entries to reflect on the complexities of cross-cultural collaborative research and "to bring life to research and bring research to life" (Ellis, 1998). Like Humphreys, we hope that our autoethnographic narratives can "connect the personal and the cultural" and place ourselves within the social context of our research (Humphreys, 2005, p. 841).

Elsewhere (Barney & Solomon, in press) we began this story about our research journey together but only scratched the surface of our experiences. Here we want to open the door further to "look into the trochus shell" and expose our experiences working together. Rare and unique, trochus shells are found in the Torres Strait region. The mottled red, green and white shells are often difficult to find and contain a thick inner layer of mother-of-pearl. We use this as a metaphor to think about what lies within, to expose the pearl under layers of "the messiness of lived experience" (Ellingson, 1998, p. 4).

Like others we are "struggling with the dilemma of how to position" ourselves "within our research project to reveal aspects of our own worlds, challenge our assumptions, locate ourselves through the eyes of the others and observe themselves observing" (adapted from Ellis & Bochner, 1996, p. 28). Following Holman Jones's footsteps (1998), in this chapter we want to make visible rather than conceal the fleshy issues and challenges we face, puzzle out the complexities and possible benefits of non-Indigenous and Indigenous research collaborations, and highlight the interpersonal, engaged, and lived nature of this research process.

A Dialogue about the Project

Katelyn and Lexine are at Katelyn's place in the lounge room. Katelyn's dog Sacha is sitting on the chair, resting her head against her legs. Lexine lies comfortably on the couch, feeling full from lunch.

They are taking a break from working on a presentation that they are preparing for a conference.

"We really need to add a section in the presentation describing what exactly the project is about," Katelyn says.

"Yes, you're right," Lexine pauses, "do you want say that bit or should I?" she says lifting herself up to sit on the couch.

"We could divide it up. I guess I could talk about how we began this project in 2007 to interview 20 Torres Strait Islander women who perform in contemporary music contexts. We focused on the issues of identity, representation, and how Torres Strait Islander women performers have been marginalised by academic studies and the music industry and together we travelled across Australia to conduct interviews with performers," suggests Katelyn.

"It's also important to tell people exactly where the Torres Strait is because some people still don't seem to know," Lexine comments, and moves a little on the couch to get comfortable.

"Yes, so we'd better show a map to demonstrate where it is situated between Cape York and Papua New Guinea, and maybe you could talk about how although Islanders are recognised as having strong ties to the Torres Strait Islands, many have moved to mainland Australia to further their education and employment opportunities after World War II. What do you think?" Katelyn takes a notepad and starts making notes.

"That's important to include, and maybe we could include in a PowerPoint slide that approximately two thirds of the population of Torres Strait Islanders, total population 33,100, now live on mainland Australia," Lexine adds.

Katelyn looks at her bookshelf and sees books about Aboriginal music by Dunbar-Hall and Gibson, Ellis, Marrett, Mackinlay, Magowan, Stubington, Neuenfeldt, and others. "And we need to acknowledge that although there has been a long history of research with Aboriginal people in Australia, there has been relatively little research on the contemporary music-making of Torres Strait Islander women."

"That quote from Shnukal is so true, isn't it?" Lexine says. "They are 'a minority within a minority and the women a minority again — triply marginalised' (Shnukal, 1999, p. 180). Our project aims to allow Torres Strait Islander women performers to voice their experiences and be recognised as a unique part of Australia's diverse Indigenous population."

Katelyn jots down more of their ideas on the notepad. "We could also mention that many Torres Strait Islander women performers were keen to see the project happen, and we were lucky to gain funding from the Australian Institute of Aboriginal and Torres Strait Islander Studies too."

"Yes, and the outcome of the project will be that they are provided with recognition through the creation of a written report and a DVD which will be given to the performers and housed in AIATSIS. Yes, that should do." Lexine settles back on to the couch for a snooze.

The Politics of Representation: Being a Non-Indigenous Woman Representing Indigenous Women

Katelyn's Vignette

It is October 18, 2008. I am presenting a lecture to a small group of students undertaking the course "Working with Indigenous People" at The University of Queensland. All of the students are non-Indigenous and are mostly studying anthropology and Indigenous studies. The PowerPoint slides are projected on the wall with pictures of the Indigenous women I've worked with, and I tell the students about my PhD research: "I have been working with Indigenous Australian women since 2002 when I began my PhD. I interviewed 20 Indigenous Australian women who perform contemporary music, travelling to Sydney, Melbourne, Darwin, Adelaide, Alice Springs and Gold Coast to conduct interviews. I focused on non-Indigenous expectations of Indigenous Australian women who perform contemporary music and how Indigenous women perform around, within, and against these expectations and stereotypes through their music."

I look at the students and they seem to look blankly at me so I quickly go to the next slide with a picture of Lexine and I sharing a watermelon together.

"I'm currently working on a collaborative research project with Indigenous Australian performer Lexine Solomon." I look at the picture of us and I notice how white my skin looks next to her black skin. "I'm a non-Indigenous researcher and very aware of the uneasy history of research between Indigenous and non-Indigenous people. Because I am non-Indigenous I realise I'm complicit in that history. I'm constantly wondering: "How do I 'unlearn' my privilege as a white woman scholar" (Holman Jones, 1998, p. 17) and keep Indigenous women's voices at the fore?"

"*Why are you so apologetic?*" The voice whispers.

Sorry? What? Who is it? I can't see them but their voice permeates through my mind.

"*Your discussion of your research,*" the internal voice continues a little louder, "*You are apologising for not being Indigenous and it verges on the mea culpa that is itself patronising.*"

"What do you mean?" I ask.

"*You talk as if Indigeneity is a priori some guarantee of 'authenticity' and wisdom. It sounds like an apology,*" the internal voice says.

"But I'm not trying to apologise for being non-Indigenous but just acknowledge it," I interrupt. "Huggins and others talk about the importance of acknowledging your speaking position, and speaking from your own experiences. That's one of the reasons collaborative research holds so much promise, and Lexine asked me if I wanted to work on a project with her so ...".

Another voice cuts in, "Some of us will be more open and tolerant than others." This voice I recognise: It's of Indigenous activist and my colleague at The University of Queensland, Jackie Huggins. "There is a long history of violence, mistrust, guilt and fear that cannot be erased overnight. Know when you are becoming an intruder rather than an accomplice" (Huggins, 1998, p. 84).

Before I can respond, another voice chimes in. "Look at the reality of your own life," says Indigenous writer Anita Heiss from her position sitting up the back of the room with Jackie, "your invisible whiteness" (2007, p. 42).

"But, I'm trying to acknowledge my whiteness, make it visible," I say.

Anita continues, "You will never know what it's like, to walk in our shoes. No matter how long you research, no matter how many interviews you do, notes you take, videos you make, opinions you form" (2007, p. 85).

I swallow hard, unsure of what to say. I realise the students are all looking at me expecting a response. I am visible, present, and feel vulnerable.

Being a non-Indigenous researcher working with Indigenous people is a complex issue. There has been a long history of non-Indigenous people researching Indigenous people, and as Smith notes (1999), research has been "one of the dirtiest words in the Indigenous vocabulary" (p. 1) because of the exploitation that has occurred. Indigenous Australian perspectives on whether or not non-Indigenous people should research and write about Indigenous people are diverse. Phillips notes that non-Indigenous people "are writing as outsiders to that culture and their representation would be vastly different to the representation defined, developed and refined by an Indigenous writer" (as cited in McDonald, 1997, p. 13). Huggins (1998) takes a different stance and believes that, in some instances, non-Indigenous people can write on Indigenous issues, and notes the importance of acknowledging one's speaking position.

Non-Indigenous researchers working with Indigenous Australian performers have discussed, and continue to discuss, their position in different ways. Dunbar-Hall and Gibson "acknowledge that as non-Indigenous researchers, with security of income and housing, we remain in positions of privilege in comparison to many of the subjects of this book", and hope to improve "general understanding about Aboriginal culture" (2004, p. 22). Mackinlay has written extensively about her position as a "halfee" — wife to an Indigenous man, mother to two Aboriginal sons, but at the same time a non-Indigenous female academic (2007, p. 15). Reed (2002) writes openly from her position as a non-Indigenous scholar and acknowledges she is striving towards a better future between Indigenous and non-Indigenous Australians. Similarly, I feel it is important to acknowledge my own positioning. It is my voice present in my writing yet I aim to incorporate the voices of Indigenous Australian women performers in an effort to keep their perspectives to the foreground — to tell their stories with their words. I hope to empower them and hopefully benefit them by providing access to their music for a wider audience. Collaborating through research with Lexine has been a way of including an Indigenous person as co-researcher and collaborator. As Dyck, Lynham and Anderson demonstrate, "power differentials between researcher and researched" can be minimised through collaborations among women (1995, p. 622). However, they note that continually negotiated interactions and appropriate methods are essential if we are to "give voice" to women who are usually silenced by academic discourse. There are no easy answers but I continually strive to find a way forward which is useful and beneficial to the Indigenous women I work with.

An Insider Outside: A Torres Strait Islander Performer Researching 'Other' Torres Strait Islander Women Performers

Lexine's Vignette: Have I Betrayed Someone?

During June 2000 while still residing in Brisbane, I was interviewed by a researcher collating information from Indigenous performers in South East Queensland. Little did I know that interview would be the beginning of so many more interviews. People wanted to know what I thought, what my experiences have been and what I had to tell the world of music research. One of these people was PhD student Katelyn Barney. I thoroughly enjoyed the experience of being interviewed by her, and from this I embraced an opportunity to become "the researcher".

In 2005 I relocated to Canberra and undertook my own research project, to produce a resource kit to empower Indigenous women across the nation. I interviewed 25 Indigenous women from my life — friends, family, and mentors — and then when finalising this project I got the idea of working with a qualified researcher. I thought of Katelyn and e-mailed her about my interest. We talked about a lack of research and information regarding Torres Strait Islander women performers in contemporary music. Before we knew it, funding was secured and we began the project. We interviewed my fellow Torres Strait Islander women to find out their perspectives — these connections came from my family circles and from links Katelyn had developed through other research she had completed.

While collaborating with Katelyn on our research project, I have discovered that I am on both sides of the fence. I have become the researcher, yet I am also a Torres Strait Islander, female, and a performer of contemporary music. I have a voice in the research and I must ensure that I reach the right outcome. Does my voice have the right approach? Will my identity still be represented and will the women we have interviewed have representation? Have I betrayed my community by becoming a researcher? Will the project separate me from my fellow Torres Strait Islander women performers?

~~

The blurrings between insider/outsider in research have been explored by many, yet Somerville and Perkins note that although the challenges of research collaboration is often discussed by non-Indigenous people, there are very few reflections on the research process from the perspectives of Indigenous people. As Haig-Brown questions: "Does the process of doing research separate a researcher from the community?" (2001, p. 21). For me (Lexine) there are many obligations — to fellow Torres Strait Islander women performers, to family, to community, to the university, and to the funding body, and I must cross many borders to negotiate these roles.

A number of scholars discuss cross-cultural research as "border work" which involves border maintenance, a focus on difference and border crossing (Haig-Brown, 2001). Homi Bhabha calls the zone of cultural contact "the cutting edge of translation and negotiation, the in-between space — that carries the burden of the meaning of culture" (1994, p. 141). Similar notions have been developed by other cultural theorists to describe aspects of cultural contact: Anzaldua (1987) as the "borderlands", hooks (1990) as the "margins" and the "edge", Giroux (1992) as "border crossing", and Soja (2000) as the "third space". The multiple speaking positions I assume as insider (Torres Strait Islander woman, community member, and performer) and partial outsider (researcher in Indigenous Australian performance) must be continually negotiated.

Non-Indigenous/Indigenous Collaborations

There are many examples of collaborations between non-Indigenous and Indigenous Australian people in a number of settings including film (e.g., *Ten Canoes*, 2006), historical accounts (e.g., Roe with Muecke, 1983; Pederson & Woorunmurra, 1995), and auto/biographies (e.g., Flick & Goodall, 2004). There are also examples of music collaborations including Barwick's recording with Warumungu women of Tennant Creek (Yawulyu Mungamunga, 2000), Corn and Gumbala (2002), Marrett's recordings with Maralung (Maralung, 1993), Mackinlay's research with the Yanyuwa women of Borroloola (2007), and Neuenfeldt's recording projects with Seaman Dan (Dan 1999, 2001, 2004, 2006) and his recording work with other Indigenous Australian performers (e.g. Paipa, 2003; Sailing the Southeast Wind, 2003; Saltwater Songs, 2005; Strike Em!, 2000). However, with the exception of a few scholars (e.g. Mackinlay, 2002; Neuenfeldt, 2001, 2007) there is little discussion of how collaborative research processes between Indigenous/non-Indigenous people in music research work in practice.

There is a growing body of research on cross-cultural collaborative research (Bochner, 1982; Hooker, 2003) and also more specifically between Indigenous and non-Indigenous people in many settings outside of Australia. This includes Canada (Haig-Brown, 2001; Haig-Brown & Archibald, 1996), Bali (Dunbar-Hall & Adnyana, 2004) and New Zealand (McLean, 2003; Nunns & Thomas, 2005). Yet as Somerville and Perkins point out, the literature on research collaboration is largely prescriptive rather than analytical and many examples of collaborative research "gloss over the negotiations of collaboration. They fail to account for the power relations that saturate the research site and are the conditions of knowledge production" (2003, p. 255). Goodall notes that "the challenge for all of us … is to find ways to represent such relationships in our writing, rather than to make them disappear from our pages and to retreat them from our life and work" and "it is critically important to take an active role in a collaborative relationship, throughout its phases" (2005, p. 80). We are attempting to take up Goodall's challenge to write and speak openly about our collaborative research process, our relationship, and our experiences with performers. There are of course always "potentially thorny issues" (Dyck, Lynham & Anderson, 1995, p. 611) that arise in collaborative research, yet we believe it is important to acknowledge the good with the bad as "in hiding from uncomfortable experiences, we do our work less well" (Selby, 2004, p. 143).

Fieldwork Experiences: Collaborators, Companions and the "Discomfort Zone" (Somerville & Perkins, 2003)

Katelyn's Journal Entry: Thursday Island

December 12, 2007. At 4 pm Sylvia, Lexine's contact, rang to say she would meet us in 10 minutes and we would follow her to Ina's place — one of the famous Mills Sisters. We arrived at Ina's place — children and grandchildren seemed to live there. Ina was sewing in the lounge. Pictures of family, the Mills Sisters and other family on the walls, including her sister Rita Mills's album launch poster. Ina was friendly and had her walker next to her, she's just turned 80. We set up the video and laptop and then did the interview. We asked all the questions, she answered, and we got the audio and video footage. Yet I felt like we hardly scratched the surface. She seemed to steer clear of certain topics and didn't go into too much depth. But it was great to interview her. She gave us each a homemade tea towel and Lexine bought a sarong.

Figure 1
Katelyn and Lexine cool off with watermelon on Thursday Island, December 2007.

Lexine's Journal Entry: Thursday Island

December 12, 2007. Thank God for companions on the journey. Today when Katelyn and I stepped off the ferry that brought us and all other arrivals from Horn Island, my friend Mrs Gear[2] was standing on the wharf ready to show us life on Thursday Island. Mrs Gear is so excited to have visitors. We got Katelyn checked into her motel and then we did a quick look around the island. This is my second trip to the Torres Strait Islands. My first trip was in the 1990s but I didn't know too many people. I am learning that my friend, Mrs Gear, has connections all across the island; being seen with her opens doors. She lends us her car and willingly shares about who to talk to, where to find them, how to get a look into life on the island, hear about cultural ties and most importantly, share food with family.

She has been one of the most hospitable people on this research journey. I met Mrs Gear, a Torres Strait Islander woman, through the university course we are studying. I feel I am accepted as a Torres Strait Islander by someone who is a true "Torres Strait Islander". It's her birthplace and she lives up here. The Torres Strait Islands could be misconstrued as being a different country. Life runs to a different pace and today Mrs Gear showed us the value of family by including both Katelyn and I on our short visit to Thursday Island. This companion is helping me link with a nation of people, and invested into the project a sweet serenity that fills our hearts and our bellies.

Lexine and Katelyn drive in the hire car to Healesville outside Melbourne to interview Torres Strait Islander performer Topaz. They drive slowly through into the cul de sac and find the house. As they are parking outside, Topaz comes out, her wild fuzzy hair standing on end.

Lexine whispers to Katelyn, "If there's food provided we have to eat it. Torres Strait Islander women are great cooks!" Topaz has a few missing teeth and is wearing a NAISDA Dance College T-shirt. There is graffiti on the side of the house, kids walk around outside on the street. Katelyn decides to take all her stuff inside rather than leaving anything in the car.

Topaz greets them warmly, hugging Lexine. "Ah Aunty," Lexine says, "This is Katelyn, my researcher."

Topaz turns to Katelyn, "Hi Katelyn, nice to meet you," and hugs her. "Come in, come in," she says.

The fan is on and as they pass a room, the TV is blaring with football on. As they enter into the kitchen the smell of cooking envelopes them. Lexine feels a little hungry and light headed so is pleased there will be food. There are pictures of numerous children on the fridge.

"I've made a stir fry, shall we eat first?" Topaz says as she gets plates out of the cupboard, not waiting for an answer.

Lexine looks at Katelyn, winks and then says to Topaz, "Okay, that would be great."

Lexine and Topaz talk about different families and people they know. Katelyn listens, nods, but doesn't know the people they are talking about.

"Hey Camera Girl," Topaz suddenly calls to Katelyn. "Shall we start soon?"

Katelyn doesn't really mind being called "camera girl," and begins setting up the video camera. As she sets up, Topaz turns to catch a glimpse of the TV in the other room.

"No offence to you," she says glancing at Katelyn, "but there are too many white girls on TV. They're all blonde, blue eyes."

⌐✑

Katelyn's Vignette: "That White Girl: Dr Katelyn"

I dream I'm at a gig with Lexine. We are watching Stacey Lui from Thursday Island perform at an open air performance space and as we sway to the music Lexine sings along to some of the words. Another Torres Strait Islander performer walks past and Lexine calls out to her, "Hey, Selena over here!"

"Lexy, sistagirl! How are ya?"

They laugh and embrace. I clear my throat, "Hi Selena," I say but she doesn't look at me.

"How's your uncle?" Selena asks.

"Ah esso, he's alright," Lexine says in Torres Strait Creole.

"Good good."

"You get my e-mail?" Lexine asks.

"Yes, sis sorry I haven't replied. Been so busy. What was it about?"

"Ah well, I'm doing research with Katelyn Barney. You know her?"

"Hello?" I say again.

"I think so, she that white girl?"

"Yep that's her. She's Doctor Katelyn now."

"Doctor Katelyn, wa? Since when she a doctor?"

"For a little while, she interviewed me for that project."

"Hm, she interviewed me too. Interviewed me and then got a doctorate. What did I get?"

I try to get their attention, try to say something. But I suddenly realise this is a dream and they can't hear or see me. Still I am a little annoyed and hurt by their comments. I want to tell them, I didn't "get" a PhD because I interviewed them. In fact I interviewed 20 Indigenous women performers but then I had to transcribe, find themes, analyse the data, find a theoretical framework, write up the project, and ask for the approval of performers to include their comments. Nevertheless I still feel guilty and think: what did they get out of the project? How did it benefit them? But they can't see me and I am unable to respond. I am invisible — like Indigenous women often feel.

≈

Lexine's Journal Entry: Canberra

February 15, 2009. I'm sitting at home in the kitchen, going to do some writing for this paper Katelyn and I are putting together. When I think of our research together, there are many good memories but at the same time I can't help but think of what Margaret Somerville and Tony Perkins call the "discomfort zone" that sometimes occurs in the negotiations of the research process. As a mainland Torres Strait Islander, discomfort has several layers. I was raised by a South Sea Islander mother in her North Queensland country hometown, with a Torres Strait Islander father whose values were embedded in how I was raised as the eldest daughter of seven children. When I first saw Thursday Island and the Torres Straits, I was already in my 20s. Sometimes I wonder if Dr Katelyn Barney has wasted her time connecting with me — forming alliances. She may think I tolerate her — but I am taunted by the feeling that she tolerates me.

I admit I toy with words talking to Katelyn about her heritage, calling her a "skinny white girl" — we've got this friendship now but thankfully she hasn't replied the opposite, calling me a "big black girl" — well okay — it's all truth after all.

I am wearing a couple of hats in my role as researcher and artist and I am using my Torres Strait Islander heritage to connect the relevance of these roles. I was told by a Torres Strait Islander raised and residing in the islands that Torres Strait Islanders from the mainland do things differently to them up in the islands. Because I had to be told that information, I knew I had offended someone. You see the layers must have respect and I can't afford to jeopardise my link to all Torres Strait Islanders for the sake of the research. I never mean to offend anyone but the discomfort zone shows boundaries and it depends on my approach to all those concerned. As I've been learning about the performers, I've discovered some home truths about myself. It's diffi-cult to express and the research journey is never easy. Perhaps a poem might help me express these complexities ...

> *A Difference*
>
> *I embark upon a journey*
> *To see from the other side*
> *I thought I'd make a difference*
> *Reveal the truth, not lies*
>
> *I didn't see this travel*
> *Held any good or bad*
> *Can I be the difference?*
> *Show that truth resides*
>
> *The road can seem too hard*
> *Running out this race*
> *Who said there's a difference?*
> *I noticed who set the pace*
>
> *Though weary from the task*
> *Not sure why or what for*
> *We can make the difference*
> *Hand in hand, yearning for more*
>
> © Lexine Solomon

Conclusion

We have attempted to tell autoethnographic vignettes of our journey together to make visible our experiences undertaking collaborative research. The trochus shell we have peered inside unveils the unex-pected joys and generosity of our research companions but also we hope has uncovered some of the uncomfortable realities of cross-cultural research. We have written openly about our experiences in the hope of telling a story about how Indigenous and non-Indigenous researchers can come together through a collaborative approach to research. Like Haig-Brown, we think it's important to "be brave and curious enough to open the door" (2001, p. 31), to explore the possi-bilities of writing about our research experiences. We continually nego-tiate and renegotiate the research process and the key is to be open with each other about our goals, the skills we bring, our thoughts and feelings. Like any relationship it is about give and take.

We hope you as the reader can relate our narratives to your own experiences and relationships. We have attempted to speak from our individual perspectives, and also at times together, to illustrate the complexities and messiness of cross-cultural research. Our vignettes have revealed many issues and questions regarding the difficulties and discomforts of Indigenous and non-Indigenous research and relations in Australia. How can research on Indigenous music benefit Indigenous performers? How can Indigenous researchers undertake research which satisfies their responsibilities to their community and family, as well as to funding bodies and universities? How can collaborative research help reconcile some of these tensions? These questions are on-going and there are no easy answers, yet together we will continue to search for ways to work through them in our research and writing towards a better future between Indigenous and non-Indigenous Australians.

~~

Lexine and Katelyn have just finished their presentation at Griffith University and have answered many questions. It has gone for one and a half hours and Katelyn looks at Lexine. She looks weary from the long presentation. They are both relieved they're finished but there are a couple more questions from the audience:

"Have you published this anywhere?" asks a man with glasses sitting up the back of the room.

Lexine looks at Katelyn to answer. "No, we haven't yet," says Katelyn, "but we hope to."

Katelyn's friend and mentor Liz Mackinlay has a final question and raises her hand. Smiling at Katelyn and Lexine, she asks: "You obviously have a really great connection and that came across in your presentation. How do you think you'll represent that in your writing?"

"Yes, it's difficult to bring that to life in writing, I think," Lexine comments. "Our subjectivities are ever present in research. We'll have to do some experimenting. Perhaps autoethnography might offer a creative format for exploring this further."

The audience claps. Lexine and Katelyn embrace; someone takes their photo. Katelyn unplugs the memory stick from the computer and Lexine begins to gather her things.

"Let's go get some dinner. I'm hungry," Katelyn says to Lexine.

"Ah Katelyn, you skinny white girl, at least you like to eat! We've got lots to talk about and all our best discussions happen during meals." They both laugh and walk towards the open door.

Acknowledgments

We are grateful to AIATSIS and the Aboriginal and Torres Strait Islander Studies Unit at The University of Queensland for their generous funding support. Many thanks also to our Torres Strait Islander research companions and friends for their participation in our research.

Endnotes

1 This was a comment said to Katelyn by one of the performers she interviewed during her PhD research.

2 In this chapter in some cases we have used the fictitious names Mrs Gear, Topaz, Stacey Lui, and Selena in order to protect their identities and because of the sensitive and personal nature of some of the material.

References

Akeroyd, A. (1984). Ethics in relation to informants, the profession and governments. In R. F. Ellen (Ed.), *Ethnographic research: A guide to general conduct* (pp.133–154). London: Orlando: Academic Press.

Anzaldua, G. (1987). *Borderlands: The new mestiza = La frontera.* San Francisco: Aunt Lute Books.

Barney, K., & Solomon, L. (in press). "The memories linger on, but the stories tell me who I am": A conversation between an Indigenous Australian performer and a non-Indigenous Australian music researcher. In E. Mackinlay, B. Bartleet & K. Barney (Eds.), *Musical islands: Exploring connections between music, place and research.* Cambridge: Cambridge Scholars Press.

Bhabha, H. K. (1994). *The location of culture.* London: Routledge.

Bochner, S. (Ed.) (1982). *Cultures in contact: Studies in cross-cultural interaction.* New York: Pergamon Press.

Castellano, M. B. (2004). Ethics of Aboriginal research. *Journal of Aboriginal Health, 1*(1), 98–114.

Corn, A., & Gumbula, N. (2002). Nurturing the sacred through Yolngu popular song. *Cultural Survival Quarterly, 26*(2), 40–42.

Dan, H (Seaman). (1999). *Follow the sun* [CD]. Spit Junction: Hot Records.

Dan, H (Seaman). (2001). *Steady, steady* [CD]. Spit Junction: Hot Records.

Dan, H (Seaman). (2004). *Perfect pearl* [CD]. Spit Junction: Hot Records.

Dan, H (Seaman). (2006). *Island way* [CD]. Cairns: Steady Steady Music.

Dunbar-Hall, P., & Gibson, C. (2004). *Deadly sounds, deadly places: Contemporary Aboriginal music in Australia.* Sydney: University of New South Wales Press.

Dunbar-Hall, P., & I Wayan Tusti Adnyana. (2004). Expectations and outcomes of intercultural music education: A case study of teaching and learning a Balinese *gamelan* instrument. *Proceedings of the XXVIth Annual Conference of the Australian Association for Research in Music Education,* 144–151.

Dyck, I. J., Lynham, M., & Anderson, J. M. (1995). Women talking: Creating knowledge through difference in cross-cultural research. *Women's Studies International Forum, 18,* 611–626.

Ellingson, L. (1998). "Then you know how I feel": Empathy, identification and reflexivity in fieldwork. *Qualitative Inquiry, 4*(4), 492–514.

Ellis. C. (1998). What counts as scholarship in communication? Autoethnographic responses. *American Communication Journal 1*(2), 1–5.

Ellis, C., & Bochner, A. (Eds.). (1996). *Composing ethnography: Alternative forms of qualitative writing.* Walnut Creek: AltaMira Press.

Flick, I., & Goodall, H. (2004). *Isabel Flick: The many lives of an extraordinary Aboriginal woman.* Sydney: Allen and Unwin.

Fluehr-Lobban, C. (Ed.). (1992). *Ethics and the profession of anthropology: Dialogue for a new era.* Philadelphia: University of Pennsylvania Press.

Giroux, H. (1992). *Border crossings: Cultural workers and the politics of education.* New York: Routledge.

Goodall, H. (2005). Writing a life with Isabel Flick: An exploration in cross-cultural collaboration. *The Public Historian 27*(4), 65–82.

Haig-Brown, C. (2001). Continuing collaborative knowledge production: Knowing when, where, how and why. *Journal of Intercultural Studies, 22*(1), 19–32.

Haig-Brown, C., & Archibald, J. (1996). Transforming First Nations research with respect and power. *International Journal of Qualitative Studies in Education, 9*(3), 245–267.

Heiss, A. (2007). *I'm not racist, but ... A collection of social observations.* Cambridge: Salt.

Holman Jones, S. (1998). Turning the kaleidoscope, re-visioning ethnography. *Qualitative Inquiry, 4*(3), 421–439.

Hooker, J. (2003). *Working across cultures.* Stanford: Stanford Business Books.

hooks, b. (1990). *Yearning: Race, gender, and cultural politics.* Boston: South End Press.

Huggins, J. (1998). *Sister girl: The writings of Aboriginal activist and historian Jackie Huggins.* St Lucia: University of Queensland Press.

Humphreys, M. (2005). Getting personal: Reflexivity and autoethnographic vignettes. *Qualitative Inquiry, 11*(6), 840–860.

Kvale, S. (1996). *InterViews: An introduction to qualitative research interviewing.* Thousand Oaks: Sage Publications.

Mackinlay, E. (2002). Engaging with theories of dialogue and voice: Using Bakhtin as a framework to understanding teaching and learning Indigenous Australian women's performance. *Research Studies in Music Education, 19*, 32–45.

Mackinlay, E. (2007). *Disturbances and dislocations: Understanding teaching and learning experiences in Indigenous Australian women's music and dance.* Berlin: Peter Lang.

Maralung, A., with Manuberu, P. (1993). *The world's musical traditions, Vol. 4: Bunggridj-Bunggridj: Wangga songs: Northern Australia* [CD]. Smithsonian Folkways.

McDonald, W. (1997). Tricky business: Whites on black territory. *Australian Author, 29*(1), 13.

McLean, M. (2003). *To Tatau Waka: In search of Maori music 1958–1979.* Auckland: Auckland University Press.

Neuenfeldt, K. (2001). Cultural politics and a music recording project: Producing Strike Em!: Contemporary Voices from the Torres Strait. *Journal of Intercultural Studies, 22*(2), 133–45.

Neuenfeldt, K. (2007). Notes on the engagement of Indigenous peoples with recording technology and techniques, the recording industry and researchers. *The World of Music, 49* (1), 7–21.

Nunns, R., & Thomas, A. (2005). The search for the sound of the Putorino: 'Me Te Wai E Utuutu Ana.' *Yearbook for Traditional Music, 37*, 69–79.

Paipa (Windward). (2003). *Paipa (Windward)* [CD]. Canberra: National Museum of Australia.

Pederson, H., & Woorunmurra, B. (1995). *Jandamarra and the Bunuba resistance.* Broome: Magabala.

Reed, L. (2002). Singing the land. *Philosophy Action Nature, 2,* 65–71.

Roe, P., with Muecke, S. (1983). *Gularabulu: Stories from the West Kimberley.* Fremantle: Fremantle Arts Centre Press.

Sailing the Southeast Wind. (2003). *Sailing the Southeast Wind* [CD]. Rockhampton: Central Queensland University.

Saltwater Songs. (2005). *Saltwater songs. Indigenous maritime music from Torres Strait* [CD]. Rockhampton: Central Queensland University.

Selby, J. (2004). Working divides between indigenous and non-indigenous: Disruptions of identity. *International Journal of Qualitative Studies in Education,* 17(1), 143–156.

Shnukal, A. (1999). Review of *Torres Strait Islander women and the Pacific war. Journal of Australian Studies, March,* 180.

Smith, L. T. (1999). *Decolonising methodologies: Research and Indigenous peoples.* Dunedin: University of Otago Press.

Soja, E. W. (2000). *Postmetropolis: Critical studies of cities and regions.* Malden, MA: Blackwell.

Somerville, M., & Perkins, T. (2003). Border work in the contact zone: Thinking Indigenous/non-Indigenous collaboration spatially. *Journal of Intercultural Studies,* 24(3): 253–266.

Strike Em! (2000). Strike em! Contemporary voices from Torres Strait [CD]. Thursday Island: Torres Strait Islander Media Association.

Yawulyu Mungamunga. Dreaming Songs of Warumungu Women, Tennant Creek, Central Australia. (2000). [CD]. Tennant Creek: Festival Records.

Chapter 14

In Memory of Music Research

An Autoethnographic, Ethnomusicological and Emotional Response to Grief, Death and Loss in the Aboriginal Community at Borroloola, Northern Territory

Text and images by Elizabeth Mackinlay

Right now I am trying to puzzle out what I will write for Brydie and Carolyn's book on music research and autoethnography. Brydie asked me if I would write something about Borroloola and all I can think about is how my music research role as an ethnomusicologist has come to an end. I thought I might feel sad about that but I don't. I actually feel quite relieved because I don't have to dance around anymore. My role as an ethnomusicologist — a midwife for musical cultures as Robertson (1993) so eloquently put it — is finished. I have hung up my tape recorder and moved on. There are any number of reasons why and none of them negative. So many of my kundiyarra — my Yanyuwa, Garrwa, Mara and Kudanji "most necessary companions" — have passed away, I'm not quite sure what my research all means now that they are no longer here to give it life. It's not that preservation or even documentation was my main agenda — I could never wear that hat for very long. I hate wearing hats, and this one was always too tight, the wrong style, in a shade that gave my skin a greenish tinge, and made of material that gave me hives that itched and burned for days. There is another much more personal explanation though and it drowns out any others I thought might have meant something. My research is no longer professional and if I am honest with myself, it never really was. The moment I boarded a plane from Armidale in northern New South Wales to travel to the remote Aboriginal community of Borroloola in the south-west Gulf of the Northern Territory, or perhaps even before that, when I walked into my first tribal singing lesson at the Centre for Aboriginal Studies in Music at the University of Adelaide and laid eyes upon the man who would become my husband, my life had already changed. My research became personal then, very personal. Over the past 15 years, the gentle hands, hearts and harmonies of so many Yanyuwa, Garrwa, Mara and Kudanji women — and sometimes men — have guided, "grown me up", and put me through women's Law the proper Aboriginal way. They also made certain that I would walk with them, sing, dance and follow them with love, respect and commitment for them, for my husband, for our two sons and for our family. Now I can sing, I can dance but I can no longer speak or write — my kundiyarra tell me that that knowledge is not research, it is not for everyone, it never was for Dr Elizabeth Mackinlay — it was always and will always be for me (Journal entry, February 8, 2009).

I look into the mirror of research
And see music
She glares back at me and accusingly screams,
"You didn't hear me!"
And then so forlornly,
"Such beautiful songs I sang for you, why did you leave me?"
I turn my head away
Even then she keeps on
With a tight voice,
pursed lips and teeth clenched,
"Why did you stop singing with me?"
I put my head down ashamed
She shouts at me
"What is this performance you call research", she pauses
And then comes a soft and sad whisper, "And why did he replace me?"

I cannot bear her sadness
I know what I must do
I lift my head up and look
bravely into the mirror
I stop seeing research
And now I see music
I wonder how I could have
ever let her fade away
I hear nothing but her
And I open my mouth
As I open my mouth to sing
with her.
(Journal entry, 18 February, 2009)

Endings and Beginnings, Death and Life, Research and Relationships at Borroloola

The tardis-like phone box at Wandangula station where I have been doing my "fieldwork" rings out plaintively in the early crispness of a Sunday morning in the bush. I am sitting quietly on the porch, contemplating life, and enjoying a hot cup of tea while I watch the world around me wake up. At first I don't want to answer it, who would be ringing so early anyway? But then, something stirs inside me, and I know instinctively that the phone call is for me. It's my Dad. His voice is strange, strangled; he tells me that my grandmother has died. I cannot speak; I drop the phone and run for the hills. I stand on top of that rocky outcrop where only the day before we had looked for porcupine and scream, my voice cries out until it can be heard no more. My voice is gone. I leave Borroloola, my baba (sister) Jemima speaks for me — she hears the words that I cannot say and speaks for my heart. I go back to Melbourne. I see myself standing at the grave of my grandmother and still I cannot speak. I cannot say goodbye to her, I refuse to say goodbye to her. I close my eyes to shut out what I know must be done and I can hear the old men at Borroloola singing around the Yalkawarru funeral pole, feet thumping in the sand, firesticks flying in the air, and all around me the haunting sounds of grieving. Someone close by is crying in rasping gasps and for a while I am unsure of where I am. I look up and see that it is my father. His entire body is shaking uncontrollably and my mother weeps beside him as death becomes us.

I rush into the house from outside to answer the phone. It is my baba Jemima in Borroloola. I look at the calendar on the fridge, the clock on the wall and fleetingly wonder whether she has received my most recent parcel of second hand clothes and toys, before grabbing the handset. "Hello wunhaka (little sister)," she says, and I immediately know that something is wrong. "It's your kardirdi (mother's brother), that old man who sang Kalwanyarra and kujika for you, he passed away", and the sound of her wailing sends me sobbing to the floor.

I walk into my department at the University. It's a little after 9am in the morning and I remember that I need to call Jemima at Borroloola — she will be there at the Language Centre with my marruwarras (female cross cousins) Dinah and Mudinji, my kulhakulhas (daughters) Rosie, Joanne and Topsy, waiting for me. I quickly dump my bag and dial the number. "Yu Maryanne! Yamulu bajinda? Ngalhi baba Jemima?" I ask. She calls out to Jemima and while I am waiting for her to come to the phone, Maryanne asks, "So you've heard the news then?" "My heart drops heavily into my stomach, "No, what news?" I reply, trying hard to control the looming sense of dread and loss. "I'll let your baba tell you" she says and hands the phone over. "Baba?", Jemima speaks softly. "Yes, what's happened? What's wrong?" "It's your wukuku (maternal grandson), that old man McDinny, he died this morning". And all of the songs he ever taught me, sang to me and shared with me build inside me as a high-pitched keening.

"Hello kujaka (mother), it's me Rachel," she says. "Kulhakulha", I answer excitedly, "It's so good to hear your voice! What's happening?" There is a pause before she asks, "Can you come? It's your sister, she's in the hospital and we don't think she's going to make it". I board the next plane to Darwin and race to the intensive care unit to see her. She is lying in a bed, her chest rising and falling in quick short breaths, her black skin in opposition to the white sheets on which she lies. She has tubes and bandages all over her arms and chest. I run to her and her eyes open slowly. At first she doesn't recognise me and then I speak. She hears my voice, smiles but then her face changes. She tries to sit up and becomes agitated. Her eyes are wild and now I see that she is not smiling at all, but she is frightened, shit scared of what is happening around and to her. I hold her hand and sing to her, the same songs she sang to me. After a while she seems to calm down and closes her eyes to sleep. It is the last time I see her alive.

I drive apprehensively into the Gravel, the Mara camp, at Borroloola looking for her, my kulhakulha Joanne. "Over there mar-ruwarra," Dinah whispers to me as she points. I can see a small group of women sitting outside a red corrugated iron house. Small children play around outside in a puddle of water as dogs watch lazily from the shade. I look anxiously for her and my kulhakulha stands up. I cannot bear the pain on her face. Last year her only son died tragically from a heart attack and now her oldest grandson, her ngabuji (son's son) has passed away suddenly. He was only 11 years old, and fell down on the school cricket pitch and could not be revived. I wrap my arms around her and together we cry. Another pair of arms encircle us; it is my daughter who lost her son. She doesn't speak; she can only weep for the loss of her child.

I sit quietly on the hard wooden seat and feel the coolness of the cathedral begin to soothe me. My mother is next to me, holding my hand and equally as silent. I left my Christian faith on the side of the Western Highway a long time ago but this sacred sanctuary of faith and spirit seems like the only place I can be. The smell of incense wafts through the air and every now and then, the muffled sound of a car on the busy roads of Bologna outside interrupts our reverie. The old but sturdy pew we are resting on faces the small chapel of Mary Magdalene. There is a painting of Mary Magdalene on the wall behind a simple altar. Mary is pictured with a plain scarf over her head. She is sitting in a peaceful garden and she is gently wiping a tear from her eye. The emotion, love, grief and loss that is depicted in that one gesture is incredibly moving, and it is some time before I realise that I too am crying. I think to myself how alike Mary Magdalene my marruwarra Mudinji Isaac was. Both women loved men and were devoted completely to those that they loved. They both walked a pathway that was not for everyone, and showed themselves to be strong and courageous women, not of their time, but for eternity. I think to myself that my marruwarra would be pleased that I had come to sit at the feet of this risky, astonishing and beautiful woman. I stand up and walk softly towards a basket of thin white candles. A sense of ritual overcomes me as the wick catches fire and I gently place the burning flame in front of the Magdalena. Images of my marruwarra singing, dancing, laughing, talking, shouting, crying and sleeping around other types of fires swirl inside my head and my heart whispers goodbye.

I first encountered Aboriginal women's performance culture under the guise of anthropological and musicological research when I first went to Borroloola in the south-west Gulf Carpentaria of the Northern Territory in July 1994. I went with a mission to record and document the songs and ceremonies of Yanyuwa, Garrwa, Mara, and Kudanji Aboriginal peoples living there, and I chose Borroloola because little was known about the musical culture of this region by white researchers. I was an enthusiastic, wide-eyed and bright-minded 23 year-old girl who thought that I could change the world by becoming a "song catcher". In my ethnomusicological suitcase I had carefully and safely packed a three-year music degree, an honours degree in eth-nomusicology, the authority of a doctorate in progress, notebooks, and all kinds of recording equipment. I also carried with me a number of non-tangible but completely visible items of baggage that I didn't realise I had brought — my white skin, the history of black and white relations in Australia, the legacy and ongoing trauma of colonisation, and a power and privilege bestowed upon me because of my white sub-jectivity that I was blissfully unaware of.

My memories of becoming an ethnomusicologist lazily intermingle and blur many events, people, places and performances, so much so, that I cannot say exactly when it might have happened, or if in fact it did at all. Was it when old man McDinny asked me excitedly when we first met whether or not I had brought my tape recorder with me and then sang non-stop every day for three months? Perhaps it was while recording the Yalkawarru funeral ceremony? Or maybe it occurred while I sat cross-legged around a campfire, one eye on my notebook and the other on the tape recorder, as the silhouettes of my baba Jemima a-Wuwarlu Miller and daughters Nancy, Myra, and Rachel McDinny danced gracefully in front of me? I cannot be sure but in 1994 I began to believe that I was an ethnomusicologist. I went into the "field", I made tapes of ceremonies and songs, copied these onto CDs, learnt how to sing and dance Yanyuwa way; I presented lectures as a white expert, and wrote academic papers about the musical culture from this remote place in Australia. By the end of my first trip to Borroloola, something had changed, and the labels on the fancy dresses I called ethnomusicology and music research did not fit so snugly and comfortably on my white body. Even though I had always thought of ethnomusicology as progressive in philosophy and practice, there was something about the narrow style, the sharp and unflatter-

The research of music sings loud and strong the song wants to be heard the listener waits to be sung until both meet on a blank page and the song becomes a story of two/to/too the listener becomes a researcher and the music becomes research is something wanting and waiting needing an answer or perhaps even a new question everything the sounds, the singer and the self spins around like a record all that you hear me now as I create new melodies of understanding that a chorus of voices will soon be compelled to sing as the research becomes music the research of music. (Journal entry, 17 February, 2009)

ing cut, the stark and stiff clothing of music research which no longer suited me; my body was now embodied with sensate memories, emotions, understandings and relationships which my current wardrobe could not cater for. As I wriggled my legs around to try and make my favourite pair of denim jeans fit, slow recognition and a certain sense of shame overcame me as I realised that this kind of fashion and my obsession with it was no longer appropriate. The old Liz who wore these clothes slammed the back door as she left and it was time to find something new to wear.

In this chapter, I want to use autoethnography to perform a ritual for sending away someone, somebody or something that has died in my practice as a music researcher and ethnomusicologist. As the narratives at the beginning of this paper allude, death has seeped into and flooded my work and relationships with people at Borroloola so frequently with sadness, grief and loss that at times it is too difficult to bear. When so many people I have known — some close family, others good friends, young people and older members of the community, and some I spoke to only once — have passed away, how am I to respond? What does my music research mean in the context of so much trauma, grief and loss? What role can music research play in the face of so much dispossession, oppression and struggle for daily existence? Does my music research *have* a role in Borroloola or has it died too? Do I even have a right to research, and if not, why I am still doing it? The feeling that my responsibilities, roles, relationships and research with Aboriginal people at Borroloola must be something more than black musical marks on a white page grows stronger and stronger each day. Words like social justice, ethics, compassion, love and heart stand poised on the tip of my tongue, ready to make a grand entrance. I know soon that I will have to open my mouth and give them voice or else they will be swallowed whole. If I don't bring them out of the dark, how else can my music research live

An Interruption: Another News Story About Indigenous Australians

As I walk into my home and sit heavily onto our soft blue couches, I realise what a long day it has been. My head is ringing with all of the questions students fired at me during my lecture on "Gender, kinship and performance". My feet are aching from the incessant prowling I tend to do while I am talking to a class, and my mind is already a buzz with the material I want to present next week. "Hey babe!" I call to my husband, who is dutifully preparing a stir-fry for our dinner in the kitchen.

A Poem called "She"

She saw the straight and seemingly endless Carpentaria Highway
    stretching out in front of her
 saw a sign that said 398 kilometres to go to Borroloola
She saw herself driving down the same road 15 years ago
She saw a young naive girl whom *she* hardly recognises

She heard the steady lull of big wheels on black bitumen
She heard a chorus of Yanyuwa, Garrwa, Mara and Kudanji voices
    join the gentle hum
She heard them calling her
She hard singing drawing her to a place *she* has come to call home

She went as an ethnomusicologist, trying to catch songs of the Others
She went with her husband's maternal Grandmother Mudinji Muir
    and her mother-in-law Jeannie
She went knowing that Mudinji was stolen from Burrulula because
    she was a "half-caste"
She went hearing the tears of grief as *she* told her traumatic story
    of forcible removal from her country, her culture and her family

She wanted in the beginning to fill the gap in the musicological record
She wanted to record and preserve, to document and understand
She wanted all of these things for herself and her research
She wanted more of the Others and less of herself
She took with her the tools of her trade
She took with her a notebook, camera
    and tape recorder
She took with her, her stark white skin
She took with her power and privilege
    that *she* had not yet thought to question

She was called Mijiji, white woman
She was called Nungarrima, the "right way"
    skin name from the Rrumburriya semi-moiety
She was called a-Yakibijirna, a bush name
    linking her to the country of her husband's
    great grandmother and the Tiger Shark
    Dreaming
She was called Kundiyarra, a partner in song

She smiles as *She* remembers how *she* has become what *she* is now
She smiles as *She* anticipates the warmth of the women who will
wrap their arms around her when *she* arrives
She smiles as *She* sees them singing and dancing around fires at night
She smiles as familiar feelings of belonging, friendship and love
embrace her

She asks who am I in relation to Yanyuwa, Garrwa, Mara and
Kudanji people?
She asks what place does a white woman like me have working in
this community?
She asks what role does an Aboriginal man's non-Aboriginal wife
and mother to his children have?
She asks what do I think I am doing here?

She decides perhaps *she* is not out of place but in many interlinked
subject positions
She decides *She* is a white middle-class woman,
She decides *She* is an ethnomusicologist, a singer, and a researcher,
She decides *She* is a wife and a mother to an Aboriginal man and
our sons
She decides *She* is a border crosser

She knows that *She* dangerously sways and trips over the colour line
She knows that *She* often sits "in between"
She knows that this positioning can be uncomfortable and unforgiving
She knows that her "in-between-ness" intersubjectively frames her
work as musical-political-personal
She knows that her border crossing drives her commitment to an
engaged ethnomusicology

She hears words like social justice linked with ethnomusicology
engaged
She hears words with feeling that are embodied and emotioned
linking her mind to her spirit
She hears Ruth Behar's voice gently remind her, "If you are not performing an ethnomusicology which breaks your heart Elizabeth,
why do it?"
She hears herself make a promise to do ethnomusicology differently.

"Hi Mac!" he calls back. "How was your day?" I pause a minute, wondering whether I should give him the short answer or the long. I opt for the abbreviated version and simply shout "OK, but I'm absolutely exhausted! Do you mind if I just chill out in here and watch the news until tea time?" I have already nestled into the cushions on the lounge when he reaches down to give me a cuddle and a kiss on the cheek. "You've got about 15 minutes," he tells me kindly. I look up at him and smile gratefully, "Thanks — you're a domestic god in the making!" I turn my attention back to the television as he leaves the room and see that the ABC news has just started. The newsreader begins, "And now for tonight's top story. The Australian Bureau of Statistics summary of Indigenous Health was released today in Canberra and reports that Indigenous people are much more likely to die before they are old than people in the rest of the Australian population" (Australian Bureau of Statistics, 2007). In an instant, the faces of all the Aboriginal women, men, boys and girls I have known who have died too early, too violently, or from too many curable diseases flash before me. The newsreader continues, "The statistics paint a grim picture of the status of Indigenous health with life expectancy of Aboriginal women and men at least 17 years lower than the non-Indigenous population" (Australian Bureau of Statistics, 2007). The report then cuts to an interview with the president of the Australian Medical Association, Dr Rosanna Capolingua, outside Parliament House in Canberra. Her face is serious and concerned when I hear her repeat a familiar lament — that the statistics present a disturbing picture of health conditions and outcomes for Indigenous peoples in Australia "more commonly associated with the Third World than with a wealthy nation such as ours" (Australian Medical Association, 2008). The television cuts back to the newsreader: "There have been a staggering number of inquiries, commissions and reports written about Indigenous health in Australia — no less than 25 in the past 30 years, and yet the situation is not getting any better" (Webb-Pullman, Nethercote & Vorrath, 2007). "Lynne Malcolm spoke with Professor Ian Anderson earlier today and filed this report on behalf of the ABC." I see Lynne on the screen. She is dressed in a frilly white shirt and her hair blows around in the breeze as she talks. "Professor Ian Anderson, today the health of Australian Aboriginals, their life expectancy is still 17 years behind the rest of the population. What suggestions do you have for tackling this problem?" (Malcolm, 2007) The camera cuts to a casually well dressed man, with a neat haircut and a beard: "Yes um thanks for that question Lynne." I have heard a lot about Ian

Anderson, a very well known and respected Indigenous academic, and I lean in closer to the set box so that I can hear his response. "There are a number of complex things that we need to do in order to tackle this kind of social inequality," he begins. "There are issues … that suggest that housing will make a difference." I think about how long my baba Jemima and marruwarra Dinah have been waiting to move out of their temporary corrugated iron houses into a home that gives them access to power, safe drinking water, and washing facilities, and that can sleep more than a nuclear family comfortably — how much longer will they have to wait I wonder? Ian is still talking: "There are issues around quality of care both in terms of primary health care … There are issues around alcohol supply, there are a number of clear cases where if we actually reduce the number of takeaways we reduce the number of alcohol outlets so that you have less drinking." I feel a lump form in my throat as I think about my granddaughter at Borroloola who recently passed away from a skin cancer on her cheek. She kept on going to the health clinic asking for treatment and to have it looked at "properly" but the nurses kept on giving her Panadol and telling her to sober up. It was only when she started bleeding from her nose and eyes that they realised she needed more *care* but by then it was too late — she was dead within three months. I feel angry knowing that hers is just one story in a storm of others (e.g., Biddle, 2002). "There are also issues though that relate to dealing with educational disadvantage and poverty but also to a range of issues which are about empowering individuals and families to actually look after their hygiene, to manage alcohol responsibly, to look after their chronic disease and also to deal with domestic violence" (Anderson in Malcolm, 2007). When Ian finishes speaking, Lynne nods and asks, "We've been struggling with these things for really a very long time, what's the key thing to have all those things addressed and actually make a difference?" (Malcolm, 2007). Ian pauses a moment before answering and I immediately know what he is about to say will make an impact. He looks directly at the camera and says "I think that one of the critical factors is around Aboriginal self-determination. We've got to support Aboriginal decision-making around how we deal with these issues within our local communities. We've also got to support the delivery of effective and appropriate services and often they aren't services that are managed and run by Aboriginal people. And we've also got to find pathways for Aboriginal engagement in the policy process" (Anderson in Malcolm, 2007). I think that is where the news story ended but I could not be sure. I am lost in my own thoughts about how easily the words "health", "services" and "care" could have easily been replaced by "research" — my research — in this story, and still have the same meaning. I look up and Gordon is standing in front of me. He smiles, puts his hands on my shoulders and tells me, "Dinner is ready when you're ready." I slowly lift my face up and his face crumples with concern, "Hey, what are those tears in your eyes? Are you OK?"

A dialogue

(Please note: This transcript can be read forwards and backwards)

Dr: Well, what seems to be the problem?

Dr Liz: I don't feel myself at all

Dr: And you're ... what?

Dr Liz: Well, I'll be 38 in May

Dr: No, no. That's not what I meant. I mean, what are you, who are you?

Dr Liz: I thought I was a musicologist, no wait, an ethnomusicologist ... I mean, a music researcher

Dr: What? You mean to say you aren't sure?

Dr Liz: See, that's just it. I don't know.

Dr: I see ... well (He raises his eyebrows). Let me ask you some questions.

Dr Liz: OK (she sits up straight in her chair)

Dr: When does the Romantic period finish and end in music?

Dr Liz: (looks blankly in disbelief)

Dr: Can you name the four big B's in music?

Dr Liz: Boomerang clapsticks — my husband has a pair with his Dreaming on them; belly-dancing, I've always wanted to try it; and then there's bell (yes, bell hooks) you couldn't possibly leave her out; and of course the final one would have to be black — which I'm not.

Dr: (He is looking at me wide-eyed, his mouth hanging open) ... Ahem ... well, we've answered one question – you're definitely not a musicologist are you!

Dr Liz: (A smile of relief washes over her face but somewhere deep inside she wonders if this is an appropriate response).

Dr: What is the latest transcription and analysis technique for Aboriginal music and would you say you are competent in this regard?

Dr Liz: Honestly? I'm not sure — I can do it and have done it, and I could do it again if I wanted to — but what and who for?

Dr: (He places a red cross against the label "ethnomusicologist") Right! What is meant by the saying, "If you can't teach me to fly, teach me to sing!"

Dr Liz: Music transforms you!

Dr: that's an unusual response — most people usually say something about the fact that everyone can sing – it's possible, unlike flying.

Dr Liz: Dr? (she can't understand what he is saying)

Dr: What would you do if one of your students was tone deaf, couldn't stamp in time and only wanted to sing hip-hop music in class?

Dr Liz: I'd shout "Break it down baby" and get my feet grooving with them!

(Journal entry, 9 February, 2009)

Singing and Writing a Life that is Gone: Ethnomusicological, Anthropological and Ethnographic Laments

Our work as ethnomusicologists, anthropologists and ethnographers leads us into the communities, homes and lives of many different people. Many of us work in the same community for many years and it is inevitable that we will experience the full cycle of life with people we may also have come at most to love and at least to call our friends. Sometimes our encounters with death are of the ceremonial kind and our in-the-field journals and out-of-the-field papers, and seminars about this type of musical and cultural phenomena become the stuff of textbooks and discourse in our disciplines. Indigenous Australian anthropology, ethnomusicology and ethnography is certainly no different, and I can recall the morbid fascination I experienced as I read some of the classic and more recent academic readings and representations about funerals, mortuary rites and ceremonies in general in Aboriginal and Torres Strait Islander communities. Ronald and Catherine Berndt's *The World of the First Australians* (1988, 5th ed.), Strehlow's *Songs of Central Australia* (1971), Elkin's *The Aborigines and How to Understand Them*, Kaberry's *Aboriginal Woman: Sacred and Profane* (1939/2004), Morphy's *Ancestral Connections* (1991), Bird-Rose's *Dingo Makes us Human* (1992), Bell's *Daughters of the Dreaming* (1983) start a list of essential reading which is seemingly endless. Australian Aboriginal ethnomusicology was nurtured by equally distinguished scholars such as Alice Moyle (e.g., 1964), Catherine Ellis (e.g., 1985) and Trevor Jones (with Elkin, 1958), and today others such as Stephen Wild (1975), Jill Stubington (2007), Allan Marett (2005), Richard Moyle (e.g., 1979), and Fiona Magowan (2007) have followed their lead. These scholars have all chosen to focus on slightly different regional areas of musical performance, slightly different aspects of musical culture, and positioned themselves in sometimes slightly and sometimes vastly different personal-political-musical agendas. However, there is absolutely no doubt that the work of these scholars has and continues to contribute an enormous amount of musicological and anthropological knowledge about Indigenous Australian forms of song, dance and ceremony. I do not want to suggest that the work of these researchers has not been loved, appreciated, requested, supported and/or undertaken in collaboration with Aboriginal and Torres Strait Islander performers and communities, nor that because a music researcher does not write about their emotions, it necessarily follows that they do not experience, feel or have them. I am aware that such vulnerable writing is *not* for everyone, and I would be arrogant to think it was. For me the job that I do as an ethnomusicologist "in-out-in-and-out-never-really-out-of-the-field" makes my-self visible *and* vulnerable — it is emotional work which remains, as hooks (1994) asserts, a "location of possibility" for music and other research practices in Indigenous Australian Studies to privilege a generosity of self, an ethical sense of responsibility, and an engaged, embodied and emotioned performance of relationship.

It is perhaps not surprising then that I first look to the writings of the professors and peers I have mentioned to gain a sense of how they have responded to the deaths of people they have worked with. One of the laws about death in many Indigenous Australian communities, and Borroloola is no exception, is that you do not speak about the dead — it is taboo speak the deceased person's name for an undetermined time after. Many of us learn how to speak and write around the person's name and I have been taught to use words such as *Mudinji*, Yanyuwa avoidance language to use instead of a person's name. But I am desperate for something to hang onto, and given that books and other printed materials usually take several years to churn through the publication system, how *did* the ethnomusicologists, anthropologists and ethnographers feel? What did they do? How did it affect their research? How did it affect them personally? As I open each book, I am sure that I will find something — there must be something because we as ethnomusicologists spend a long time getting to know and living beside the singers and performers we record on tape — don't we? I see dedications at the beginning of books, chapters, theses, and papers to performer/s that ethnomusicologists feel they owe their life's work, and who have now passed away. Australian ethnomusicologist Kirsty Gillespie (2007) provides us with a beautiful example in her doctoral thesis of an ethnomusicologist responding personally to grief. She devotes an entire chapter of her work to a Papua New Guinean friend she had worked with who had passed away during her fieldwork. Gillespie openly talks about her friendship, and how she felt, cried and grieved for her when she passed away. Similarly, Helen Reeves Lawrence (1995) writes about the death of a singer she worked closely with; and I read entire chapters devoted to the documentation of funeral ceremonies which were performed not as a "show" for the researcher, but as a real life rite of passage to send spirits of dead people back to their traditional country. The ethnographic detail is astounding, but the emotional engagement of the ethnographer in these events, is for the most part, absent. I am reminded of Hortense Powdermaker, who struggled with witnessing the raw emotion of her "informants" while trying to perform her ethnographic duty of documentation at the same time. Writing about her fieldwork in Lesu, she noted:

> "How can you take notes midst human sorrow? Have you no feelings for the mourners?" I had a quick vision of a stranger walking into the living room of my Baltimore home at the time of a death. The notebook went back into my pocket. But I continued "Are you not an anthropologist? ... A knowledge of these rites is absolutely essential!" I took the notebook out and wrote what was happening ... The Lesu people understood. (Powdermaker, 1966, pp. 84–85)

One heart-warming-breaking exception to the emotional estrangements of ethnomusicologists, anthropologists and ethnographers in response to death, is the vulnerability and honesty with which Jennifer Biddle (2002), an Australian anthropologist who worked with Warlpiri people, tells of how her fieldwork abruptly ended when she was badly injured on a bush road in a 4WD accident. A death was not involved but Biddle instead speaks to the end of her own research practice. As I read Biddle painfully give a witness to her work, that is, the way she came to identify, feel empathy and generosity for her Warlpiri family and friends, I find myself becoming more and more in awe of this woman whom I have never met. She gives testimony to her story through a narrative and theoretical process that provides us with a rare glimpse of how anthropological work is lived, embodied and emotioned. Biddle tells of learning to speak to, to speak with, not to speak about Warlpiri and she ultimately tells of the sense of failure she feels as anthropologist. After her accident, Biddle kept in touch with but did not return to the Warlpiri community she had become so much a part of. For her — perhaps like me — something had died because she saw all too clearly her own failure in

> what took place before and has since taken place: the violence involved in the [anthropological] imperative — and my failure in the face of it — to live in the place of another. The failure of my self-in-relation-to; the destructive effects of that failure on others, and on myself. (Biddle, 2002, p. 108)

As I close each book, I find myself becoming less and less hopeful, and more and more alone. I read pages and pages of descriptions about how funeral ceremonies are enacted, how death and dying are ritualised and vocalised, and Indigenous words for these musical cycles of life, but very little about how ethnographers themselves respond to grief and loss in formal academic settings, and how it might affect their work.

Surely, their experiences are not so different to mine, I ask myself? It is then that I hear Ruth Behar — one of the few ethnographers I know to write powerfully with intellect *and* emotion about the death of a colleague — whisper in my ear: "[Liz, listen to me]. There is a snag: death is the most difficult subject to write about ... even 'ordinary death' leaves us on the brink between silence and speech" (Behar, 1996, p. 84). Death harbours in other unwanted and uninvited guests to our dinner party of life such as distress, despair, disorder and the body of a person who is now more vile, disgusting and disembodied dead than s/he ever was alive. In sustaining a strained and uneasy quietness about death in our writing, Behar continues, "We collude in the silence our society would have us maintain about death in order not to wake ... we also maintain the fenced boundary between emotion and intellect that is the academic counterpart to the practices that make dying 'obscene'" (Behar, 1996, pp. 85–86). Death is something we cleverly deny and run away from in Western understandings and in a cowardly rush, seek safety in rational thought that automatically kicks into gear all of the tricks it knows to repress any thought of death. The significance of the often acquainted words *death* and *silence* is not lost here either — we perhaps fear silence just as much as we fear the loss of life — and death is often described as "traumatic" for those who remain. Following Caruth's definition and theorising about trauma as an "interactive and intertwined physical and mental distress" which has a loose temporality and exists very much as a type of "ghost" (1996, p. 3), it is perhaps easy to understand why the living do not want to keep on conjuring up such pain, anguish, hurt and sorrow. Death in Indigenous Australian communities, for Indigenous Australian peoples and their families, is generationally, inherently, violent and frequently traumatic. What can, are and sh/could our responses to these traumas as music researchers be? Do we have a response-ibility to response-d? McConaghy poignantly asks, "How do we bear witness to trauma? ... Should we be silent or active witnesses?" (2003, p. 14).

Conclusion

> I meant to write about death, only life came breaking in as usual.
>
> Virginia Woolf, Diary entry: 17 February 1922, in A. Bell (1977).

Jemima has been in Darwin the last few days. She went back to Borroloola by plane this morning. She was flown up by charter to the hospital on Wednesday morning because her heart is in trouble. After three days of specialists and small operations, they've given her some tablets to fix a leak in her heart — her heart is bleeding from inside. She has lost a lot of weight and as I look at her skeletal frame I can't help but sense her slipping away. Her skin has gone a very deep black and the whites of her eyes are yellow. The night before she came to Darwin, I had dreamt about her. She was in the hospital on a bed sitting next to me and I was crying in her arms. She was holding me so tightly in her bony arms, gently stroking my hair and telling me it would all be OK. I was almost relieved when she phoned the next day to say she was in Darwin — I was expecting some bad news all day. I sat with her at the hospital when I could, making small and big talk while she waited for the doctors to say she could leave. She came to our place for a cup of tea the afternoon before she left, and then she said goodbye. Will I see her again? I am not sure — life is so delicately poised in a place like Borroloola. The inevitably of death is difficult to grasp, a certainty that I don't want to reach out for and cannot embrace. There are so many parts of me—thoughts, experiences, feelings, memories and knowledges—that I have shared with her. This woman I call self is inextricably intertwined with my baba Jemima. What, where, who and why will I be when she is gone? (Journal entry, 17 February, 2009).

In this chapter I feel like I have been dancing a different and almost dangerous be-bop or ballet style; isn't a dance with death inherently risky, even if it is but words neatly and thoughtfully choreographed on a page? I wanted to share the experiences of loss, grief and death that I encounter in my personal-political-musical life as an ethnomusicologist, in the hope of having a conversation with other music researchers working in Indigenous Australian and other communities who are faced with similar situations. Now that this dance of words has been performed, I am not so sure about the worth, wisdom or perhaps if I even *really* want to share these thoughts about death, research, music and self with others. Can you see how sustaining, nurturing and loving my Aboriginal family at Borroloola have been of me in all of my guises? Can you imagine being me and not having these relationships, roles and responsibilities with the people I work with? Am I naive to hope that you will understand why I must now cross one final border from intellect into emotion to become who I am? I see the futility of so much of my earlier music research, dotted quavers on white pages trying to capture the sung magic of black singers — too many dots I painstakingly plotted so that I could take an understanding and text it into shape for a Western academic audience so that they too may have this understanding which was never given in that way. I think to myself how ironic it is that I began my work as an ethnomusicologist with the credo of preservation firmly in my front pocket. I am reminded of summer time at home with my Mum and my sister. We would stand in the cool kitchen and help Mum carefully cut and peel boxes and kilos of stoned fruit — peaches, apricots, plums — and delicately arrange them in glass vacola jars to preserve them for winter. We wanted to savour the flavour of these summer fruits for as long as we could, even though we knew they wouldn't taste quite the same. When children are hungry, when my kundiyarra cannot keep themselves safe, warm or healthy; when grog and so much other violence kills too much of life; when the words and ceremonies of ancestors can no longer be heard or sung because whitefella business steals, colonises, interrupts and destroys — any dots on a white page I may write, fancy presentations at conferences I may give, and written papers in academic journals I publish, are just not enough for me anymore. The intellectual thirst, greed and desire for more of the Others squeezes the life, the song, the voice, the essence out of what I do. The music becomes lifeless because the singers cannot take breath. Their mouths are smothered by the heavy blankets of analysis, transcription and theory. The less they breathe, the more we as researchers take — selfishly and without care for life, committing a further act of dispossession. These words, stories, reflections, poems and sketches are my way of trying to make sense of why I feel that the type of music research I began doing at Borroloola 15 years ago, has died so that I may live. These are harsh words — I can feel their sting as they spew forth from my pen. But make no mistake, they are meant for me — if they mean something to you as a reader, then catch from them what you will but do not waste anything you take. There is room in what we do for both intellect and emotion — if matters of the heart cannot beat to their own rhythms, how can what we do live?

References

Australian Bureau of Statistics. (2007). *Deaths Australia 2006.* Accessed 1 March, 2009, from http://www.abs.gov.au/AUSSTATS/abs@.nsf/39433889d406eeb9ca2570610019 e9a5/CB2739310CEF4F8ACA2574390014C35A?opendocument).

Australian Medical Association. (2008). *Ending the cycle of vulnerability: AMA Indigenous Health Report Card 2008.* Retrieved March 1, 2009, from http://www. ama.com.au/node/4341.

Behar, R. (1996). *The vulnerable observer: Anthropology that breaks your heart.* Boston, MA: Beacon Press.

Bell, A. (Ed.). (1977). *The diary of Virginia Woolf.* London: Hogarth Press.

Bell, D. (1983). *Daughters of the Dreaming.* Melbourne, Australia: Spinifex Press.

Berndt, R. M., & C. H. (1988). *The world of the first Australians: Aboriginal traditional life, past and present* (5th ed.). Canberra, Australia: Aboriginal Studies Press.

Biddle, J. (2002). Bruises that won't heal: Melancholic identification and other ethnographic hauntings. *Mortality, 7*(1), 96–110.

Bird-Rose, D. (1992). *Dingo makes us human: Life and land in an Aboriginal Australian culture.* Melbourne, Australia: Cambridge University Press.

Caruth, C. (1996). *Unclaimed experience: Trauma, narrative, and history.* Baltimore, ML: Johns Hopkins University Press.

Elkin, A. P. (1964). *The Australian Aborigines: How to understand them* (4th ed.). Sydney, Australia: Angus & Robertson.

Ellis, C. J. (1985). *Aboriginal music: Education for living, cross-cultural experiences from South Australia.* Brisbane, Australia: University of Queensland Press.

Gillespie, K. (2007). *Steep slopes: Song creativity, continuity and change for the Duna of Papua New Guinea.* PhD dissertation, Australian National University.

hooks, b. (1994). *Teaching to transgress: Education as the practice of freedom.* New York: Routledge.

Jones, T. A., & Elkin, A. P. (1958). *Arnhem land music* (North Australia). Sydney, Australia: University of Sydney.

Kaberry, P. (2004). *Aboriginal woman: Sacred and profane.* London: Routledge. (Original work published 1939)

Lawrence, H. R. (1995). Death of a singer. In L. Barwick, A. Marett & G. Tunstill (Eds.), *The essence of singing and the substance of song: Recent responses to the Aboriginal performing arts and other essays in honour of Catherine Ellis* (pp. 185–188). Sydney, Australia: University of Sydney

Magowan, F. (2007). *Melodies of mourning: Music and emotion in Northern Australia* (World Anthropology Series, W. James & N. J. Allen, Eds.). Perth, Australia: University of Western Australia Press.

Malcolm, L. (2007). The "thrifty gene" hypothesis and indigenous health. *The health report* [Radio program]. Sydney, Australia: Australian Broadcasting Corporation. Retrieved March 1, 2009, from http://www.abc.net.au/rn/healthreport/stories/2007/1913092.htm.

Marett, A. (2005). *Songs, dreamings, and ghosts: The Wangga of North Australia.* Middletown, CN: Wesleyan University Press.

McConaghy, C. 2003. Pedagogy, trauma and difficult memory: Remembering Namitjira, our beloved. *Australian Journal of Indigenous Education, 32,* 11–20.

Morphy, H. (1991). *Ancestral connections: Art and an Aboriginal system of knowledge.* Chicago, IL: University of Chicago Press.

Moyle, A. M. (1964). *Songs from the Northern Territory [sound recording]: An ethnomusicological study.* Canberra: Australian Institute of Aboriginal Studies.

Moyle, R. M. (1979). *Songs of the Pintupi: Musical life in a central Australian society.* Canberra: Australian Institute of Aboriginal Studies.

Powdermaker, H. (1966). *Stranger and friend: The way of an anthropologist.* New York: Norton.

Robertson, C. E. (1993). The ethnomusicologist as midwife. In R. Solie (Ed.), *Musicology and difference: Gender and sexuality in music scholarship* (pp. 107–124). Berkeley, CA: University of California Press.

Strehlow, T. G. H. (1971). *Songs of Central Australia.* Sydney, Australia: Angus and Robertson.

Stubington, J. (2007). *Singing the land: The power of performance in Aboriginal life.* Strawberry Hills, NSW: Currency House.

Webb-Pullman, M., Nethercote, J., & Vorrath, S. (2007). *30 years of reports into Aboriginal Australia.* Retrieved March 1, 2009, from http://www.crikey.com.au/Politics/20070622-30-years-of-reports-into-Aboriginal-Australia.html.

Wild, Stephen A. (1975). *Walbiri music and dance in their social and cultural nexus.* Bloomington, IN: Ann Arbor.

Chapter 15

A Way of Loving, A Way of Knowing
Music, Sexuality and the Becoming of a Queer Musicologist

Jodie Taylor

Almost 10 years ago, when I first began to take an interest in musicology as an undergraduate, I never imagined that music research would lead me towards a deeper understanding of gender, sexuality and my sexual self. The purpose of studying music at a conservatorium, so I thought, was to learn more about musical formalism, style, history and technical practice. This thought was reified by detailed musicological instruction on the inner workings of music — how it is put together and makes sense melodically, harmonically and rhythmically — as opposed to how people make use of music and how music potentially affects our bodies, emotions and desires; that is, how it makes sense personally and socially. For quite some time I remained largely unaware that a purpose of studying music could also be to learn more about gender performance, sexual identity performance and the ways that people use music to facilitate these expressions of identity. And as such, it was not until some years later, when I could no longer resist questioning myself about the nature and construction of my own queer gender and sexual identity that the same questions began to matter to me as a musicologist.

In the early stages of my doctoral candidature, I took great interest in the gendered and sexual history of Western music, particularly how music has marked gender, signified the feminine and aroused sexual suspicion. What I soon uncovered was a sizable body of feminist and popular writing on the topic, none of which had ever been brought to my attention as an undergraduate student. The associations that music shares with the gendered, the sexual and the intimately pleasurable was evident both in historical and contemporary accounts of music's affect, its social significance and cultural constructedness. The fourth-century writings of Augustine of Hippo suggested that he was very much aware of the seductive persuasions of music upon the flesh, and thus he begged God to release him from the dangers that lay in the gratification of musical pleasure (Augustine, 1961). As such, Saint Augustine warned that all musical practices (even the sacred) must be undertaken with acute moral questioning. In reading Cusick's work I found similar arguments which suggested that for centuries music has been scrutinised because of its physical and emotional appeal: "From Plato to Artusi to Hanslick" she proposed, "anxieties about music's power have been elaborated through metaphors of gender, sexual difference, and sexual allure" (1999a, p. 478). While McClary, advocating for contemporary studies of music that recognise the culturally constructed and "ideological basis of music's operations," also argued that music's power "resides in its ability to shape the ways we experience our bodies, emotions, subjectivities, desires, and social relations" (2000, p. 7).

Music is intimately connected to our gendered and sexual selves, just as our gendered and sexual selves are contingent upon the ways in which we listen to, perform and write about music. In this chapter, I wish to draw upon the powers of music as outlined by Cusick and McClary, contextualising them within a queer framework of identity construction and performance. I begin by exploring the anxious history that surrounds music, gender and sexuality, arguing that the discipline of musicology is one that, for many years, sought to exclude gender and sexuality from the study of music. A theoretical discussion of queer and musical identities follows, the purpose of which is to expound some of the complexities of gender and sexual identity performance according to queer theory. The subsequent sections entitled "Coming Out" and "Going Out" respectively offer an intimate and detailed reflection on my personal experiences and musical negotiations of gender and sexuality, foregrounding my ethnographic work as an "insider researcher" or "complete member" (Adler & Adler, 1987; Bennett, 2003; Brewer, 2000; Hodkinson, 2005; Merton, 1972; Sprague, 2005; Wolcott, 1999) of a local queer music scene. Employing an autoethnographic approach positions me, the researcher, within the broader social context of this work and attempts to connect my very personal experiences with the cultural milieu in which they occur. Moreover, autoethnography celebrates the vulnerable, personal and emotional qualities that are deeply embedded in my work and challenges the dichotomies between subjectivity and objectivity, locating me in the field of queer musicological enquiry (Coffey, 2003; Chang, 2008; Denzin, 1997; Ellis & Bochner, 2000, 2006; Reed-Danahay, 1997).

It is not without fear and trepidation that I weave myself into this text in such an undisguised way. As I sit here writing, my thoughts stray toward memories of my grandparents: What would they have made of all this, I wonder? If they were still alive I am fairly certain I would have kept this and most of my other research publications from them. Even though I trusted their love as kind and forgiving, I doubt that they would have accepted my queerness, particularly such a public expression of it. I would not have wanted them to think about my sexual relationships — the ways of loving that are implicit in my work. Yet, I freely offer my work and myself for you to read, for you who I do not know, who I cannot see, and whose criticism I cannot hear. To you, I am at once an anonymous face and a naked heart, and in this strange mix of anonymity and nakedness, there is an awkward comfort. Somewhat akin to the confessional, the black and white spaces on this page afford just enough camouflage so that I can be honest and feel safe in my honesty. Because, you see, writing about queer desire and sexual bodies — specifically my queer desire and sexual body — is still rather confronting, but overcoming this sense of confrontation and fear is an important step toward queer visibility and an important step in the advancement of anti-oppressive and multi-vocal academic discourses.

Fearing the Flesh

Since the postmodernist turn in scholarship which brought about "new" or "critical" forms of musicology in the 1980s (Kerman, 1985), discussions regarding gender, sexuality and their relation to music have emerged with vigour, effectively reminding musicologists that "whatever else music is 'about', it's *inevitably* about the body" (Leppert, 1993, p. xx, emphasis in original). Prior to this, however, musicology's patriarchal institutions fostered a discourse that can be seen as characterised by absolutism, autonomy and transcendence. By establishing a musical canon that was hypothetically untainted by corporeality and its trivial desires, the modernist (and overwhelmingly male) academy attempted to expunge the flesh, and thus the feminine, from the high ground of canonical music (Brett, 2002b; McClary, 1991; Solie, 1993). It was this fleshless, desireless and loveless form of musicology that I first came to know as an undergraduate and honours student; a form of musicology built upon a fear of femininity and queerness.

Since the fall of Eve (in Christian dogma), women have worn the mark of sin to a greater extent than men, their bodies coming to symbolise an undisciplined sexuality and corruption. According to Peraino "'woman' was understood as sexuality incarnate; and furthermore, all sources of sensory pleasures, such as music, poetry, visual arts, and even food, came to be gendered as feminine" (2006, p. 45). Solie points to this in her introduction to *Musicology and Difference,* noting the "long-standing trope of European culture ... in which music is understood to occupy the female position vis-à-vis the male composer" (1993, pp. 13–14). And finally, Dibben, in her work on music and gender also argues that, in Western culture, music's corporeal alliances, its emotional and physical appeal, "predispose[s] it to be assigned to the feminine" (2002, p. 121).

The gendering of music in this way has been historically viewed as a threat to the "normal" male body and the masculinity, heterosexuality, rationality and intellect of male musicians, composers and music scholars. This is because, as Leppert notes, "music constitutes the putative agent in the feminisation of men" (1993, p. 180) and by extension, as Butler (1990, 1993) in her theory of heterosexual hegemony and the bogus logic of sexual inversion suggests (Davidson, 1987), the feminisation of men equally constitutes the homosexualisation of men. Fearful of intellectual "castration," men sought to keep women from scholarly pursuits of music as the presence of women was thought to agitate further crisis on the position of men and the "naturalness" of their masculinity (Cusick, 1999a; Solie, 1993). Moreover, it was in these authoritative roles that men were able to control and maintain their masculinity and thus their heterosexuality.

Little did I realise, when I set out to become a musicologist, that my female body (let alone my sexuality) was so imposing; so poisonous and foul-smelling to the history of the discipline I loved. Moreover, I had never really thought of music as exclusively feminine or feminising because for me music encompassed all manner of gender and sexual expressions, especially those that compelled the most unspoken of desires. Looking back over my youth I can see this now: in my pre-adolescent school days I had witnessed boys being teased for singing in the choir. However, it never occurred to me then that their sweet unbroken voices were perceived by the other boys as a weakness in the fabric of their maleness, a sign of "sissyness" and thus of suspect sexual "deviance". I guess I had simply written off this kind of gender slander as idiocy on the part of the perpetrators — the same perpetrators who teased me for being fat and teased other children for wearing glasses or for being diligent students. My body has always been a "musical body" and at times I have felt it to be musical more than female. Maybe this was because my musical body didn't have excess puppy fat, or because at times people have found my music far more attractive than the physical reality of me. For whatever reason, I had always felt a profound connectedness between music and my body and for that reason, feminist musicology became highly appealing some years later.

At first, I revelled in the feminist understanding of music as "sensually powerful, socially constructed, and socially constructing" (Cusick, 1999a, p. 484) and feminist attempts at examining music's role in the affirmation of pleasure and in the construction and maintenance of gender and sexual identity, as these same questions were close to my heart also. Yet, I was quickly disappointed to discover the abject position of queerness within music and musicological history, especially given that, as a queer female, I had found no other medium so well suited to self-articulation as music. While both feminist and popular criticism have been instrumental in remedying the historical treatment of music as formally self-contained and socially detached, they both — for quite some time — ignored those genders and sexualities that did not line up in the socially prescribed way, favouring a rather "straight" approach to discussions of sexuality and eroticism. For popular scholars in particular this is a peculiar omission, given, as Morris points out, that "an enormous number of figures in popular music are known to have had elaborate gender identities, intense physical relationships with members of their own sex, or sexual tastes outside the mainstream" (2006, p. 22). It was not until the early 1990s that gay, lesbian and queer scholars of music began writing queer musicology. Since its beginnings, queer musicology has proven itself particularly adept at declaring self-identity (be it directly or indirectly) and providing a context for musicologists to "come out" within their scholarship (see key texts by Brett, Wood & Thomas, 1994; Fuller & Whitesell, 2002; Gill, 1995; Hadleigh, 1991; Koestenbaum, 2001; Peraino, 2006; Whiteley & Rycenga, 2006).

Recently, I completed a PhD in the area of musical performance and queer sexualities (Taylor, 2008a). This was driven in equal parts by academic aspirations and a desire to better understand who I was. Writing this dissertation was a reflexive project: It forced me to question my gender, sexual and musical identity and disclose my private self to my institution, my peers and the wider community of scholars. Personally, I did not fear rejection when I embarked on my own queer scholarship, but I did fear that people would misinterpret me after I had spent so long figuring out who I was for myself. I feared that my colleagues and students would assume I was a lesbian, when in fact, I strongly identified as queer.

At first I was cautious not to give too much of myself away. Being "out" was not a problem, as there were numerous "out" lesbian and gay scholars at my university, but being "out" as a lesbian is something entirely different to identifying as queer — well, for me anyway — something that many people still do not seem to understand. I wondered if people were judging me behind my back or scorning my "loose" morals? I feared losing the respect of my supervisors and peers by researching and subsequently admitting attendance of BDSM[1] and sex-on-site spaces and involvement in drag and queer punk scenes. I feared that my research and I myself therefore would be rejected, given the conservative history of my discipline. Fear very nearly held me back, as it took me a year to work up the courage to tell my supervisors that what I really wanted to study for my Ph.D. was queer sexualities and queer musical performance and not the disparities between conservatorium training and community music practice which was my original — and far less personally motivated — topic. Eventually this fear of judgement and rejection subsided, and I realised that it was only through talking and writing about my ways of loving that I would be able to uncover new ways of knowing music and new ways of articulating what music means to other queer people like myself. Being a musician, a musicologist, and having lived as a queer identified person — one who exhaustingly performed her queer female identity through music — provided me with a unique opportunity to write about others like myself, and to enact change within a form of scholarship that had feared the flesh — both of women and of queers — for the larger part of its history.

Queering the Flesh

Borrowing most notably from the work of Foucault (1979) and Butler (1990), the discourse of queer theory emerged in the early 1990s as a strong postmodern and poststructural critique of identity. Queer theory is radical, subversive and disruptive in the way it problematises historical meta-narratives and deconstructs hierarchies, emphasising the marginal and the liminal. It resists prevailing heteronormative constructs of gender and sexual identity (Berlant & Warner, 1998; Corber & Valocchi, 2003) and more recently, the emerging homonormativity of assimilated lesbian and gay minorities (Duggan, 2002; Halberstam,

2005). In 1993, Doty's ground-breaking book, *Making Things Perfectly Queer*, demonstrated how queer can be conceptualised as something different, something more than lesbian and gay: the "intersecting or combining of more than one specific form of nonstraight sexuality" (1993, p. xvi). Queer is not a monolithic category in itself, nor does it function solely as a substitute, or a collective term for lesbian and gay identity. Rather, it is an argument against the specificity of both heterosexual and homosexual identities and the presupposition that gender and sexuality is performed in a socially prescribed manner (Butler, 2001). Queer poses a challenge to binary labelling philosophies — masculine, feminine, heterosexual and homosexual — and essentialist notions of fixed, coherent and universal subjectivity (Gamson, 2000; Halperin, 1995; Jagose, 1996; Meyer, 1994; Phelan, 1997; Sullivan, 2003; Warner, 1993, 1996). Queer theory supposes that identity is located in a performative nexus, arguing that the self is by no means stable but rather constituted in time via stylised acts (Butler, 1988, 1990, 1993; Sedgwick, 1993). Therefore, queer critique rejects a social identity based solely upon material sexual practices, acknowledging that identities (be they gendered, sexual or otherwise) are accompanied by non-sexual enactments and public signification in a variety of forms — such as signification and enactment through music.

It is well established within musicological and sociological studies that music is an important resource in the construction and articulation of identity (DeNora, 1998; Frith, 1996; Hargreaves, Miell & McDonald, 2002), and this applies equally to queer identities (Brett, Wood & Thomas, 1994; Fuller & Whitesell, 2002; Peraino, 2006; Whiteley & Rycenga, 2006). Music, like gender and sexuality, is also performative in that it constitutes a set of acts that are attributed to one's identity, and it is at the site of performance that we find Butler's thinking about sex, gender and sexuality intersecting most poignantly with theories of musical identity. As Cusick explains:

> These performances of a gendered and sexed self are partly, but certainly not entirely, performances of and through the body. It is at this point in Butler's notion of gender and sex as performative that I think to be most promising for thinking about musical performance. For musical performance, too, is partly (but not entirely) the culturally intelligible performance of bodies ... Musical performances, then, are often the accompaniment of ideas performed *through* bodies by the performance *of* bodies. (1999b, p. 27, emphases in original)

Music acts as an aesthetic channelling of the performer's body. For queers, music offers us an opportunity to (re)create and perform our bodies in ways that may be unavailable to us in daily life. Moreover, it is often through music that the fear of expressing a queer body can be greatly reduced.

The aesthetic and performative qualities of music, coupled with its fluidity, temporality and looseness of meaning, make it well suited to expressions of queerness, moreover providing a "safe space" for these expressions because of music's theatrical and fanciful nature. Music, and the world of entertainment more generally, have long been hospitable to gender and sexual misfits because in music you can get away with exaggerated and "artificial" effect; you can "try on" different modes of self-presentation; you can "come out" and reveal yourself through music, lessening the risk of persecution, because music itself is a mysterious and implicit form (Brett, 1994; Hadleigh, 1991; Koestenbaum, 1993; Morris, 2006; Peraino, 2006). The exploration of pleasures and potentialities afforded by music has often made it a pursuit of the socially deprived and liminal body. We only need think of Tchaikovsky, Bessie Smith, Boy George, k.d. lang or Antony Hegarty to understand how this is so. Fuller and Whitesell propose that, historically, "music [has] provided the accompaniment for confrontations between disparate conventions of social propriety in general, and in particular, for encounters between diverse idiolects of sexual identity" (2002, p. 12). Koestenbaum further emphasises this, suggesting that:

> Forbidden sexualities stay vague because they fear detection and punishment. Historically, music has been defined as mystery and miasma, and implicitness rather than an explicitness, and so we have hid inside music; in music we can come out without coming out, we can reveal without saying a word. (1993, pp. 189–190)

Music can be a powerful social agent: It can potentially soothe uncomfortable subject matter that disrupts social norms. As such, music often provides a refuge for queers (those who are particularly disruptive to normativity) and a space in which queer bodies can tolerably skew the margins of acceptable gender and sexual identity.

For me, this has long been the case, as music accompanied my earliest experimentations and performances of gender and sexuality. Music provided me with a temporal space in which my sexual desires could be safely unveiled, effectuated and cryptically shared. And although I am now very secure in my queerness — having no desire to soothe anyone's discomfort with my sexuality — I continue to return to music, for I have noticed that many of my recent experimentations cannot be considered musicless. In private sexual spaces there is almost always recorded music playing and in public spaces there is usually a deejay or band playing live. This music, then, becomes part of my aural memory; it marks the experience in a similar way to people, places and feelings. It not only accompanies my sexual experiences, but in many ways, it has become a significant part of my sexual identity. Because it is, and has long been, with and through music that I create desire, channel it and enact it.

Coming Out (A Way of Loving)

From the time we are born (and in some cases prior to this), our sex, gender and sexuality is imprinted upon us by our parents, our communities and our cultures. At that moment when our parents utter the deceptively simple words "it's a girl" or "it's a boy" what they are also doing is declaring their expectations for how and whom we will love. When someone tells their friends and family that their new baby is a girl, they are not simply telling these people that their baby has female anatomy, but they are also (implicitly) declaring that their baby — who happens to have a womb, a vagina and so on — will in fact *become* a girl who will *become* a woman. In order for a girl to become a woman she is taught femininity and heterosexuality by default. Girls should like pink, they should like nurturing artificial children of their own and they should learn to "like" boys. I always despised pink, I never liked those blinking, crying and defecating dolls but I did learn to "like" boys. However, I also learned to "like" girls.

Coming out as a 15-year-old, practising bisexual, feminist, goth in the mid-1990s was not so great a problem for me personally; I actually drew a lot of strength from these identities; they made me feel distinguishable and independent; they seemed to me a perfect set of traits for someone who romanticised notions of becoming a singer, philosopher and political anarchist. Trying to be all these things did, however, raise a lot of suspicion and grief among friends at my all-girls high school and among the three 20-something-year-old-boys with whom I played in a band — one of whom was my boyfriend. The problem most of my friends seemed to have with me was not whether I was gay or straight, it was my inability to choose. This choice was complicated not least by my sexual desires but also by the rigid gender stereotypes that (I thought) went hand-in-hand with sexual identity. I didn't look or act like a lesbian: I didn't know you could be a velvet skirt-, fishnet tights- and make-up-wearing lesbian who ate meat and wanted to sing opera. Moreover, I didn't act like the straight girls I knew: I didn't want to get married or have children, I didn't like any boys my age. I owned a copy of *The Female Eunuch*, I had hairy armpits and I wrote songs about suffragettes and played in a hard rock band.

Eventually, the social pressure to fix my identity became too much. My boyfriend threatened to leave me, my girlfriend decided she was straight, and I felt isolated from the rest of my peers. I felt that the only way I could relate to people was through music. My musicality was the only thing that brought me respect and admiration from my peers, so I retreated into music, using it as a way to deflect unwanted attention from my fluid and multiple sexualities. It was in music and only in music, that I could perform all the roles necessary to satisfy me. In music I could compose, perform and listen; I could play multiple instruments; I could perform and appreciate various styles. It was only as a musician and music lover, that I was allowed to be fluid: to interpret and reinterpret, to create and recreate.

As a weekday student of classical voice and weekend singer in a hard rock band, I found the freedom in music to explore my sexual desires. I was the diva one moment and a rock'n'roller the next. As an enthusiast of opera and musical theatre, I discovered that the diva was often the object of male desire, just as I longed to be. Her femininity was robust and disciplined. It was captured in her costumes, in the roles that were written for her, in the curves of her body and in her voice, which gave a powerful blast and refused containment. In my eyes, her own voice was the key to her sexual prowess, and thus she became a personal icon: she was a woman in control, a woman who regulated her own pleasure. In contrast, the masculinity encapsulated in playing the rock star afforded me the public expression of aggressive sexuality. It made me feel like the object of female desire while also covering up my gaze upon other women.

The rock star was a fugitive of definition and self-control. In this role, it became perfectly acceptable to flaunt my sexuality, to adorn my body in piercings and leather, and to say and act in whatever manner pleased me. While many people still found it unusual that I possessed an equally intense passion for the genres of opera, musical theatre, industrial rock and metal it seemed that expressing conflicting taste in music did not attract nearly as much scrutiny as expressing conflicting sexual desires. This is because unlike the supposedly natural and thus "normal" expression of gender and sexuality, musical taste is not understood to be in any way natural, normal or innocent but rather a self-determined and defining mechanism of identity. Music allowed me to perform gender and express sexuality in multiple non-normal ways that were unavailable to me in daily life. Furthermore, it allowed me to do this "under the radar" — to explore the spaces in-between masculine, feminine, gay and straight without fear of rejection. An expert in border crossing, I "played it feminine" with the men and boyish with the girls and managed for quite some time to stay sexually vague — to stay "musical" — escaping detection and punishment.

It was not until some years later — when I discovered queer theory in my postgraduate studies of music and sexuality — that I realised my sexual negotiations through music were not uncommon. In fact, my experiences were similar to many others who had also lived inside the "musical closet" — a space which allows us to come out, to play, to perform, to queer and to be queer, under a guise of frivolity and entertainment. Having lived this, I was thoroughly elated to find a handful of musicological texts around the topic of queerness in music. Seeing these published words legitimised my own musical queerness and gave me the necessary courage to pursue a queer musicology of my own.

Going Out (A Way of Knowing)

Part of the process of coming out, is going out — out to find other people with whom one can be queer — and the most prominent social spaces in which queers go out to be with one another are bars and nightclubs. These spaces are significant, not least in that they facilitate meeting and socialising among sexual minorities, but that meeting and socialising is almost always accompanied by music and dancing. In the latter part of the twentieth century in particular, music has played a significant role in the organisation and marking of queer scenes (see discussions on a variety of queer scenes in Buckland, 2002; Ciminelli & Knox; Currid, 1995; Halberstam 2005). While music often differentiates queer clubs from straight clubs, it also works as a way of differentiating divergent scenes among the broader queer community (Taylor, 2008b). This is just one of the many facets of queer life that I was completely unaware of until I started actively researching lesbian, gay and queer socio-musical spaces.

My first experience of local queer scenes was as a naive eighteen year old who would drag her straight female best friend to gay dance clubs on nights when her disapproving boyfriend was visiting his parents. Sexual curiosity clearly played a large part in me wanting to go to these spaces; however, the music — and the freedom with which everyone moved to it — was just as intriguing to me. Prior to going out with other lesbians, gays and queers, most of my social musical experiences had been through singing in choirs, playing in school instrumental ensembles, performing with my rock band, attending musical theatre and opera productions and the occasional rock concert, none of which involved the sexually energised displays of music and dance I experienced here.

As an 18-year-old, I could have never imagined that 10 years later, writing about my experiences and the experiences of other queers would earn me the award of PhD. Nor could I have imagined that in doing musicology — a kind of musicology that compelled me to seriously consider queer musical production and performance, queer feelings and queer love — I would come to know my gendered, sexual and musical self so much better. Through this I have also become (and I am still becoming) a different kind of musician and musicologist, one who has been deeply and irreversibly affected by critically engaging with the theories and histories of queerness; one who has been sincerely and gratefully affected by the people she met along the way. In gaining a deeper understanding of queer theory and through the personal connections that I made during my doctoral research, I was able to once again reconfigure my self-image, taking another vital step towards knowing myself better. I now see more clearly the multiple subjective positions that I assume — positions that cannot be described as one thing or another; positions that flow between multiple times, spaces, histories, affiliations and styles of self-perception. I had always felt the connectivity between my queerness and musicality, but in doing queer musicology I now have greater understanding of this connectivity and the power that it yields.

Through conducting an ethnographic study of my local queer scene I heard new music, witnessed new gender and sexual performances through music and made new friendships. I saw from multiple perspectives the joys and pains of being and doing queer, and of living as an out and proud queer person. People shared with me their experiences of family rejection, of contracting and living with HIV, of drug overdose, of queer bashing and discrimination. I saw how important music was to all of them and through music — through dancing with them, listening to and watching them perform, and talking with them about our musical stories — I connected with other queer people and their histories, and many of them connected with me.

One night almost two years ago, my partner said to me on a living room dance floor, "Babe, if this is the queer scene then we're right in the middle of it". The next day I wrote this down and reflected on what it meant. It felt monumental. I felt as if my presence in this very private space signified that I was "accepted" by some of the people who I had been observing and probing for some years prior. When I came to the end of my doctoral research and began looking over all the personal notes I had made in my research journals, I came to realise that what really excited me about this comment — why it has stuck in my head for so long — was not a feeling of acceptance but a feeling of multiple and ineffable difference. I felt privileged to be invited into the private space of this particular queer group that I was researching, but I had in fact been a part of something "queer" all along. This was not a profound moment of queer acceptance; this group of people was no more or less queer than others I knew — they were just a different kind of queer, one I had limited experience of, and that is what I felt in this moment: the vast and awe-inspiring differences in the ways that people express and perform their queerness and the willingness of these people to share themselves, in their private moments, with me.

In the final paragraph of my doctoral dissertation I used the "journey" cliché which lacked the profundity I was hoping to evoke in my final lines of text; however, when I looked up this word and all its synonyms in the dictionary, it was clear that "a gradual passing from innocence to mature awareness" was the most honest description I could attach to the process of conducting queer musicology. Through my scholarly engagements with queer people and their music I have indeed become more maturely aware: aware of my disciplines; aware of methods and processes; aware of theories, histories, styles and sensibilities. But most of all I have become more aware of other queer people, their histories, styles and sensibilities. I feel more connected to my own history and culture; I am more aware of myself, my potential and the complications of desire, of feeling and of being queer. As such, I have come to believe that this is the most significant "truth" and value of my work as a queer musicologist.

References

Adler, P. A., & Adler, P. (1987). *Membership roles in field research*. Newbury Park, CA: Sage.

Augustine, Saint. (1961). *Confessions*. (R. S. Pine-Coffin, Trans.). Harmondsworth, UK: Penguin.

Bennett, A. (2003). The use of insider knowledge in ethnographic research on contemporary youth music scenes. In A. Bennett, M. Cieslik & S. Miles (Eds.), *Researching Youth* (pp. 186–200). London: Palgrave.

Berlant, L., & Warner, M. (1998). Sex in public. *Critical Inquiry*, 24(2), 547–566.

Brett, P. (1994). Musicality, essentialism, and the closet. In P. Brett, E. Wood & G. C. Thomas (Eds.), *Queering the pitch: The new gay and lesbian musicology* (pp. 9–26). New York: Routledge.

Brett, P. (2002). Musicology and sexuality. In S. Fuller & L. Whitesell (Eds.), *Queer episodes in music and modern identity* (pp. 178–188). Urbana, IL: University of Illinois Press.

Brett, P., Wood, E., & Thomas, G. (1994). [Preface]. In P. Brett, E. Wood & G. C. Thomas (Eds.), *Queering the pitch: The new gay and lesbian musicology* (pp. vii–ix). New York: Routledge.

Brewer, J. (2000). *Ethnography*. Buckingham, UK: Open University Press.

Buckland, F. (2002). *The impossible dance: Club culture and queer world-making*. Middletown, CT: Wesleyan University Press.

Butler, J. (1988). Performative acts and gender construction: An essay in phenomenology and feminist criticism. *Theatre Journal, 40*(4), 519–531.

Butler, J. (1990). *Gender trouble: Feminism and the subversion of identity*. London: Routledge.

Butler, J. (1993). *Bodies that matter: On the discursive limits of sex*. New York: Routledge.

Butler, J. (2001). The desire of philosophy. *Lolapress 2*, Retrieved July 7, 2006, from http://www.lolapress.org/elec2/artenglish/butl_e.htm

Chang, H. (2008). *Autoethnography as method*. Walnut Creek, CA: Left Coast Press.

Ciminelli, D., & Knox, K. (2005). *Homocore: The loud and raucous rise of queer rock*. Los Angeles: Alyson Books.

Citron, M. (1993). *Gender and the musical canon*. Cambridge: Cambridge University Press.

Coffey, A. (2003). Ethnography and self: Reflections and representations. In T. May (Ed.), *Qualitative research in action* (pp. 313–331). London: Sage Publications.

Corber, R., & Valocchi, S. (2003). [Introduction]. In R. Corber & S. Valocchi (Eds.), *Queer studies: An interdisciplinary reader* (pp. 1–17). Oxford, UK: Blackwell.

Currid, B. (1995). "We are family": House music and queer performativity. In S. E. Case, P. Brett & S. Foster (Eds.), *Cruising the performative: Interventions into the repression of ethnicity, nationality and sexuality* (pp. 165–196). Bloomington, IN: Indiana University Press.

Cusick, S. (1999a). Gender, musicology and feminism. In N. Cook & M. Everist (Eds.), *Rethinking music* (pp. 471–498). Oxford, UK: Oxford University Press.

Cusick, S. (1999b). On musical performances of gender and sex. In E. Barkin & L. Hamessley (Eds.), *Audible traces: Gender, identity, and music* (pp. 25–48). Zurich: Carciofoli Verlagshaus.

Davidson, A. (1987). Sex and the emergence of sexuality. *Critical Inquiry, 14*(1), 16–48.

DeNora, T. (2000). *Music in everyday life*. Cambridge, UK: Cambridge University Press.

Denzin, N. (1997). *Interpretive ethnography: Ethnographic practices for the 21st century*. Thousand Oaks, CA: Sage Publications.

Dibben, N. (2002). Gender identity and music. In R. MacDonald, D. Hargreaves & D. Miell (Eds.), *Musical identities* (pp. 117–133). Oxford, UK: Oxford University Press.

Doty, A. (1993). *Making things perfectly queer: Interpreting mass culture*. Minneapolis, MN: University of Minnesota Press.

Duggan, L. (2002). The new homonormativity: The sexual politics of neoliberalism. In R. Castronovo & D. Nelson (Eds.), *Materializing democracy: Towards a revitalized cultural politics* (pp. 175–194). Durham, NC: Duke University Press.

Ellis, C., & Bochner, A. P. (2000). Autoethnography, personal narrative, reflexivity: Researcher as subject. In N. K. Denzin & Y. S. Lincoln (Eds.), *Handbook of qualitative research* (2nd ed., pp. 733–768). Thousand Oaks, CA: Sage Publications.

Ellis, C., & Bochner, A. P. (2006). Analysing analytic autoethnography. *Journal of Contemporary Ethnography, 35*(4), 429–449.

Foucault, M. (1979). *The history of sexuality: Vol. 1. An introduction*. (R. Hurley, Trans.). London: Allen Lane. (Original work published 1976.)

Frith, S. (1996). *Performing rites: On the values of popular music*. Oxford: Oxford University Press.

Fuller, S., & Whitesell, L. (2002). [Introduction]. Secret Passages. In S. Fuller & L. Whitesell (Eds.), *Queer episodes in music and modern identity* (pp. 1–21). Urbana, IL: University of Illinois Press.

Gamson, J. (2000). Sexualities, queer theory, and qualitative research. In N. K. Denzin & Y. S. Lincoln (Eds.), *Handbook of qualitative research* (2nd ed., pp. 347–365). Thousand Oaks, CA: Sage.

Gill, J. (1995). *Queer noises: Male and female homosexuality in 20th century music.* London: Cassell.

Hadleigh, B. (1991). *The vinyl closet: Gays in the music world.* San Diego, CA: Los Hombres Press.

Halberstam, J. (2005). *In a queer time and place: Transgender bodies, subcultural lives.* New York: New York University Press.

Halperin, D. (1995). *Saint Foucault: Towards a gay hagiography.* New York: Oxford University Press.

Hargreaves, D. J., Miell, D., & MacDonald, R. A. R. (2002). What are musical identities, and why are they important? In R. A. R. MacDonald, D. J. Hargreaves & D. Miell (Eds.), *Musical identities* (pp. 1–20). Oxford: Oxford University Press.

Hodkinson, P. (2005). 'Insider research' in the study of youth cultures. *Journal of Youth Studies, 8*(2), 131–149.

Jagose, A. (1996). *Queer theory.* Melbourne, Vic: Melbourne University Press.

Kerman, J. (1985). *Musicology.* London: Fontana.

Koestenbaum, W. (2001). *The queen's throat: Opera, homosexuality, and the mystery of desire.* Cambridge, MA: Da Capo Press. (Original work published 1993.)

Leppert, R. (1993). *The sight of sound: Music, representation, and the history of the body.* Berkeley, CA: University of California Press.

McClary, S. (1991). *Feminine endings: Music, gender and sexuality.* Minneapolis, MN: University of Minnesota Press.

McClary, S. (2000). *Conventional wisdom: The content of musical form.* Berkeley, CA: University of California Press.

Merriam, A. (1964). *The anthropology of music.* Evanston, IL: Northwestern University Press.

Merton, R. K. (1972). Insiders and outsiders: A chapter in the sociology of knowledge. In R. Merton (Ed.), *Varieties of political expression in sociology* (pp. 9–47). Chicago: University of Chicago Press.

Meyer, M. (1994). [Introduction]. In M. Meyer (Ed.), *The politics and poetics of camp* (pp. 1–22). London: Routledge.

Morris, M. (2006). Stories coming out. [Review of the books *Love saves the day: A history of American dance music culture, 1970–1979* by T. Lawrence; *The fabulous Sylvester: The legend, the music, the seventies in San Francisco* by J. Gamson; *Listening to the sirens: Musical technologies of queer identity from Homer to Hedwig* by J. Peraino]. *Journal of Popular Music Studies, 18*(2), 220–240.

Peraino, J. A. (2006). *Listening to the sirens: Music technologies of queer identity from Homer to Hedwig.* Berkeley, CA: University of California Press.

Phelan, S. (1997). [Introduction]. In S. Phelan (Ed.), *Playing with fire, queer politics queer theories* (pp. 1–8). New York: Routledge.

Reed-Danahay, D. E. (Ed.). (1997). *Auto/ethnography: Writing the self and the social.* Oxford, UK: Berg.

Sedgwick, E. K. (1993). *Tendencies.* Durham, NC: Duke University Press.

Solie, R. A. (1993). On difference [Introduction]. In R. A. Solie (Ed.), *Musicology and difference* (pp. 1–20). Berkeley, CA: University of California Press.

Sprague, J. (2005). *Feminist methodologies for critical researchers: Bridging differences.* Walnut Creek, CA: Altamira Press.

Sullivan, N. (2003). *A critical introduction to queer theory.* Armidale, Vic: Circa.

Taylor, J. (2008a). *Playing it queer: Understanding queer gender, sexual and musical praxis in a 'new' musicological context.* Unpublished doctoral dissertation, Griffith University, Brisbane, Australia.

Taylor, J. (2008b). The queerest of the queer: Sexuality, politics and music on the Brisbane scene. *Continuum: Journal of Media & Cultural Studies, 22*(5), 647–661.

Warner, M. (1993). [Introduction]. In M. Warner (Ed.), *Fear of a queer planet: Queer politics and social theory* (pp. vii–xxxi). Minneapolis, MN: University of Minnesota Press.

Warner, M. (1996). From *fear* of a queer planet. In D. Morton (Ed.), *The material queer* (pp. 286–291). Boulder, CO: Westview Press.

Whiteley, S., & Rycenga, J. (Eds.). (2006). *Queering the popular pitch* (pp. xiii–xix). New York: Routledge.

Wolcott, H. (1999). *Ethnography: A way of seeing.* Walnut Creek, CA: Altamira Press.

Chapter 16

In Music and in Life
Confronting the Self Through Autoethnography

Colin Webber

The Triple Trials

Three years ago, at the time when the topic of my doctoral thesis was new and fresh and unavoidable, I was advised not to let my autoethnographic research become my therapy. My doctorate was examining the ways in which heightened autistic traits affect musical practice in composition and collaborative arts. Specifically, *my* autistic traits. However, it seemed like bad advice at the time — surely self-knowledge is just what I needed: "To know me is to love me" in a very literal (my favourite) way. This advice didn't initially deter me, but in time I soon came to discover, the problem with autoethnography is that everyone ends up knowing your secrets. I guess that's the point really — we write having asked the question "what can someone learn by reading about me?" Anyone who writes their own story has to deal with this; how much to reveal — where to draw the line, lift the veil, don the mask. This chapter highlights three aspects that I have found myself confronting in my autoethnographic research/therapy; the triple-headed dragon of Obsession, Depression, and Defence.

Music

I remember as a child lying on the floor of the primary school music room listening to some orchestral piece, the teacher asking students what the piece made them feel. I must have been about 10. I don't recall what the piece was, but I vividly remember him telling us that we might all feel something different, that music was for everyone. I think

I took that to heart because I could not define the feelings I had. I took up the saxophone and recorder at about this age — previous schools having had no instrumental music program — then moved on to the trombone the next year.

I enjoyed the role of second trombone — playing the harmonies — being inside the music, aware of the interplay and vertical structures. Lots of rests too — time to listen to the little details in the parts. Another teacher pointed out that many of the great arrangers of big bands and jazz have been trombonists — I took that one to heart too. By the time I went to university to study music I wanted to write, rather than play, but I rebelled against formal harmony lessons, preferring to rely on my ears and what I experienced inside my head, along with the (now mostly atrophied) ability to hear full orchestrations "off the score". I left the course in 1985 when I discovered the creative control that the studio, the new MIDI electronic instruments, and music technology could give me.

Some people describe being swept along by the structural tide of a piece, anticipating the return of a theme in another guise, but for me, music is a place to retreat into a moment, where I can stop time and be fascinated by some tiny accident or design, where I can marvel at the very intimacy of a moment frozen. I am also fascinated by extreme slow motion and macro photography — maybe the two are related. Many individuals with autistic spectrum disorders (ASDs) describe their attraction to the making of music, theatre and other arts as a means to "practise spontaneity" (Müller et al., 2008, p. 185) and social interaction, where the activity is in a sense mediated by a script, or a scripted context and its conscious expression. It is a chance for meaning-making to be slowed down, examined and pulled apart.

There are two principle aspects to music making that appear to be affected by the way my brain works: compositional method and practice, and collaborative practice. Different processes and sets of autistic traits appear to be at work.

Composition Practice

The practice of creating the music is surely the crux of the matter at hand, but it is certainly the hardest to write about, and the hardest to observe. Perhaps an exposé of eccentric creativity, an exploration of new ways of hearing is more viable. This chapter is concerned with the method of discovery, not the discoveries themselves, so I'll restrict myself somewhat. Here and there I have scattered some of the personal insights that self-examination has uncovered.

I love detail. I want to look deep inside the moment, hear it again and again, look for and revel in the tiny changes. I want to hear the micro-rhythm in the note, the catch of dissonance in that first hundred milliseconds of an erstwhile pure sound — and if it's not there I'll put it there — I don't care if you can hear it or if it will ultimately disappear beneath melodic narrative or theatrical dialogue. I want the details to have something tying them, an over-arch but not a structural integrity. It is still about the moment, not the form. I need to hear the sonic moment as it grows, to take the sound and shape it, to make aural sculpture and to match the developing sound in my head with that in my ears. I don't imagine music fully formed and then create it. I like it to grow in some organic way and put roots into the rock. I can lose myself in that.

A Little about Asperger's

In 2005, at the age of 39, I received (attained, discovered, was gifted with) a diagnosis of Asperger's syndrome in residual form. Asperger's syndrome is one of the autistic spectrum disorders with specific deficits in social cognition, executive function, central coherence, processing of emotion, empathy and non-verbal communication (American Psychiatric Association, 1994). These are the "deficits", but there are also "assets", including strong discrimination of detail, ability to lock into a topic or activity, logical responses rather than emotional ones, above average intelligence, good facility with systems and a strong ability to analyse and see patterns. Asperger's is sometimes referred to as "Wrong Planet Syndrome" (Jones et al., 2001, p. 396) because the unwritten rules and non-verbal nuance of social interaction can be a complete mystery — rather like a culture shock that goes on forever.

MRI and electrical function tests indicate the autistic brain functions differently from the "neurotypical" one (Baron-Cohen et al., 2006; Brieber et al., 2007; Deeley et al., 2007; Lotspeich et al., 2004; Murphy et al., 2002; Nieminen-von Wendt et al., 2002; Sokol & Edwards-Brown, 2004; Sugihara et al., 2007), and there is also a reduction in the average size of the cerebellum (Hallahan et al., 2008). The "intuitive" and "emotive" parts of the brain are less active, and stimuli that normally generate activity in these areas instead cause activity in the cognitive zones. However, the full mechanisms of autistic thinking (indeed typical thinking) are still little understood.

Table 1 indicates a subset of the *Diagnostic and Statistical Manual of Mental Disorders* (DSM-IV) diagnostic criteria for Asperger's Syndrome (American Psychiatric Association, 1994) and some ways that the various traits can manifest, both positive and negative. I have adapted these to focus on music and collaboration but the descriptions draw heavily from Gray and Attwood's "discovery" criteria (Gray & Attwood, 1999; Willey, 1999).

It is interesting to note that the aspects of autism tabled above are defined largely by external parameters. These are things that are readily observed and measured by psychologists using controlled tests. Research on autism in adults is lagging behind the understandings of children, in particular the compensatory mechanisms that adults develop, and which traits remain "in residue." The views of autistic persons, when they are available, point to some slightly different "priorities" in the symptomology. Brigitte Chamak recently led a team of sociologists and psychologists in examining the biographies of 21 authors with diagnoses of Autistic Spectrum Disorders (Chamak et al., 2008). These authors all point to sensory–perceptual idiosyncrasies and emotional regulation difficulties as being at the core of the autistic "way of being" (ibid., p. 276), and many of the DSM-IV criteria as being symptomatic manifestations of these core differences. This is a clear indicator of the value of adult autobiographic and autoethnographic writing in this field. The insight that autistic writers can offer has the potential to help redefine the very core of understanding of the condition.

Finding Out About the Self

Apparently I have always been "autistic" and always will be. I have muddled through with various successes and failures and sometimes a very strong sense of "otherness." Given a diagnosis at the age of 39 that explained so much of my life came as something of a shock and upheaval. I thought I had some hard-earned self-knowledge, except that my understanding of myself often did not fit with my understanding of others; there have always seemed to be things that other people could do that I could not, especially in relation to social interactions, some insight or "intuition". But I never talked about it. I never openly questioned my own perceptions or asked for help when I had clearly misunderstood a situation. The "residual" label in the diagnosis means that the symptomology is fully present but that, over time, I have developed sufficient coping mechanisms and cognitive strategies that the condition may not be obvious to an untrained observer or be a "problem" most of the time. Nonetheless, the condition persists and its effects become heightened under various conditions including stress. An analogy is that someone with full vision in only one eye can catch a ball because the brain learns depth perception by means other than stereoscopic vision.

Table 1
Manifestation of Autistic Traits

DSM-IV Diagnostic Criteria	Positive manifestation	Negative manifestation
Executive function deficits	• strong ability to take personal control of situations • ability to concentrate deeply on tasks such as instrumental practice, composition or software use • highly specialist and committed to field of endeavour, e.g. music, maths, computers • perseverance, loyalty, strong sense of justice and drive for task completion. Applies logical, systematic thinking to creative tasks • decisions based on fact and rational argument. Lack of emotional attachment to creative work • occasionally tangential or juxtaposing emotional response in creative work	• strong need for personal control of situations • difficulty shifting between tasks or mental focus • narrow, persistent interests • inflexible thinking, strict adherence to rules and routines • emotional disconnection from intellect • difficulty recognising emotions in self and others; difficulty with perspective taking
Weak central / strong local coherence	• focus on detail, patterns and minor inconsistencies; perfectionist drive; excellent analytical skills • strong sense of verbal humour; able to write clear, meaningful text • often unique approach to problem-solving • clarity of values unaffected by political factors	• difficulty in generalisation and gestalt; focus on parts of objects • literal interpretation of verbal and written language • may tend to insist on "own way of doing things" • rigid adherence to rules and laws
Sensory sensitivities	• highly accurate observation of visual, aural or tactile events	• hypersensitive to visual, aural or tactile stimulus
Impairments in non-verbal communication	• may not be easily offended, threatened or distracted by behaviour of others • may not need eye contact for effective communication • may be highly verbal and articulate, including analysis of subjective events • tends to be honest and direct	• may not understand meaning in facial expressions, gesture or tone of voice • may avoid eye contact or eye contact may be confusing • may rely on verbal communication for clarity • may lack tact and appear arrogant. may over-disclose personal detail
Impairments in social awareness	• likely to be trustworthy and honest • likely to be free of social or cultural bias and prejudice • may be highly self reliant • tends to treat everyone equally	• may be over-trusting or gullible and expect complete honesty • may not recognise social or cultural customs • may not "know how" to make or keep friends • may not understand social boundaries (friendships, colleagues etc)
Impairments in empathy	• may be strongly compassionate	• may not spontaneously respond to emotions of others
Impairments in theory of mind	• tends to assume others have the same understanding and knowledge as themselves	• does not spontaneously understand or adopt the point of view of others

A different part of the brain to "normal" is involved, and if that part of the brain is busy elsewhere, the ball will be missed.

So Pandora's Box has been opened and a wraithlike Thing has emerged. Its new name is Asperger's syndrome, and it becomes an omnipresent companion, a filter, a lens and a distance from which to observe. Asperger's may have given me a new way to watch myself, but the very sight of some hitherto unknown or misunderstood part of one's Self has its own sweet sharpness. The soul-sapping spectre of self-doubt and the blinding vulnerability of self-knowledge are inextricably bound together. So we lead to Obsession.

Obsession

I suspect that obsession is a necessary evil in PhD territory. Surely no-one would attempt to spend several years looking at some narrowly defined topic without a touch of it. In autoethnography, obsession brings with it the risk of insular regression, navel-gazing and egoistic fascination that students and supervisors need to be aware of and guard against. The challenge to avoid "unreflective use of personal account" (Atkinson & Delamont, 2006), to play the game properly and position the narrative against theory should be a foil to the obsession, a cognitive, conscious objectivity — but it is not. Unfortunately obsessive tendencies are a definable characteristic of Asperger's syndrome and the broader autistic phenotypes (Baron-Cohen & Wheelwright, 1999, p. 484; Soderstrom et al., 2002, p. 287) so the situation can get out of hand. Every aspect of every thought is now linked to The Research. "Did I say that, do that, think that, miss that, screw that up, make that choice, hear that detail, have that insight, because I have autistic traits? What of my past — the history that made me? How much of that is defined by this new Name? How much control did I really have then — do I really have now? How is that different to someone else?" In fact the crux of the issue is this last question, the relationship between Self and Other.

By definition, the autistic spectrum is a collection of traits, each with its own sliding scale of "severity". The various syndromes — Kanner autism; Asperger's syndrome (AS); high-functioning autism (HFA); and pervasive development disorder, not otherwise specified (PDD-NOS; love that last one!) — describe "clinically significant" manifestations of "at least X number of the following traits" (American Psychiatric Association, 1994). Well, there's a problem here. Everyone is a bit autistic (especially cats!), so the phrase, "Hey I'm a bit like that too" is one of the most common (and frustrating) responses I have heard over the last couple of years. In explaining Asperger's to patients and parents, Professor Tony Attwood uses an analogy of a 100-piece jigsaw, where each piece represents a trait and every "normal" person will have 20 or so of them. If you have 80 pieces, *including the corners*, you get a diagnosis (Attwood, 2008, p. 50). In practice things are not that simple. For a start, the pieces vary in size, and a little bit of a given trait is common. It may be enough that a person can recognize an "aspie experience" but not be clinically significant to a psychologist or cause an impairment of normal function. So in studying the condition itself and the ways in which it might affect me, I am constantly comparing myself with others, trying to *quantify* the degree or depth of a *qualitative* experience. This leads to lengthy, often one-sided conversations with pretty much anyone who will listen (assuming they *are* actually listening). Fortunately, I have other work to do to occupy my mind, but there are certainly many times when the research "crosses over" into that too. Then there's every other waking moment — family life, and social activity and music making. And sleep.

There is a strong correlation between Galbraith's "writing as knowledge-constitution" (Galbraith, 1999) and composing as music creation. It is interesting to reflect on the idea that knowledge-constitution is a process of the intellect and music-creation is a process of the emotions. The technological way of making music — computers, sequencers, synthesis, audio manipulation — appeals to my way of making meaning — it grows, it is not a process of transcription from the mind, or even discovery. It is possible that the composition process, this Moment, is the one time I can connect directly with my heart, for in much of my life, the connections from brain to heart and back again are conscious virtual constructions. "I think I feel like ..."

Depression

As has been noted by many autoethnographers before me, when one sets out to explore the self, one inevitably finds things one does not like (Denzin & Lincoln, 2000). When one's prior understanding of self has been undermined, the things one does not like can become the focus of attention, revelation can become revile-ation. Depression is a common occurrence in individuals with autistic spectrum disorders (Stewart et al., 2006; Hedley & Young, 2006; Cederlund & Gillberg, 2004), and I was not unfamiliar with it pre-diagnosis and pre-thesis. Jago writes about depression heightening one's reflexive awareness (Jago, 2002, p. 743), and it is also well understood that a primary driver of depression is the tendency to amplify negative thinking — the dam is not only half empty, but getting lower with every passing moment, there's no sign of rain, the climate change scientists say it's just going to get worse and there's nothing I can do about it, because the damage of the past is irreversible.

Autoethnography also heightens reflexive awareness. That's the point of it, observing what you are doing and how you are doing it, constantly evaluating, critiquing, comparing to others, so there can be a tendency for the two processes to feed off each other. Delamont (2007), in her article "Arguments Against Autoethnography", suggests that the method suffers in terms of its validity through its inability to escape familiarity. But without that familiarity, there is no validity at all. One cannot "situate" without intimate self-knowledge. One cannot analyse ethnographic material, auto or not, if the "subject" is unfamiliar or unconnected with their own experience. Ethnography of any name is about situating the individual experience within culture. Comparison is inevitable and necessary.

In my own case, the first comparisons have highlighted "difference" and it has not been particularly comfortable. I was always aware of some differences in my peers, but that was because *they* were a bit odd sometimes. I put that down to intra-species variation — we are all individuals according to Brian (*Life of Brian*; Gilliam, 1979) — everybody struggles to understand each other sometimes and that fact goes a long way towards explaining wars, Chinese food and modern art. It turns out though, that I am more different than I ever imagined. This revelation is partly from the process of self-learning, and partly from a parallel process of other-learning. Not being blessed with good "theory of mind" — another of those measurable deficits — I am finding myself constantly surprised at how other people actually function and the things they understand, apparently without being "taught". Theory of Mind (ToM) is that ability to spontaneously adopt the understanding of others. ToM is related to the "perspective taking" part of empathy (Rogers et al., 2006), and it typically develops in children around the age of 3 or 4. An impairment of ToM results in an inability not so much to understand another's point of view once it is articulated, but to understand that another *could possibly have* a different point of view. A typical person is not surprised to hear another person's perspective or idea. I am not "typical" and although I'm quite good at pretending to be when I have to, it is a very stressful and tiring way to be. I can "do" ToM to some degree, but it is generally not spontaneous. It requires a conscious prompt to engage a logical process: "I need to imagine I am someone else now". If the other person is actually behaving logically (according to my own logic), I'll most likely get it right. If they are responding emotionally to something there's a good chance I'll get it wrong, and if I'm distracted or stressed, that conscious effort may not occur at all. Sometimes, that's depressing.

Clinical depression manifests as an overriding negativity that a person needs help with, a deep black abyss of nothingness with sides too steep to climb without a lifeline. Imagine a state of euphoric excitement, or a fit of laughter when everything seems funny. Turn that upside down into deep sadness, where everything is a negative and make it have no end. That's depression. While depression is certainly a state of mind, it has significant chemical components. There are medicinal means to keeping the body's seratonin levels a bit more even and they do work for most people, but it is an on-going battle in the mind, requiring conscious modification of "thought behaviours" — as if I wasn't doing enough of that already! So in short, depression is pretty common among PhD students, very common among autistics and may be accentuated by the processes of autoethnography. Great!

Defence

"You can't do 'good' autoethnographic work without constantly questioning the ethics of your pursuit. As soon as you put that "I" on the page, you can't avoid asking if your revelations might be harmful to you or anyone else" (Jago, 2002, p. 753). Delamont puts this dilemma just as strongly, stating that autoethnography is almost impossible to publish ethically (Delamont, 2007, p. 2), in part because the reader demands that the story be "true". It is an issue that authors wrestle with in all forms of personal narrative, whether telling their own stories or those of others. "Do no harm" is a nebulous and inadequate concept in the place of guidelines, and the requirement to judge each instance on its merits leaves the door wide open to ethical errors, concerns, and criticism.

Anonymity is the first issue here, protecting individuals from the critical gaze of others. Everyone is innocent until exposed, but at what point are the characters we portray identifiable? In an ethnographic narrative about some extraordinary experience, it can be difficult to cloak the individual in anonymity, especially given the pervasive nature of the media and the public thirst for "human interest stories". Of course if the "lead character" is identified as the author, the problem just gets worse. How does one protect one's "significant others" from identification, and is it necessary anyway? If an author's condition is genetic, what will the story imply about familial generations in both directions? Will a relative want anyone else to know in 10 years' time? Who is going to read the work? Statistically, it may be unlikely that people reading a given academic work will know the people portrayed — but will that be enough? At some point, it seems inevitable that the people around the author will have to be asked for their reactions and their consent.

The second aspect of Defence concerns the revealing of things hitherto unknown within existing relationships. Ellis (2007) discusses "relational ethics" in this context, bringing friends both old and new, colleagues, and family under the umbrella of significant others. There are moments reading her work when I think the ethic is misplaced, or perhaps simply that her understanding has developed and changed over time, and indeed this is recognised in her later work (ibid.) and her criteria has become more stringent. The ethics of informed consent will necessarily influence what we tell and how we tell it (Adams, 2008, p. 12), whether we choose to reveal or withhold and this may also have implications for the conclusions we draw. As I study the effects of my autistic traits on my musical practice, I am increasingly finding that the real learning about these things is coming from other aspects of my life in both past and present. In some cases there are things that may have enormous impact but I feel may be inappropriate to reveal, for fear of hurting others (Ellis, 2007, p. 17). Do the conclusions then become less valid because the means of reaching them is undisclosed? Do I need to go back and look for other, more benign, evidence elsewhere, and what do I do if I can't find it?

It struck me just the other day that my practice in collaborative arts may be linked to a desire for a safer intimacy, a thirst for the mind-meld. Friendships are not easy for me, their initiation and maintenance is some mysterious magic. In the studio, in the theatre rehearsal room, in the *making of meaning together* there is a shared experience, an intimacy that is defined by its content, mediated by its context and completely safe within its own boundaries. The environment of collaborative music-making in the studio gives an opportunity to *talk about the music* and the emotional content and context of the moment in a way that I have not experienced elsewhere. If one is playing jazz, one is expected to *feel* the music, to respond intuitively to the changes and the ebb and flow of the other musicians. Well, I tried it and it didn't work for me. In larger ensembles it is the conductor, to a large extent, who plays the music — the musicians are themselves the instruments under her hands.

In "real life" the moment is gone, it cannot be replayed and analysed but in these studio moments I can bring my life experience to a discussion about the heart, *speak my mind*, say what I think and probe the thoughts and feelings of the other participants directly through language and the recorded coding of the music itself. These realisations are a direct result of the process of self-observation and of writing about the experience. The concept of writing bringing knowledge *into being*

(Galbraith, 1999) becomes clear as a cycle of knowledge-constitution via an internal dialectic. The parallels between this and the ways in which I make music are not lost on me, and it is an aspect that I will be devoting some space to in my doctoral thesis.

These creative partnerships highlight another trait that is not uncommon in the general population but tends to be heightened in Asperger's Syndrome (Müller et al., 2008; Soderstrom et al., 2002; Baron-Cohen & Wheelwright, 2004; Tantam, 1992). I like to have as many of the interpersonal aspects of my life as possible nicely compartmentalised, and I become confused and frustrated when the boundaries are blurred. Clearly this means that I am frustrated and confused about a lot of things and my anxiety levels are consistently high. What happens when we leave the contextual safely of the studio, the rehearsal space or the classroom? How have the roles changed? When I have spent two years in and out of the studio with someone, what is the nature of our relationship? Defining boundaries around relationships and people, and trying to keep track as they shift, sometimes goes in the "too hard" basket and that's when mistakes can be made. Charlotte Davies discusses this issue, indicating that for the ethnographer it is important to be aware that the ambiguities in such social relationships are "sometimes misleading and readily misinterpreted" (Davies, 2008, p. 92) warning that the research process involving people who were close prior to the research can adversely affect the relationship. This is very scary stuff — see "Depression" above.

Ellis uses the term "appropriate" in her writings about ethics, not least in the "Telling Secrets" article (2007), so I will appropriate the term here. Definitions of the word include "suitable", "fitting", "proper", "correct", "right", or "OK". All of these have value judgments attached — they are not absolute, they require a defence, not least to those involved and to the university ethics committees. Some of these aspects of my own research are, as yet, unresolved. There are things that I will write "for myself" and figure out later how much needs to be revealed to keep the story "true". Already there are relationships that have changed as a result of harsh discovery and the vulnerability that goes with the territory.

Conclusion

There doesn't seem to be a good way to end this chapter, perhaps because the process itself is ongoing in my own work. The trials come and go, one recedes and another edges closer. One thing I can say is that you have to work with them — working against them is too hard! They can each have their own virtue as well as fearsome claws.

Obsession is your friend because without it there is nothing but apathy. Obsession is the driving force of enquiry and the way to the truth. Depression is your companion because it forces you to ask "why". It demands a deeper satisfaction with the answers and it cries for change. Defence is your own armour and protection. It reminds you of the people you love and the reasons you love them. It connects your Self to the Other.

References

Adams, T. E. (2008). A review of narrative ethics. *Qualitative Inquiry, 14*, 175–194.

American Psychiatric Association (1994a). *Diagnostic and statistical manual of mental disorders: DSM-IV* (4th ed.). Washington, DC: American Psychiatric Association.

American Psychiatric Association (1994b). *Diagnostic criteria from DSM-IV.* American Psychiatric Association.

Atkinson, P., & Delamont, S. (2006). Rescuing narrative from qualitative research. *Narrative Inquiry, 16*, 164–172.

Attwood, T. (2008). *The complete guide to Asperger's syndrome.* Philadelphia: Jessica Kingsley.

Baron-Cohen, S., & Wheelwright, S. (1999). 'Obsessions' in children with autism or Asperger syndrome. Content analysis in terms of core domains of cognition. *British Journal of Psychiatry, 175*, 484–490.

Baron-Cohen, S., & Wheelwright, S. (2004). The empathy quotient: An investigation of adults with Asperger syndrome or high functioning autism, and normal sex differences. *Journal of Autism and Developmental Disorders, 34*, 163–175.

Baron-Cohen, S., Ring, H., Chitnis, X., Wheelwright, S., Gregory, L., Williams, S., et al. (2006). fMRI of parents of children with Asperger Syndrome: A pilot study. *Brain and Cognition, 61*, 122–130.

Brieber, S., Neufang, S., Bruning, N., Kamp-Becker, I., Remschmidt, H., Herpertz-Dahlmann, B., et al. (2007). Structural brain abnormalities in adolescents with autism spectrum disorder and patients with attention deficit/hyperactivity disorder. *Journal of Child Psychology and Psychiatry, 48*, 1251–1258.

Cederlund, M., & Gillberg, C. (2004). One hundred males with Asperger syndrome: A clinical study of background and associated factors. *Developmental Medicine and Child Neurology, 46*, 652–660.

Chamak, B., Bonniau, B., Jaunay, E., & Cohen, D. (2008). What can we learn about autism from autistic persons? *Psychotherapy and Psychosomatics, 77*, 271–279.

Davies, C. A. (2008). *Reflexive ethnography: A guide to researching selves and others.* New York: Routledge.

Deeley, Q., Daly, E. M., Surguladze, S., Page, L., Toal, F., Robertson, D., et al. (2007). An event related functional magnetic resonance imaging study of facial emotion processing in asperger syndrome. *Biological Psychiatry, 62*, 207–217.

Delamont, S. (2007). Arguments against auto-ethnography. *Qualitative Researcher, 4*, 2–4.

Denzin, N. K., & Lincoln, Y. S. (2000). *Handbook of qualitative research.* Thousand Oaks, CA: Sage Publications.

Ellis, C. (2007). Telling secrets, revealing lives: Relational ethics in research with intimate others. *Qualitative Inquiry, 13*, 3–29.

Galbraith, D. (1999). *Writing as a Knowledge-Constituting Process.* In D. Galbraith & M. Torrance (Eds.), *Knowing what to write: Conceptual processes in text Production* (pp. 139–160). Amsterdam: Amsterdam University Press.

Gilliam, T. (Director) (1979). *Life of Brian* [Film]. London; Los Angeles: Handmade Films.

Gray, C. & Attwood, T. (1999). Discovery of "Aspie" criteria. Retrieved 1 December, 2004, from http://www.tonyattwood.com.au/articles/archivedpapers8.html.

Hallahan, B., Daly, E. M., McAlonan, G., Loth, E., Toal, F., O'Brien, F., et al. (2008). Brain morphometry volume in autistic spectrum disorder: A magnetic resonance imaging study of adults. *Psychological Medicine, 39,* 337–346.

Hedley, D., & Young, R. (2006). Social comparison processes and depressive symptoms in children and adolescents with Asperger syndrome. *Autism, 10,* 139–153.

Jago, B. J. (2002). Chronicling an academic depression. *Journal of Contemporay Ethnography, 31,* 729–757.

Jones, R. S. P., Zahl, A., & Huws, J. C. (2001). First-hand accounts of emotional experiences in autism: A qualitative analysis. *Disability & Society, 16,* 393–401.

Lotspeich, L. J., Kwon, H., Schumann, C. M., Fryer, S. L., Goodlin-Jones, B. L., Buonocore, M. H., et al. (2004). Investigation of neuroanatomical differences between autism and Asperger syndrome. *Archives of General Psychiatry, 61,* 291–298.

Murphy, D. G., Critchley, H. D., Schmitz, N., McAlonan, G., Van Amelsvoort, T., Robertson, D., et al. (2002). Asperger syndrome: a proton magnetic resonance spectroscopy study of brain. *Archives of General Psychiatry, 59,* 885–891.

Müller, E., Schuler, A., & Yates, G. B. (2008). Social challenges and supports from the perspective of individuals with Asperger syndrome and other autism spectrum disabilities. *Autism, 12,* 173–90.

Nieminen-von Wendt, T., Salonen, O., Vanhala, R., Kulomäki, T., von Wendt, L., & Autti, T. (2002). A quantitative controlled MRI study of the brain in 28 persons with Asperger syndrome. *International Journal Circumpolar Health, 6,1 Supplement 2,* 22–35.

Rogers, K., Dziobek, I., Hassenstab, J., Wolf, O. T., & Convit, A. (2006). Who Cares? Revisiting Empathy in Asperger Syndrome. *Journal of Autism and Developmental Disorders, 37,* 709–715.

Soderstrom, H., Rastam, M., & Gillberg, C. (2002). Temperament and character in adults with Asperger syndrome. *Autism, 6,* 287–297.

Sokol, D. K., & Edwards-Brown, M. (2004). Neuroimaging in autistic spectrum disorder (ASD). *Journal of Neuroimaging, 14,* 8–15.

Stewart, M. E., Barnard, L., Pearson, J., Hasan, R., & O'Brien, G. (2006). Presentation of depression in autism and Asperger syndrome: A review. *Autism, 10,* 103–116.

Sugihara, G., Ouchi, Y., Nakamura, K., Sekine, Y., & Mori, N. (2007). [Advances in neuroimaging research on Asperger syndrome]. *Nippon Rinsho, 65,* 449–452.

Tantam, D. (1992). Characterizing the fundamental social handicap in autism. *Acta Paedopsychiatr, 55,* 83–91.

Willey, L. H. (1999). *Pretending to be normal: Living with Asperger's syndrome.* London: Jessica Kingsley.

CPSIA information can be obtained at www.ICGtesting.com
Printed in the USA
BVOW06s1403120116

432640BV00001B/1/P